PRAISE FOR
Brad Burns & *Maine to Montauk*

"*Maine to Montauk* is the story of the evolution of an angler (and man) and the highs and lows of an enigmatic-yet-wholly-captivating fishery. Filled with fascinating characters and intriguingly fishy settings, this book is an absolute must for anyone who loves fishing for striped bass."

— **Monte Burke**
author of *Lords of the Fly* and *Saban*

"Few folks have fished as hard for striped bass as they have fought to conserve them. Equal parts diehard angler and devoted conservationist, Brad Burns has put these experiences on paper for the rest of us. It's all here, from eel-skin plugs to the Eel Skin Inn. Meet the heroes of the sport, land a sixty pounder (or two), witness the rise (and fall) of the striper population, and share one man's passion for the fish that unites us all."

— **David DiBenedetto**
author of *On the Run: An Angler's Journey Down the Striper Coast*

"A comprehensive and entertaining portrait of the pursuit of America's iconic gamefish the Striped Bass. *Maine to Montauk* is a wonderful romp over time up and down the East coast. Filled with people and the places all Striper addicts only dream of. Golden nuggets of knowledge lie between the lines, with a message that should resonate with all. Bravo Brad Burns!!"

— **Captain Paul Dixon**, Montauk

"Brad Burns ranks high in the history and lore of legendary striped bass fishermen. For 60 years he has pursued stripers with remarkable energy and skill, all the while keeping detailed fishing logs which form the basis of this narrative describing his adventures on the famed fishing grounds of the northeast, and the cast of characters that he met. There's plenty of how-to details about landing and releasing an astonishing number of large bass up to 63 pounds, and there is the sobering timetable of the species' declines in the past and again today, as well as the author's conservation efforts to help create a breeding stock in Maine's Kennebec River and making stripers a gamefish in Massachusetts. As a bonus there are numerous drawings by famed illustrator John Rice and a forward by Rip Cunningham. This book is a keeper for all of us who are involved in the striped bass fishery."

— **Kib Bramhall**, Artist and Author of
Bright Waters, Shining Tides: Reflections on a Lifetime of Fishing

MAINE *to* MONTAUK

MAINE *to* MONTAUK

A Striped Bass Journey
1950 to 2021

Brad Burns

Foreword by Rip Cunningham

Maine to Montauk—A Striped Bass Journey 1950 to 2021

Published by Burns Fly Fishing
http://www.bradburnsfishing.com

Copyright © 2021 by Brad Burns

Illustrations by John Rice

All rights reserved. No part of this book may be reproduced or transmitted in any form or by any means, electronic or mechanical, including photocopying and recording, or by any information storage and retrieval system, without permission in writing from the publisher, except for brief quotations in critical reviews and articles.

ISBN: 978-0-9908626-5-9 (softcover)
ISBN: 978-0-9908626-6-6 (Kindle)

Book Design and Production by
Desktop Miracles Inc., Stowe, Vermont

Contents

Foreword   7

Chapter 1   My Early Years, Friendship, and Damariscotta   10

Chapter 2   Reawakening, the Portland Surfcasters, Old Orchard Beach, and the Graveyard   70

Chapter 3   The Kennebec River, Part I   100

Chapter 4   The Kennebec River, Part II   128

Chapter 5   Martha's Vineyard and Block Island   198

Chapter 6   Cape Cod and the Elizabeth Islands   256

Chapter 7   The Glory Years of the 1990s   290

Chapter 8   The Unraveling and the Future   322

Foreword

Webster's dictionary defines addiction as "a strong inclination to do, use, or indulge in something repeatedly." In my mind an addiction does not necessarily have to be a bad thing. I came from a family where fishing addiction was prevalent and gracefully accepted. My father enthusiastically passed along his dependency. I married into a family where sporting pursuits came first. My mother-in-law feared dying in either the fishing or hunting season as my father-in-law would have her put on ice until the season ended. I now understand that Brad has always been an addict.

When I first met Brad Burns under the old Route 1 Martin Point bridge over the Presumpscot River in Falmouth, Maine, I was with my father, who had befriended Brad. We were scrambling around the riprap, fishing the outgoing tide for striped bass. The exact date escapes me now, but I did not initially recognize that I was rubbing elbows with another addict. It would soon become apparent. That night was the beginning of a lifelong friendship and feeding off each other's addiction to and binding interest in all things piscatorial.

In many ways our lives have had similar paths, and in many ways they have been different. While my fishing life started almost entirely with my father, as Brad so easily relates in this book, his was a lot more self-directed in the early years. He quickly spread his fishing wings and branched out with a growing list of fishing companions. And a damn impressive list it is.

This book is not so much about striped bass as it is about a man's journey through life centered around the pursuit of the often-elusive *Morone saxatilis*. It is about the progression anglers make from simply wanting to catch and keep as many fish as possible to wanting to catch and release just the bigger fish. Then to learn how to do this with technically difficult tackle. This is partially a progression of maturity but also a progression of the mind. We start out simply looking for as many fish as possible, and we progress to understanding the value of these fish in our world. We ultimately see the world in which we pursue these fish in a new way. We understand there is existential value in sustaining our natural world, not only for aesthetic reasons, but because our world is so interconnected. We begin to understand that a true conservationist is someone who knows the world is not given by our ancestors but borrowed from our children. Brad's long history of promoting conservation-minded management of fish resources is a testimony to this philosophy.

Brad did not write this book about bass to teach technique, but for those who pay attention, he has weaved technique into much of this. There are also bits and pieces of the history and evolution of saltwater fishing tackle. Stan

Gibbs, Art Lavallee, Lefty Kreh, the Alou eel, the needlefish, the Striper Swiper are all part of this fun journey. The long list of folks who fished with Brad is a who's who of the early pioneers of the striped bass fishery. One needs to remember that when Brad started this journey, saltwater sport fishing was in its infancy. It became popular only after World War II, when many of the GIs returned home and wanted something beyond the forty-hour workweek. The 1950s and the 1960s were the years when the sport began to take off.

Life is an evolution and so is a fishing life. As we mature, we begin to focus on those parts of the fishing experience that most interest us. As for the parts we set aside, there is a little bit of the "been there, done that" attitude. Brad points out it is okay to be content merely seeing that the fish which demanded our attention are still there. We can also watch as our grandchildren now get excited about catching them.

The one thing that is very evident in this book is that Brad, in the lingo of a poker player, is "all in!" when he gets interested in something, from fishing to making a living. After reading this book, I thought the title should be "All In: A Life in Pursuit of All Things Fish." Brad is likely not done with striped bass, but his having had a taste of Miramichi salmon fishing, he went all in as dictated by his normal operating strategy. Here's to Brad and his addiction, which he lays out in full detail in the following pages.

> C.M. "RIP" CUNNINGHAM
> Former owner and publisher of *Salt Water Sportsman*
> Inductee, Fishing Hall of Fame

Chapter One

My Early Years, Friendship, and Damariscotta

Friendship, 1950

After my grandfather Curtis Winters passed away, my grandmother Edith lived with us in the red Cape Cod–style house my parents built in 1949 in Friendship, Maine. Edith had been a schoolteacher in her preretirement life in Framingham, Massachusetts, and long before I started grammar school in 1957, she had taught me to read. To encourage my reading, my other grandmother, Louise Burns, who lived directly across Harbor Road, bought me a subscription to *Outdoor Life* magazine, and I read every issue cover to cover. She kept that subscription going all the way through my college years.

There were two columns I really looked forward to every month, and those were Jack O'Connor on guns and George Heinold writing about saltwater fishing. Heinold, I learned thirty years later from fishing friend Pat Abate (who you'll

hear more about later in the book), was a policeman in Madison, Connecticut. His writing was mostly about New England, especially the area from Long Island Sound to Cape Cod. Heinold was also primarily a surfcaster. Through him I heard about some of the famous striped bass surfcasting grounds such as Point Judith, Jamestown, and Newport in Rhode Island and the Cape Cod Canal, Cape Cod National Seashore, and Plum Island in Massachusetts many years before I would see them all for myself. George even wrote about a bass safari he took to what he thought were the unexplored waters of Maine. I remember the story about Maine because it included a photograph of him at York Beach holding up a low-fifties striped bass he had taken using a metal spoon for a lure. He also visited Popham Beach, where he caught nothing, but a man told him about a local angler who fished there and caught striped bass using a wooden lure as "big as a cucumber."

O'Connor's column was just as interesting to me, and until late in my college years, hunting was as important to me as fishing. Then, for some reason I've never been able to put my finger on, I no longer had any stomach for the killing part of the sport. Most of my fishing friends who had also been hunters eventually came to that point too, but many years later in their lives. Intellectually I see nothing wrong with hunting. It is the natural harvest of a renewable resource. My distaste for killing spoiled what could have been a lifetime of great outdoor experiences. Every fall, for ten or fifteen years after I last shot a deer, I had the itch to hunt when autumn rolled around. Several times I actually bought a license, and a few times I went into the field. I did shoot some sea ducks when I was in my late twenties; I always loved to eat sea ducks. I think it is in the DNA of people brought up along the Maine coast. My friend, the late Ransom Kelly of Boothbay Harbor and Merrymeeting Bay, used to outfit for sea ducks in the 1960s and 1970s and swap them with the local lobstermen for lobsters. My poor wife June had to air out her kitchen for days after roasting eiders stuffed with apples and onions, but I ate them right down to the skeletons.

Shooting a handful of sea ducks was as close to being rekindled as my hunting urge ever recovered to, and eventually I no longer wanted to do that either. The evolution of my interest away from hunting, though, has proved to be a valuable legacy in itself. The birds and animals I so admired as game during my youth—black ducks, white-tailed deer, ruffed grouse, moose, Canada geese, woodcock, and sea ducks of all kinds—have been a lifelong source of pleasure, and my knowing a little extra about their habits has added a great deal to my enjoyment of things to do with the outdoors.

I'm not sure to what it is that I owe my lifelong passion for fishing. I have two brothers who grew up in the same era and under the same roof as me. They both ended up loving boats, the ocean, and the New England countryside just as I have, but neither developed any interest in either hunting or fishing. I was the firstborn son, and perhaps it all stems from there.

My grandfather Melvin Burns Sr. was a lobsterman, as were about three-quarters of the men in Friendship. Mel grew up in a small house on Hatchett Cove, situated on the other side of the peninsula from the comfortable home he lived in during my youth. He'd been on the water his whole life. When Mel was thirteen, he lied about his age to get a job as a fisherman hand-lining for haddock from a dory on Georges Bank. Mel was very independent, and except for a few hours in the evening, when he had a good belt of whiskey and watched television, he thought of little besides the ocean and lobster fishing. In the winter he built traps, on stormy days he worked on his gear in his workshop down "under the shore," and on every other day from early March until early December, he lobstered.

On fishing days he rose long before light, cooked and ate the breakfast that Louise had laid out for him the night before, and went down to the shore. Louise had also made his lunch. Anything that didn't need to be kept cold was wrapped in wax paper and already packed in his lunch box, which was setting open on the kitchen counter. The latches on this lunch box had long since worn to the point of being undependable, and Mel had wrapped a piece of heading twine—a nylon string used in those years to knit the netting the lobster crawled through into the trap—around the lunch box and used some special fishing knot to take the strain off the worn hinges. Mel also added to the lunch box a sandwich from the refrigerator—also premade and wrapped by Louise—and a thermos of coffee. The thermos was already in position on the counter, beside the stove, and it contained the proper amount of instant coffee to go with the hot water. He topped this off with evaporated milk from the can that perpetually sat on the kitchen table, sometimes requiring that the skin in the opening be punctured with the tip of the yellow-handled jackknife he always carried in his pocket.

Mel's fingers were so tough from constant bathing in cold salt water and hard physical work that, while he watched television in the evenings, he would whittle back the calluses with the same jackknife. As I remember, his fingers were incredibly rough, more like claws than fingers. On mornings when breakfast contained bacon or a piece of meat, he would simply reach into the sizzling skillet and turn it over by hand.

Baseball was one of the few things outside of fishing that interested my grandfather. I don't know how much attention he paid to the names of the players, and I don't remember him rooting for any particular team, but he did like the game. As soon as I was big enough to swing a bat and throw a ball, Mel spent an hour or so almost every spring and summer evening pitching balls to me or playing catch. I don't believe my grandfather showed any favoritism toward me; he loved my brothers just as much. But from my earliest recollections it was me who loved the things that were also at the center of his life. So in the summers before I began school, I would spend quite a few days aboard the boat with my grandfather. I learned to bait the iron, peg lobsters, and clear the decks of all the various marine life that came up in the lobster traps.

When my youthful attention span to these work details inevitably ran out, I would fish. In the wake of hauling lobster traps and throwing over old bait, there comes a following of fish and marine birds. Of these the most plentiful fish were harbor pollock. The occasional one of these would be as large as twenty-four inches or so and put up a great scrap on light tackle. The great prize of the day, though, were mackerel.

As my grandfather worked his way down the Meduncook River and out into outer Muscongus Bay, we passed the Gardens, Wreck Island Ledges, Harbor Island, and Franklin Light, and later in the morning we eventually came to the Egg Rocks. Near the Eastern Egg Rock, during the summer, there were always large shoals of mackerel. The average of these mackerel was bigger than the ones that hung around the docks back in Friendship harbor.

"You know, boy," my grandfather would say, "first comes mackerel, then comes all the other fish in the ocean."

Mel ate a mackerel or two every day when they were in season, fed the extra ones to the family of cats that lived in his fish house down under the shore, and Louise canned up a good supply for every winter. I remember them cut in big chunks, with their sides split, sitting row after row in Mason jars on the shelves in the basement.

In the entranceway to those cellar stairs was another constantly available food staple of 1950s life in Friendship: dry, salt cod. The fish were split, the backbone removed, covered with salt, spread apart by tying the pectoral fins to ends of a stick, and hung by the tail with a piece of twine. The fish houses down along the wharves always had some codfish hanging out to dry, and we never walked by one without grandfather carving off a chunk of it with his thumb and jackknife. I think I was also the only one of what Mel called "his boys" to ever care for the stuff.

One time, when I was perhaps eight or so, I went fishing particularly early in the morning with my grandfather. We were down near Franklin Island gully to set a tub trawl for haddock that he had heard were running. My grandfather was no stranger to tub trawls. There were several of these stacked here and there around his fish house. Each of these was a wooden washtub in which a long, heavy, tarred cod line was coiled. Every fathom or so along this main line a short piece of somewhat lighter line, called a gangion, was seized on. Before setting out the line, each of the large hooks was baited with something, often freshly dug clams.

This morning, like all mornings, we got away from the mooring early, and Mel was paying the hooks out before it was fully light. The baited hooks all rested on the rim of the tub, and as the line came to each one, the hook was carefully lifted off the edge by a long stick and held out of harm's way until it had harmlessly been pulled over the side. An hour or two later we were hauling this set up back up to the boat, a very dangerous undertaking, considering that every few feet there was another big sharp hook tied on to the main trawl line. To my grandfather's great displeasure, most of the catch were dogfish, a small shark that he mercilessly hacked off the hooks to save time. Every second of delay in carefully winding the trawl back into the wooden tub and placing each hook with the point carefully embedded in the wooden edge was a potential problem, because of the great risk of sticking one of these hooks in yourself with all the rest of the gear dragging along the ocean bottom.

About halfway through retrieving the trawl, my grandfather began to struggle with something big on the end of the line. I don't think he was initially sure whether he had a fish or the bottom on the other end, but he was unable to gain ground by pulling the line in by hand, so he finally took a couple of turns around the pot hauler. The pot hauler on board the *Riptail* was a brass-sheathed device shaped like a short stovepipe hat that revolved around the end of a rugged shaft driven by a belt coming off the engine. To make this device work, one wrapped a loop of line around the brass hat and pulled on it. As the line became tight, the power of the engine helped haul the heavy, water-soaked wooden lobster traps from the bottom. This setup, which could twist off arms if the wrong moves were made, was eventually replaced with hydraulic haulers. My grandfather, though, had a long relationship with this device, and he wasn't about to spend any money on some new equipment he didn't understand.

With the power of the pot hauler in Mel's favor, the object resisting him soon began to give way. Suddenly beside the boat appeared a huge fish.

"Stand aside, boy!" roared my grandfather.

With a deft move he simultaneously flipped the loops of line off the top of the pot hauler and sank a gaff into the head of the halibut thrashing in the water beside the boat. My grandfather wasn't a big man, but he was all muscle, and over the side of his lobster boat slid a halibut that I would now guess to be about eighty pounds. The huge flounder landed on the bottom of the boat and began to pound away on the floorboards with its massive tail. The fish also made a sort of croaking or groaning noise. My grandfather grabbed one of the spare elevator weights that were used to weigh down the lobster traps and soon beat the hapless fish out of its misery. All this was against the background of the sea pounding in frothily against the rocky shore around Franklin Light while the foghorn moaned and the beacon shown brighter then dimmer as it revolved overhead. It was a setting equal to anything Hollywood could create, including a backdrop of screaming seagulls, diving gannets, and surface-pedaling storm petrels. When I look back on it, my grandfather was supremely competent in his element. And it all made a great impression on me, since other clear memories from that part of my life are few and far between.

But while it was mackerel and local groundfish species that characterized my early fishing years, it was striped bass that I read about. In 1955, just as they are today, striped bass were the most pursued and desired species that lived along the northern half of the East Coast of America. I read about fifty- and sixty-pound striped bass being taken by anglers in exotic-sounding places such as Sow and Pigs Reef off Cuttyhunk.

While striped bass were the fish of my dreams, I was a kid growing up in rural Maine, and I had no way to participate in that fishery. When I began to hear about stripers starting to return to Maine's waters in the late 1950s, I never actually saw a bass in the flesh until one day in 1960 at the Reversing Falls on the Sheepscot River. This fish was caught by Bill Hayward, a friend of my father. I owe Bill a debt of gratitude since my dad's friend got him interested in fishing again.

Dad had worked with my grandfather, hauling traps prior to marrying my mother, but that life wasn't for him. I remember he had an old metal tackle box in the basement that I used to paw through every now and then. It had a collection of mostly old mackerel fishing hooks and a few odd lures that someone had given him. While I learned to fish, I lost most of these by snapping them off on bad casts or by hooking the bottom.

In the late 1950s, my family spent a week's vacation in Sandwich, Massachusetts, with my mother's sisters and their children. People were fishing from the beach while we were there, but I don't remember much about their catches. I do remember them launching and retrieving a dory through the surf. It was really my first close-up experience with a sand beach and the surf. The trip kindled my father's fishing interest too, and he bought a large compartmentalized plastic box full of lures for mackerel and striped bass.

When we came home from that trip, striped bass fishing was on the agenda. There weren't many opportunities to fish for stripers near Friendship that I knew of then, but my grandmother said she had heard of some being caught at a place called Salt Pond in nearby East Friendship. One summer day we put my fishing rod in her car, and she drove us up to where the Salt Pond emptied into the Friendship River. The outflow from the pond on the dropping tide looked very fishy, but we never got a bite.

That trip to Cape Cod came around the time that our family moved from Friendship to Damariscotta, Maine, so my father would be closer to his job at the Bath Iron Works. Damariscotta was only about thirty-five minutes away from Friendship, but we were no longer on the coast. Like a lot of larger Maine towns, Damariscotta was situated where the first bridge across the river, coming inland from the ocean, was sited. Frequently this first bridge was near the head of the river's navigable waters. At one time this gave the town some importance as a port, and lumber was loaded onto Maine schooners at these places and shipped around the world. The bridge in town that crossed the Damariscotta River was to have an important place in my fishing development over the next ten years.

Damariscotta and Sheepscot, 1959

Among my close childhood friends were John and James Gallagher. They were twins, and I became one of the few people who could easily tell them apart. To me they really weren't so identical, but they did both love fishing and hunting. During the long portion of Maine's year that doesn't qualify as summer, we hunted squirrels and songbirds with our BB guns along the hedgerows in back of the Gallagher property on Bristol Road, not far from my house. We made plans for fishing during the next summer.

The Gallaghers also had a cottage on Long Point in Chamberlin. Long Point is a thin finger of ledge that sticks out at a forty-five-degree angle into the North Atlantic. From time spent around this area, the twins, like me, were familiar with Maine's native groundfish species and, of course, mackerel. But it was the experiences of John Grindell, who was a few years older than us who also lived on Bristol Road, that most interested the Gallagher twins and me. The summer before, John had seen schools of fish breaking the surface of the water in the bay just downstream from the bridge. John had a small boat and motor at the town landing and went out to see what was making the disturbance. He spent quite a bit of time that summer catching schoolie striped bass in the three- to five-pound range using mackerel jigs—a small diamond jig made to imitate sand lance, one of the stripers' favorite foods.

When John brought the first striped bass back to shore, none of the adults in town could even identify the fish. During the economic boom that followed World War II, Damariscotta attracted a few wealthy people from the New York and Philadelphia areas who wanted a quieter lifestyle and didn't need the money from high-paying city jobs, which didn't exist in Damariscotta. These folks knew what a striped bass was, and they were surprised to find they had come this far north.

A little time spent with *Bigelow and Schroeder's Fishes of the Gulf of Maine* reveals that striped bass have migrated to Maine from spawning grounds in Chesapeake Bay and to a lesser degree the Hudson River for as long as there have been records. Whether this was because the Gulf of Maine was a little colder in the middle years of the twentieth century or because of the unregulated pressure of commercial fishing in Chesapeake Bay (the more likely reason), stripers were rarely recorded east of Penobscot Bay, and none had been seen for many years in the Damariscotta River. Beginning in 1960, all of that changed.

Starting around Memorial Day and lasting until shortly after Labor Day, anglers fished for striped bass on the bridge in Damariscotta. The area beginning just below this bridge and running for the next couple of miles upriver to Great Salt Bay is relatively shallow, narrow, rocky, and fast running. It is navigable only on the upper half of the incoming tide. The river here also starts to become brackish. Alewives (anadromous herring) and rainbow smelts run up the river to spawn in Damariscotta Lake and other freshwater tributaries. There are also lots of eels, mummichogs, grass shrimp, and small sea herring. Striped bass love all this forage, and they also love feeding in the current and the rocky environment.

The bridge in town represented a significant narrowing of the river, which on the dropping tide falls very visibly from about one hundred yards above the bridge down to the bay on the seaward side. There is a large concrete center support and two channels on either side of it. At extremely low tides there is a small beach underneath the bridge on the Damariscotta side, but there's no way to walk under the bridge on the Newcastle side. This posed a real problem for the few enterprising fishermen who hooked large stripers in the shadow of the bridge on the up-current side that then ran downstream under the bridge. More on that later.

In the early years of this fishery, people stood on the bridge and, during the ebb tide, lowered hooks baited with marine worms and weighted with sinkers into one of the current streams running on either side of the center abutment. As with many kinds of fishing, there is more to know about this technique than some people immediately assume. The trick is to have your marine worm swimming naturally in the current.

If you position yourself too directly above the hard flow of the current, your worm just dances on the surface of the fast water and will never attract a fish.

If you walk over to the middle of the bridge, and stand directly between the two torrents of current, there is a large middle ground of upwellings and back eddies, where the water actually flows back upstream for a short distance. This situation also exists on the outside areas of both current streams.

If you maneuvered your rod directly upstream of either of these three areas, your rig soon settled to the bottom and became caught on a rock. Untold thousands of hooks and sinkers were lost here over the years.

If you played things right, though, and let a good quantity of line out with the rushing current, then slowly retrieved it back to the bridge, letting it swing freely when an eddy of current would swing it back and forth over the river bottom, it would hopefully be enticingly presented to a striped bass. When you did hook up, you had to move to one side or another of the bridge, go over the rail, and walk down the steeply sloped rock abutment to land your fish. It wasn't always easy. Most tides the anglers spent hours here for an occasional fish, though sometimes the fishing was hot. Word got out, and the bridge was quickly covered with people hoping to catch a hard-fighting striped bass and take it home for dinner.

There was a social aspect that went along with bridge fishing. I was there as often as my parents would let me go, and I got to know many of the local men, such as Jimmy Campbell and Kermit Clark, who fished it regularly and seemed to catch most of the bigger fish.

All that first summer, though, and most of the next, the Gallaghers and I had no luck. One of our friends, Jimmy Morin, did catch a nice one. His bass of about five and a half pounds came at night from a float at the yacht club pier, about a hundred yards downstream of the bridge. At times during the dropping tide, the current came under the bridge and swept around nicely by this float. By my experience, it was never hot fishing, but I remember Jimmy's bass curled up in a large bucket and how envious I was.

Later on, the next summer, I was fishing with the Gallagher twins from an old coastal schooner sailboat tied up to a wharf that ran out parallel to the ebbtide flow along the Damariscotta side of the river. This old schooner leaked like a sieve and was kept temporarily afloat by filling the inside of the hull with hundreds of empty Clorox bottles held in place with a shut hatch and aided by a round-the-clock battery of bilge pumps. It was a very precarious situation, and eventually the battle was lost. Sometime before they gave up, though, the owners of the sinking schooner shut off the entry plank, and we could no longer fish there. But before that, it was a good spot. You could make a very short cast and let your worm sit on the bottom, on the edge of the current. That was where the Gallaghers and I each finally caught our first striped bass.

Early 1960s: Expanding Horizons

Through various people I met, and by reading Gene Letourneau's "Sportsman Say" column in the Portland newspaper that was delivered to our house every day, I became aware of other important striped bass fishing spots in the area. These included the bridges over the Sheepscot River in Sheepscot village, the ledges near Dr. Averill's camp across from the Reversing Falls on the Sheepscot, the bridge over Cod Cove near Wiscasset, the now removed Westport Island causeway, and the Johnny Orr rapids on the Damariscotta River.

I could access the Damariscotta River areas near town, Johnny Orr included, with my bicycle. To get to the Sheepscot spots, though, I needed to enlist my father to take me. He was okay with it on occasion, but his friend Bill had moved away, and he never cared for fishing again with anything like my enthusiasm.

My dad had come from a long line of fishermen though, with his father from Friendship and his mother Louise brought up in a commercial fishing family from nearby Bremen Long Island. Even though he had little interest in spending money on all of the striped bass paraphernalia that was now becoming available locally (such as Atom Striper Swiper surface plugs, Canadian jig fly bucktail leadheads, Alou eels, and Pflueger Pal-O-Mine plugs), my dad preferred to fish with bait, such as marine worms. And he had an innate sense of where to position this bait so that he often caught a bass when I didn't. I naturally understudied his reading of the water, and I think it has stuck with me over the years.

One of our favorite spots to fish together was Sheepscot village. The village itself was an idyllic setting with the two or three streets that it comprised having a few large older homes overlooking the river and 1800s-era farms here or there on the outskirts. I think my father liked the views more than the fishing. Anything that would get him to take me there was fine with me, but I was concentrating on the fishing.

There were two bridges in the village. The first went across the main stem of the Sheepscot. The river here was divided by a large grass island over which the bridge ran. The other bridge was much smaller and spanned the Dyer River, which entered the Sheepscot from the east, just upstream of the main river bridge. I later learned that, during the late 1800s, the Dyer was the scene of a bag-net fishery under the winter ice that caught a lot of overwintering stripers that were thought to be part of the native spawning population of the nearby Kennebec River.

My father favored fishing at the beginning of the dropping tide, and I think he was right to do that. The bass that had been foraging on the tidal flats and in and around the marshy banks of the rivers would then enter the channels to hunt baitfish, since both were being forced there as the water receded from their high-tide cruising grounds. My father had found a spot on an abutment next to the small span of the Dyer Bridge, and from there he would work his sinker and worm with a bobber out into the braided currents where the two rivers came together. It often paid off for him with a striper, even when fishing was slow.

I mostly fished from the larger of the two spans over the main river. The railing along the top of the bridge was supported by concrete uprights every few yards, and I had found a favorite position next to one of them. As I walked along the side of the road over the bridge, I counted the uprights until I arrived at my spot. But I hadn't been the person who originally learned where this sweet spot was. On one of our earlier trips there, an elderly couple were fishing, and we struck up a conversation. Older folks always liked to see a youngster fishing, and the man told me that he was a retired Maine guide. He carefully let his sandworm-and-bobber rig out into a spot where the current made a nice seam, with the current coming from the other side of a bridge support, and I noticed he had caught a number of bass while I caught none. After about an hour, he went a few minutes without a strike and reeled in his rig. "We're past the point in the tide when they bite here," he said, and he and his wife left.

Not long after this, early one morning, my dad and I were back on this bridge, and I was fishing at the old guide's spot. I had a strong strike, and the handle of my dragless Penn Sea Hawk reel spun backward with an accompanying screech from the reel's clicker. I ran over to my rod, picked it up, and began fighting the striper on the other end. After a trip down over the embankment at the far end of the bridge, I finally returned with a striper that probably weighed about seven pounds. It was by far the largest I had caught to date.

My dad and I went home, and with the rest of the family in our 1957 Buick, we drove to Friendship to show my grandfather my great catch. The bass had started to dry out a bit, and my grandfather quickly put it in a bucket of water to soften the scales. A few minutes later he had cleaned the fish, including scaling it and removing all the fins and accompanying bones. He was incredibly quick and neat about it. The technique to cut on both sides of the fins and pull them out, bones and all, was one my grandfather knew well, and it made for an easy fish to handle. I've never been able to do it properly, but he made it look easy. This bass, filled with a crabmeat stuffing and topped off with a few strips of bacon, was baked for Sunday dinner, and, wow, was it good!

I heard that folks in the know had been making some big catches at the fishing ledges across from the Reversing Falls on the Sheepscot. This area was about a half mile downstream from the bridge I just spoke of. The Reversing Falls themselves were also a fishing spot, but kind of a long hike from a gravel parking area, so we didn't go there all that often. I did have, though, some very good fishing there at times, on both the incoming and outgoing tides.

At the Reversing Falls, the river makes a right-angle turn and flows over a ledge that runs straight across the river. A strong, daring wader can get way out on it at low tide. The Sheepscot River had a small run of Atlantic salmon, and for the salmon's tiny but fanatical following, the Reversing Falls was one of the favorite spots to fish. During the falling tide, an angler would wade out onto the ridge of the ledge that created the waterfall and, from there, cast toward the salmon waiting for the tide to turn so they could resume their upriver journey. Other anglers waited in a queue on a wider part of the ledge, in back of the person fishing. Each angler was given ten minutes to try his luck. As striped bass fishermen, we thought they were crazy to put restrictions like that on their time fishing. Sixty years later, I understand it a lot better.

One June evening my father drove me over to the falls, and I cast a bucktail jig into the waters of the incoming tide. I had barely turned the handle when I had a hard strike. A fish as bright as a mirror jumped clear of the water several times in front of me before coming unhooked. It was over as fast as it began. I had hooked and lost an Atlantic salmon.

On the ebb tide, the water ran over the narrow ledge at the Reversing Falls and went straight across the river to run head on into the ledged shore in front of Doctor Averill's cottage. Depending on the stage of the tide, the current divided as it hit this shoreline. A back eddy swung to the right, headed back upriver to a long shallow cove, and another current went left, along the shoreline, downriver to Wiscasset and the sea.

The exact point of that division moved slowly downriver with the tide, until the cove drained completely and the remaining current then flowed seaward. On good days, the whole area was full of striped bass feeding on baitfish pressed into the shallow waters along the shoreline. You could often see them surface, feeding in the great boils made by the conflicting currents spinning off the falls. On other days, there would only be a few fish willing to take, and the prime spot was usually the point at which the current divided.

Averill's was a great fishing spot, perhaps the best spot in the upper half of the river, and it was very popular. Years later I still encountered people who had come from all over the area to catch their first striper there. Also, all the local sharpies started their seasons here, since the Sheepscot Reversing Falls was the place where, in most years, the stripers showed up as early as anywhere along the Maine coast. Generally this occurred in mid-May, but in years when there was an exceptionally large number of migrating fish it could happen a week or so earlier. Some folks fished the bottom with sea worms in the calmer upstream reaches of this pool. During the beginning of the tide, when the water was a little deeper and the current was still flowing fairly gently, this was a very productive way to catch a bass. The real allure of this spot, though, was for casting surface plugs, which is what most people did.

As I became a more accomplished fisherman, I wanted to catch bass by casting for them. Popping plugs in particular were the rage, and I managed to put together enough change to buy an Atom Striper Swiper. Surface plugs like the Atom splash and gurgle on the surface of the water when they are retrieved by the angler. This jerky movement and the resulting splash of water are meant to convey the idea of a baitfish jumping to save its life. It could also be that the commotion mimics other bass surface feeding on baitfish, and this surface activity excites other predators to get in on the action. My experience has been that a surface plug will catch fussy striped bass better than any other kind of lure. I think the bass will take these because they can't see them clearly in the surface film, and so there is no basis to reject them. Also, the popping and splashing of the plug effectively simulates a scared and vulnerable baitfish, something that appeals mightily to the instincts of a predator.

Bob Pond, who was an icon in striper fishing from the 1960s through the 1980s, manufactured the Atom Striper Swiper surface plug, and he enclosed in the packaging instructions for using the lure. As I recall, Bob suggested you reel in your line at a slow pace, and during every third revolution of the handle, you simultaneously turn the handle with a quick movement and raise the rod tip sharply to make the lure pop. That was a little too disciplined for me as a young fisherman, and I instead constantly vibrated the tip of the rod while retrieving my line. When retrieved by me, the Atom plug swam, skipped, and splashed across the surface, creating a lot more action than Bob's suggested style. Was one way better than the other? Maybe not, but I always seemed to catch my share whenever the bass were hitting on the surface. One thing for sure about fishing, and that is that no technique is successful all the time.

Another thing that is true about fishing is that you can't know for certain how the fishing is going to be until you start trying. You can pick the best set of tides for the year, have all the best equipment and bait, seemingly perfect weather, and be fishing in a known hot spot, but you may still catch nothing. Obviously if you do have all those positive things going for you, then you will be successful more often than not, but great trips can also come out of the blue.

One day long before I could drive, my mother and one of her friends were going over to the Sheepscot area to have lunch with another friend of theirs. They agreed to take me over to Averill's and leave me to fish for a couple of hours. I can date this in 1962, because that spring I had gotten my first good-quality spinning reel: the recently introduced Penn 710, which cost them more than thirty dollars (a veritable fortune at the time). Along with it, they gave me a Browning spinning rod, which was also quite high-end for the day. Most of my fishing friends, almost all of whom were a few years older than I, had Mitchell Garcia 302 reels. I was terrifically proud of the Penn, though it ended up having a terrible fault. The bail springs in these early Penn reels were defective, and after a few hours of use, they would break and the bail would flop back and forth, making the reel unusable. I later on bought a manual conversion for this reel, but it caused me a lot of heartache in the meantime.

We arrived at the path through the woods to the fishing ledges that ran off the gravel road to Averill's cottage about an hour after the tide started to ebb. Our timing was perfect. It was in the middle of the workweek on a beautiful but very windy June afternoon. Seldom is one alone at this location, but I was on this day. From the moment I started fishing until my mother's friend was honking her horn for me to leave, I was into one fish after another. There were no size or bag limits, but after the first half dozen fish or so, I started to throw them back just because I didn't want to carry them up to the car.

I would make a long cast out into the middle of the swirling current coming across from the falls and start popping my Atom plug on the surface. The south wind was strong, and I was contending with a combination of fairly large waves and a huge bow in my line. The Atom plug would chug a couple of times, then sometimes become airborne as the plug leaped off a wave and was propelled sideways several feet by the tension in the bowed line. The stripers went crazy after it. They missed the plug ten times as often as they got it, and that was a good thing, because I was soon tired of reeling in fish, even though I had no thought of stopping to give it a rest.

I learned that afternoon just how aggressive striped bass can be. I also learned that when the bass hit the plug, you could feel it very distinctly, even with a bow in the line, but that made little difference in the percentage of felt strikes to solid hookups, whether the line was straight or bowed. In both cases there was clearly enough tension to catch the sharp hooks in the fish.

Among my catch that afternoon were several stripers that were only about ten inches long. I had never seen stripers that small, and I didn't know the significance of these small fish. In 1962 we didn't have Google, and for a kid, information about things like the relative size of striped bass wasn't all that easy to come by. I don't remember how or when I learned that these fish were just two years old rather than the much more common three- and four-year-olds that measured more like fifteen and twenty inches, but only about 25 percent of striped bass from Chesapeake Bay migrate after their second year of life. Presence in numbers of stripers this small indicates a large successful year class of stripers, and it was a harbinger of some very good years of striper fishing to come.

Cod Cove and Meeting Frank Gutek

Another location on the Sheepscot River that had quite a bit of notoriety was Cod Cove. The name is sort of a misnomer because a look at Google Earth shows that what is labeled as a cove is really just an eastern passage around Dodge Island in the middle of the Sheepscot River, across from the village of Wiscasset. At the northern or upstream end of the cove, a long causeway was built to reach Davis Island so that a shorter bridge could be built. The causeway narrows the river to just a hundred feet or so at low tide. At the southern side a much smaller causeway was built, and a tiny bridge completes the connection to the island. Almost all of the tidal flow goes in and out through the larger bridge, and that is where we fished.

While I know that small baitfish would go into the cove on the flood tide, I think the main attraction to Cod Cove is the marine worms that live in the mudflats that cover approximately 100 percent of the cove's bottom. This cove is dug over daily by a large number of marine worm harvesters, and any number of culls must be left wiggling around on these flats when they are covered with water.

At the beginning of the ebb tide, Cod Cove seems vast. The bridge opening is at least a couple of hundred feet across, and the cove itself covers many surface acres. At the start of the tide, we would fish the outflow very much as we did the Damariscotta bridge. The Damariscotta bridge, though, had a better fishing infrastructure, or at least it was safer. Damariscotta has a big, wide sidewalk and a solid waist-high steel railing with balusters every few inches. Cod Cove had a low concrete rail and no sidewalk. When you let out your line and propped your rod against the rail, the butt extended out to within a foot or so of the passing tires of cars and trucks—big trucks especially—that were moving along at fifty-plus miles per hour in busy Route 1 traffic. My father was no fan of the place, but it produced fish, and there were always a number of people fishing Cod Cove, so there was a little social fabric to the experience.

One June evening my father brought me here to fish, and we struck up a conversation with another father-and-son team fishing nearby. Frank Gutek and his son, Dickie, lived in Newcastle, the town across the bridge from Damariscotta. Frank was very outgoing and loved to talk to just about anybody. He also liked beer, and when he wasn't working, he almost always had a beer with him. Drinking a can of beer in public, and certainly riding around in your truck with one between your legs, wasn't legal in the 1960s, but no one really took notice of it. And Frank was an X-ray technician at the local hospital, and he knew every cop in the area from their coming in with automobile accident injuries. My father, on the other hand was a relatively quiet man—unless my brothers or I were driving him crazy—and Frank gladly filled the void by swilling a sixteen-ounce Schlitz while carrying on a loud and often profane conversation, with tractor trailers whizzing by just a few feet away.

When it came time for us to leave, my father urged me to reel up so we could get home before dark.

"Don't worry about the boy, Mel," bellowed Frank, "he can fish the rest of the tide with me and Dickie, and I'll drop him off safe and sound. It'll be no trouble at all."

My father was glad to get off the bridge, and I was happy to stay. With my father gone, Frank's talk switched from flower gardens and real estate—among my dad's favorite topics—to fishing. Frank really loved to fish for striped bass. Another thing about Frank was that he was such a tightly wound guy that he hardly slept.

During the summer fishing season, Frank normally worked on his yard or his enormous vegetable garden until near dark. He'd then come into the house, sit in front of the television, and doze while he mumbled a bit, sucked a few drags on a cigarette before letting it burn out in an enormous ashtray, and occasionally sip from a lukewarm beer. When the tide was right at one of the three or four spots that he frequented, he'd get in his truck and go fishing. When the best of the tide was finished, he'd drive home and sleep for whatever time was left—if any—before dressing for work and driving to the hospital.

On the way back to my house, Frank asked if I'd like to go fishing with him again. He offered to come and pick me up. He said he would call the next time he was going.

"Sure," I said. "Sounds great."

This must have been right around 1963, because I fished with Frank for a couple of summers before high school, then all through high school, and occasionally during my first year or two of college. We became very close, and over the course of our many late-night drives, I think I heard every fish story of his life, plus his personal philosophy on just about everything he knew enough about to have an opinion on.

Frank had grown up in Fall River, Massachusetts, and had spent a lot of his fishing time in town, on the Brightman Street Bridge. He had lots of stories to tell about big fish coming off that bridge and the various ways they had to fish the bridge and to handle the fish they hooked. Perhaps that is why Frank liked bridge fishing so much. When we first started fishing together, the old Wiscasset Bridge—now upgraded to a high, fancy, unfishable structure—was his favorite.

Wiscasset was only about four miles (by water) downriver from the Reversing Falls, and it was also on the Sheepscot River. The Wiscasset Bridge was .58 miles long, which was very long by local standards, and it was built over the widest part of the river. To me the idea of exactly where to fish this bridge was daunting, but Frank had it all figured out. We parked his truck on the side of the road, just before the bridge, gathered our tackle, and walked west on the sidewalk, across the bridge and heading to Wiscasset.

When we left the land and the bridge railing started, Frank stopped and said, "Take note of this spot, Brad. It is exactly two hundred and ten steps from here out to the point on the bridge where the fishing begins."

Actually I have long since forgotten how many steps were involved, but it was quite a way. When we had taken the proper number of steps, Frank stopped again and turned his headlamp on. We sometimes wore miner-type headlamps, usually down around our neck rather than on our foreheads.

"See that white paint on this piling? That's the spot," he said.

It turned out that spot more or less marked the place where the shallow flats began to drop off into the channel of the river. We would come out to this point and start fishing.

The old Wiscasset Bridge was an unusual fishing spot for a number of reasons. First, we fished it on the south side of the bridge, facing the incoming tide as it headed up the river. When I first fished it with Frank, I asked him why he fished it only during the incoming tide.

"Because," he said, "this is when the fish come through here, and you can catch them. We tried the outgoing tide lots of times, but we only caught the occasional fish."

Many nights in the early 1960s it would be hard to exaggerate how many school stripers there were to fish for from that bridge. A lot of nights in midsummer, it was foggy. Luckily we had a wide, elevated steel sidewalk to protect us from the traffic. We did have occasional late-night hecklers, mostly drunk kids hanging out the car windows and hollering at us as they went by. Sometimes Frank would holler back, but basically we ignored them.

The fog provided a surreal environment to fish in. The bridge had only occasional lights, and it is very likely that many of them didn't work. It was sometimes hard to tell where the water began, and when you'd turn a flashlight onto it, there was so much mist in the way you often couldn't see the water's surface only about twelve feet or so below. But you could hear the sounds of the bass, and that was a cool thing about fishing that bridge.

We walked out to the white spot, two hours into the incoming tide—the best fishing was from two hours after low tide to an hour or two before high—and stood quietly at the rail, looking downriver. We called the noise "slapping." Some think the stripers use their broad tails to stun baitfish, others believe it's just the energetic way the bass break the surface, but in any case, whatever they do, it often makes a distinctive slapping noise that carries a long way over the nighttime waters. Some nights it seemed the bass were everywhere, and we just began casting. More commonly you could hear schools of bass working the surface at different areas on the river, and with the incoming tide, they were all coming our way. It was exciting. We would move back and forth along the bridge, trying to intercept the schools.

The guardrail was about four feet high along the bridge, and it was ruggedly made with flat steel crossbeams supported with steel uprights. You could walk over to the bridge and cast over the top, but it was uncomfortable, especially to hold the rod and reel up high and retrieve your line. The solution was to step onto the first crossbeam, and then, with the top of the guardrail at about waist height, you had lots of room to comfortably cast and retrieve. This position allowed you to look down into the water, and often you could see the bass chasing baitfish on the surface all around the bridge pilings.

We fished the Wiscasset Bridge almost exclusively with plugs, and we tried them all. Among the best producers were the Stan Gibbs Casting Swimmer and Darter, the Spin Atom, Rebels, the Arbogast Dasher with front and rear propellers, and the Pflueger Pal-O-Mine.

The primary summer bait in the Sheepscot and in all Maine rivers during the summer are juvenile sea herring. Here is what the Gulf of Maine–New England Aquarium has to say about sea herring off the Maine coast:

> In the spring, larvae metamorphose into juvenile herring. Scales form, their bodies begin to deepen and flatten, and they are no longer transparent, taking on the silvery blue-green colors characteristic of adults. In short, they begin to look like herring.
>
> The young herring, now termed "brit," are about 40 millimeters long. The brit migrate shoreward, collecting in dense schools near the surface. Density-dependent growth is evident in schools of juvenile herring; if the schools exceed an optimal number, growth rates decline.
>
> Aggregations of brit herring enter shallow bays and inlets, where they migrate vertically in the water

column in response to light cycles. Dispersed throughout the water column during the day, they collect in surface waters at night to feed on their zooplankton prey. In the late summer and fall, when adults are migrating onshore to spawning grounds, the brit move offshore to spend winter close to the bottom.

Brit comprise an important food source for many predators and, as a result, are commonly spotted hiding under docks and piers. Mackerel, striped bass, and many sea birds including puffins, gulls, and terns focus their attention on brit herring schools.

Forty millimeters is about 1.6 inches, but there is quite a range of sizes, and by midsummer a lot of these herring are at least twice that long. The herring spend most of their time, especially at night, near the surface of the water. Plugs can be very effective. It wasn't unusual, though, to be in the middle of schools of breaking striped bass for hours and not be able to buy a hit. Usually, though, we would peck away at them, making quite a few casts for every fish hooked.

One of the big negatives about the Wiscasset Bridge was what happened when you did catch one. Our fishing zone was probably two hundred yards from the eastern shore, so it was a long way to go back to land a fish. Nonetheless that was what was required for a striper of any size, and every year it seemed a portion of these fish were getting larger. We measured everything in pounds, and seven-, eight-, and even nine-pound bass weren't uncommon.

Our solution was first to use twenty-pound test. Good twenty-pound test is pretty rugged stuff. Clark's Drug Store in Damariscotta sold Mill End lines. This was the monofilament, supposedly from top-brand manufacturers, left on the ends of large industrial spools that was then parceled out onto small spools and sold for fifty cents each. As I recall, the spools were guaranteed at fifty yards, and beyond that was the luck of the draw. Fresh twenty-pound test is very strong stuff.

When the bass were finally played out and laying on their sides on the surface below, we estimated the size of the fish, and if we thought they were less than four or five pounds, we carefully, hand over hand, lifted the fish to the bridge. We kept every one of these fish and made a sweep of the bridge at the end of the night to pick them up.

If, though, the fish were larger than that, we got down off the rail, and holding our hands up, with a good bend in the rod to keep the fish's head up, we planed the exhausted fish across the surface and headed for the shore. Sometimes the fish would get a good dose of water down its gullet, dive under the surface, and if your timing was unlucky, it would go around a barnacle-encrusted piling, and you lost the fish, lure and all.

When he concentrated on his fishing, Frank and I caught similar numbers of fish, but often he'd get a little too deep into the Schlitz, and pontificating won out over fishing. At home one day, during a period of night fishing when we were seeing lots of bass but having to work very hard for a few takers, I was playing with a couple of my Spin Atom plugs.

Years later, in the 1980s, I watched Bob Pond making these plugs in the small house that was his factory in North Attleboro, Massachusetts. Bob brewed up this horrid mixture of melted Styrofoam with specks of coloring in it. He poured this into heavy molds into which he had placed a thick wire, doubled over on one end for the attachment eye, and then let this setup cool down. He then attached the hooks and placed the finished plugs into commercial packaging. The end product looked quite professional, and the prices weren't bad. The problem with the Styrofoam was that it wasn't as tough as injection-molded products that companies such as Rebel or Cotton Cordell used. If you dropped the plug on a rock or it clicked into the steel rail of the bridge, it cracked. And we often fished with cracked plugs. The through-wire construction held the plug together, and the fish didn't care at all.

Just because I thought it looked cool and might be a little different, I bent the front eye of heavy, doubled wire upward on one of the Spin Atoms. After looking at it for a while, I was going to bend it back as it had originally come from Atom, but I got distracted and left it. That night, out on the bridge, we encountered as we had during most recent evenings one good-sized school of bass coming along on the surface after another with the incoming night tides. Frank and I stood up on the rails to cast. That night I could do no wrong. I tossed the plug out into the water where we could see the splashes of the bass beating up on the herring, turned the handle a few times, and *sock*, I was hooked up. After about the fifth fish, without Frank getting a touch, he completely lost his cool.

"Let me see that goddamned thing he bellowed," and he bent over and shined a light on my plug as I extracted it from the fish.

"You bent that eye up," he said. "You smart-ass son of a bitch, and you weren't going to tell me about it."

Frank ranted on for some time, clearly offended that, after he had generously shared with me every bit of his hard-earned knowledge about this bridge, I would hide this secret from him. I had simply forgotten I had not bent the eye back, as I intended to do.

On the ride back home, Frank calmed down, and I explained I had not hidden it from him, that I had just been fooling around with the plug at home and forgotten to change it back. It made Frank feel a lot better to know that his kid fishing pal had not somehow gained a magic touch in fishing that had escaped him over his many years of additional experience.

Westport Island

Another location in Maine that gathered a lot of attention in the early 1960s was simply called Westport by the local striped bass fishermen. Westport was a terrific striped bass fishery, perhaps the best in the region, and in a way it was man-made. The main stem of the Sheepscot a short distance below Dodge Island was divided in two by a large body of land called Westport Island. The west channel is called Cowseagan Narrows, and residents of the island accessed the mainland across this five-hundred-foot-wide waterway by a cable-car ferry until 1950, when the Westport Island Causeway and Bridge was installed. A large causeway with a road on top was built from the Wiscasset mainland to the island, but a small bridge, just under forty-feet wide was included very near the Westport shore to allow for small boat traffic. Necking down five hundred feet to forty caused an incredible restriction, and at the height of the dropping tide—dropping tidal currents are always stronger than incoming in rivers because all the fresh water that has run into the river during the previous tidal cycle must also exit—the water on the north side of the bridge was at least five feet higher than the other side, just twenty feet away. It was actually scary to be near.

At the height of its flow, the water roared out from under the bridge in several large standing waves topped with milky foam, and this current ran for several hundred yards along the shoreline. I can remember three points of land there, and as the current built, we would drop from one point to the next to escape the strongest flow. In between each of the points, the little coves became wicked whirlpools that ran backward at incredible speed to the river's main flow. After Westport, it was twenty years before I saw anything like it again, and that was at the Reversing Falls on the St. John River in New Brunswick.

I fished Westport Island with Frank and occasionally someone else many nights each summer, right up until my junior year in college. I never caught a fish as large as twenty pounds there, but for the day we did catch some good ones up into the high teens. We developed a formula for fishing there that produced a lot of fish. Just as the water started to flow out from beneath the bridge, we would start to cast slow-swimming plugs like the Spin Atom or our favorite for that spot, the Pflueger Pal-O-Mine.

This wooden swimming plug with a metal lip dated back to the 1930s, and it came in a two- and a three-hook version. We liked the three-hook version, and we liked it in the blue scale pattern. I imagine this looked like a fat herring to the stripers. The Pal-O-Mine had a big metal lip, and this caused the plug to swim with a broad side-to-side action. If you reeled fast, the plug moved more quickly and dove a little deeper into the water column. But it was when retrieved moderately slowly that the Pal-O-Mine had that seductive slow-swimming action the bass really loved.

While the current was still gentle, the bass would readily come to the surface after the plug. Frequently the biggest fish we would catch all evening was among those that came to the Pal-O-Mine at that early stage of the tide. Once the current developed some speed, which didn't take very long, the spot under the bridge became unfishable, and we moved down to the first point. Here a picket line of anglers often developed, even at 2:00 a.m.

Westport was no big secret, and it was here that I first had any experience with fishing in a crowd. I never liked fishing in crowds, still don't, and generally would rather not fish than try to fish in an environment where people are competing for space and access to the fish. We learned to simply stay away from Westport on Friday and Saturday nights during July and August.

One warm Saturday night, a little after midnight, the tide was just starting to flow out from under the bridge. Frank wanted to give the bridge a few casts, but there were a couple of loud guys drinking on the bridge, so Frank took a stroll up to see how much of a problem he would have fishing from the shore below them.

One of the men had a fishing rod, and while Frank watched, he stumbled through a big drunken heave and sent what later turned out to be a really big barracuda bucktail jig up into the night sky in the general direction of downriver. A few seconds later the jig apparently landed, and almost immediately people on the shore, down on the first point, started to holler. The man on the bridge was oblivious to the noises from the shore. He believed his lure had been taken by a fish, so he started to pull back violently to set the hook. He was successful.

The jig had landed on the rocky dry land of the first point, among the fishermen waiting there for the tide to start. The resistance the drunken caster felt was the lure sticking in the rocks, and when he gave a mighty pull, it jumped out and hit one of the fishermen below. Whether on that first big yank or another, the hook found its way into the underside of the nose of a fisherman down on the point. Successive pulls on the rod, thinking he had a big striper on the line, were done with all the gusto the drunk on the bridge could muster, and he drove the large, thick hook of the jig, beyond the barb, into the man's nose. Blood was everywhere. People were hollering and screaming, and the drunk was roaring about the huge bass on his line. Most fishermen, especially back in the early 1960s, carried a knife, and soon the drunk's line was cut.

Eventually, the drunk realized he had lost his fish, and he reeled up and staggered back to his car, already working on the story he would have for his pals at work on Monday. Down on the point, people helped the injured man toward the shore and a trip to the Miles Memorial Medical Center, where the hook was surgically removed.

Even going on weekdays, at the oddest hours, one very seldom had the first point on Westport to himself. Most of the fishermen, though, who showed up at these extreme times were dedicated anglers. There was one middle-aged husband-and-wife team that fished it quite a bit, and they were my first exposure to conservation.

Before I met this couple, I had never seen anyone release a live fish, other than maybe a tiny one, after they had caught so many they just didn't want to deal with any more. In my young life, starting in the commercial fishing village of Friendship, all fish were to eat. It was fun to catch them, no question, and that was one of the most important factors in my desire to go fishing, but we ate fish. All fish. Codfish, halibut, cusk, hake, mackerel, haddock, flounder, pollock, lobster, clams, scallops, and now striped bass. We ate fish, and it never occurred to me to release any fish that was good to eat. Everyone I knew regarded fish the same way, unless they simply didn't like to eat fish, which I found also meant they didn't like to go fishing either. In our defense, this was a time unlike today, when the number-one topic surrounding fish was not how few there were. To be sure, from everything I have read, Gulf of Maine groundfish populations in the 1960s were a shadow of what they were in the 1860s, never mind the 1760s. But there were still lots of fish out there compared to 2021, and the focus was entirely on catching them and not conserving them.

One night, shortly after we met this couple, the fishing was particularly good. In fact, the fishing was good enough that we dispensed with sweetening our Canadian jig fly, lead head lures, with sea worms. Normally we fished with a sea worm on our hook. Frank used to buy these, and if he was too busy at the hospital, I would pick them up from Carl Truhl, who shared Polish ancestry with Frank.

I always enjoyed picking up the worms. I'd knock on the door, and Carl, a big, heavily built man, would inevitably be watching television or, more commonly, napping in front of the television. Worm digging was done by the tide, and the hours could be strange. The size of the tide's range varies during the month with the stages of the moon, and some days with small tides timed in the middle of the day, you only got in a little work, because the flats where the worms lived were only exposed for a short while. Other days, with big tides in both evenings and mornings, further enhanced by Maine's long summer daylight hours, you could seemingly dig constantly. Additionally some diggers also worked at night, illuminating the mud with headlamps. The work was never-ending, and sometimes during the summer fishing season, the diggers did little but work, eat, nap, and drive back and forth to the flats.

Because of their friendly relationship, Frank was able to buy culls from his friend. Carl would take me down to the basement, where he and his father packed marine worms into cardboard flats filled with a special texture of seaweed. These were worms nicked by rake tines or broken when they resisted being pulled from the mud. They weren't good enough to send to the high-paying tackle shops in Massachusetts or New Jersey, but they were just fine for what Frank and I intended for them.

Carl put a couple of pieces of newspaper on his worm-counting bench, and then he picked up a bucket laying on the floor that contained the culls. He placed a little of the seaweed in the center of the newspaper and counted the culls under his breath as he dropped them onto the weed. He looked for some of the better ones in the tangle of injured worms, and he always raised his voice just a little as he neared the end of the counting so I could tell he had tossed in a few extra as well as a couple of prime specimens. Then he folded the newspaper over and rolled it up, securing the parcel with a piece of brown twine from a large roll suspended over the table. This source was valuable to us, because even in 1963, sea worms, both sandworms and bloodworms, were expensive.

Bloods were much tougher, but they didn't seem to attract stripers as well as sandworms, which had a pronounced segmentation and just two pincers in their mouth, instead of four. We didn't ball the worms up on a hook, such as someone might do if fishing them on the bottom. We cast and retrieved the jig flies, and we wanted the worm to trail along behind in a natural swimming presentation.

We found that if you put the hook in the side of the worm's head, very near its mouth, and then brought the hook out through the mouth that the worm would be resistant to tearing in half. That is, as long as you didn't snap the tip when you cast. Instead of ending the cast with a rapid tip turnover—giving it a snap—we developed a lobbing style of cast. Properly done, you could cast the worm for quite a while, and on many nights the worm sweetener was the difference between casting and catching.

To be really effective, the jig needed to bounce along the bottom. If you let it drag too much, you got caught up. If you reeled too fast, the bass wouldn't bother to rise up and take it. Like all fishing, after a while, you developed a feel for just how it should be done. With a little experience you could tell the taps of a striper from those of the jig bouncing off a rock.

On this night, though, there were lots of hungry bass, and without the help of worms, Frank and I were soon stacking them up on the beach. Suddenly, during the action, the husband of the fishing couple we shared the point with walked a few feet out into the water and released a two-foot-long striper he held in his hands. At first I wasn't really sure what the man had actually done, but Frank was close enough to get a good look. After releasing a few more fish, the couple had apparently had enough for one night, and they packed up their things and left the point to Frank and me. Frank then started growling about the pair releasing their fish.

"They're hypocrites," he said. "You never see anybody letting any go until they've got more than they can use. I never waste any. I throw them whole right into my big freezer and give them all away."

That was probably true, since I knew how Frank lived. His wife was a nurse at the VA hospital in Augusta, about forty minutes away, and she worked weirder hours than Frank did.

Frank lived on beer and things that he nibbled. I don't think he ever actually sat down to a regular meal.

In any case, I felt more than a little guilty about dragging off my stringer of fish that evening, and that couple's actions made a significant impression on me, which is evident because I can remember it quite clearly nearly sixty years later. It was another fifteen years, though, before releasing striped bass became the norm for me.

What I did do during those years, and it taught me a lot about striped bass and maybe a little about life and people too, was to take the extra bass I caught and peddle them around the neighborhood from my bicycle. I had a bike with two big wire baskets that straddled the rear wheel, and it made a great place to put the fish. I wish I had a photo of me from those days with the baskets full of bass, stuffed in head-first, with their tails wagging in the air. I think I normally got around fifty cents each for them, and for a quarter extra I would clean them.

The first thing I learned was that, unless they know you, people are a little nervous about having you show up on their doorstep to sell them food or probably anything. I learned that if I slowly and calmly told them who I was and exactly where I lived and how it happened that I had these fish, rather than start clamoring about the price and trying to close the deal, that my sales usually went well. I also learned that some people are just mean, and you are just better off to walk away from them.

I learned that striped bass caught in the middle of the summer usually have not much more than yellow mucus in their stomach. Of the ones with any identifiable food (I'd say less than half), the most common item was grass shrimp. There are a number of kinds of grass shrimp along the coast of Maine, and they are found just about everywhere in the inshore environment. Given their constant and widespread availability and easy-to-catch nature, it is no wonder they make up so much of the striper's inshore diet.

I found just about every creature that lived in the river that was smaller than the striped bass was in the stomachs of my catch: eels, crabs, marine worms, squid, and all kinds of small fish in various sizes. While Ernest G. Schwiebert penned his classic *Matching the Hatch* in 1955, the term was unknown in coastal Maine during the 1960s. We used lures that mimicked the things the bass would eat, but we very seldom tried to offer something we thought represented a specific prey species. To us, a Pal-O-Mine or an Atom Swimmer could have suggested just about any baitfish, and a bucktail jig represented nearly anything at all that was swimming deeply in the water column.

Stripers are opportunistic feeders, and if they are feeding, I think they are fairly easy to please. There are times we'll discuss more in later chapters when bass can selectively forage on an abundant baitfish. The so-called worm hatches are just such events. You can work away with careful presentations of accurately designed and sized flies in water that is filled with bass feeding on inch-and-a-half-long marine worms and only occasionally get a touch. But amid all that activity, someone can throw a comparatively large popping plug or foot-long eel and often get an immediate strike.

Bigger Fish

While I did a lot of striper fishing in the Sheepscot with Frank during the mid-1960s, I didn't neglect the Damariscotta River. In fact it was in the Damariscotta that we first started to see larger striped bass. One of the best local fishermen was

Jimmy Campbell. He was married to an older sister of one of my friends. They all lived upstairs in the same house on the road up Academy Hill in Newcastle.

One evening Jimmy was fishing below the Damariscotta River bridge, and there were striped bass visibly feeding on the surface a few hundred yards farther down the river. Somebody had access to a boat, and Jimmy went downriver with him to try for them. In one of his first casts he hooked and later landed what turned out to be a striper that weighed sixteen pounds. As I remember it was the first fish larger than nine pounds that anyone had landed locally since the fishery began about six years earlier.

Jimmy was a quiet, polite man and not much of a storyteller, but his unembellished recollections of how the fish fought sent a shock wave of excitement through the local community of hard-core fishers. A picture of the substantial bass made the *Lincoln County News*. It was now possible, right here in Damariscotta, to catch one of the larger stripers that local anglers had, prior to Jimmy's fish, only been able to read about.

Within a week or two of when Jimmy caught that fish, I was fishing at Johnny Orr Island. To get to the island, I rode my bicycle through Damariscotta from my house, which was not far from Miles Memorial Hospital on Bristol Road, to the estate of Edward Freeman, a retired New York businessman who transplanted himself in 1958 to five hundred acres along the Damariscotta River. Years later I became friendly with Pat Fitch, Freeman's grandson, and spent a little time at the Freeman property. Initially, though, I just hid my bicycle by the gate and walked through the field to my new fishing spot at Johnny Orr Island.

Johnny Orr is a small island about three-quarters of a mile upriver from the bridge in town. At high tide, Johnny Orr is a proper island, and you can easily run a decent-sized boat around either side of it. On the dropping tide, though, which is almost always the preferred tide for fishing the fast-flowing water in a tidal river, you can wade out to Johnny Orr in several places. The main current of the river flows very rapidly around the west side of the island, and there are lots of great places along the edges of the current that the bass like to hold. Another fishing friend, Gregg Pendleton, who was four or five years older than I, had fished this area quite a bit a few years earlier, and he had told me what a great spot this was.

One thing I had was time, and I learned about the fishing around the island by spending a bunch of time up there at different stages of the tide, fishing the point upriver of the island, the shoreline of the island itself, and then, as the tide dropped, wading downstream off the tail of the island onto a long bar with a rough, shallow bottom. Every now and then, as you waded, a rockpile would reach completely to the surface, and then it would get deeper again. But I could wade a hundred feet or more downstream from the island, and then, at the lower part of the tide, wade ashore in no more than a foot or two of water.

One afternoon I was working the bar below the island with Dickie Gutek, when I had a great strike on an Atom swimming plug. This was the strongest striper to that point I had ever had on the line, and it turned out to weigh twelve and a half pounds. I'm dating this catch as 1963, and it was the first double-digit striper I had caught.

As with that fish from Johnny Orr catches over the next couple of summers, we caught a few fish in the teens, and every now and then an even larger one would be hooked. We lost most of those because we simply weren't prepared for that much strength in the fish we were catching. We had weak, previously bent hooks on our plugs, cheap mill-end line on our reels or we hooked them in untenable places, such as the Wiscasset Bridge hundreds of yards and many pilings away from the shore, or we just panicked and pulled too hard, breaking the line.

We didn't worry too much about the drags on our reels when fishing for schoolie stripers in the rivers of Maine back in the early 1960s. Very few fish could pull hard enough to do any more than slow down the retrieve a little. But we had big-fish fever, and Jimmy Campbell's big striper really brought that to a new level.

Jimmy was a friend of Ivan Flye, a marine worm bait dealer who lived up beyond the Truhls on Academy Hill. Occasionally, if the Truhls weren't around, I'd buy worms there. Flye had a big operation, buying from many of the local worm diggers, and on a weekly basis he would drive to southern New England and deliver flats of worms to the tackle shops.

On one of these trips, Ivan brought back a fifty-pound striped bass he had purchased in Connecticut. The commercial sale of striped bass was prohibited in Connecticut, but that never stopped the trade in striper flesh. In general, the authorities looked the other way, and the men who sold their rod-and-line-caught stripers just shipped them to the New York or Rhode Island markets where commercial fishing for stripers was allowed. A striper like that wasn't very valuable in the 1960s, and the prime market size was much smaller. I don't know what Ivan paid for it, but it probably wasn't a lot.

Ivan had gotten the fish at Jimmy's request and brought it back with him from Connecticut as a present for Jimmy. I got a call from my friend Ralph, Jimmy's brother-in-law, who invited me to see the fish, which was now lying in state in Jimmy's bathtub. To say that it was an impressive sight to me would be a grand understatement. Over the next couple of days, before Jimmy filleted the fish, I think every striper fanatic in the area—of which by now there were many—came by to see this fish.

It wasn't long after my twelve-and-a-half-pounder, perhaps the next season, when a new striper fishery opened up for us on the Damariscotta, and it was completely unexpected. The exact beginning of it is now lost to history, but I remember some of the story, and it included an unlikely character named Spencer Gay.

The Gays were an old family in town, and Spencer was a tall, handsome man in his early seventies when I knew him. He lived in a beautiful old home on Water Street with his wife, who ran a boutique, upscale grocery store on Main Street. Spencer was largely a man of leisure who dabbled in a little bit of guiding from a converted lobster yacht, and he sometimes strolled among the anglers on the bridge, entertaining them and himself with fishing stories and the friendly chatter of his booming voice. He was, though, at this stage in his life, not a serious fisherman, and he seemed a very unlikely person to make the find that he was credited with.

The freshwater sources for all the rivers entering the coast of Maine vary immensely in scope and indicate very directly the size of the tidal estuary near their mouth: big freshwater source, big estuary. The Penobscot and Kennebec both drain immense watersheds with origins that come from the far reaches of Maine's and New Hampshire's interiors. Their sources are themselves mighty freshwater rivers, and in the case of the Kennebec, two of them. The Damariscotta is different in that only a relatively small stream comes out of Damariscotta Lake, and at Damariscotta Mills it enters a large tidal body of saltwater called Great Salt Bay. This bay then abruptly necks down into a fast-flowing, largely shallow river about 350 feet wide.

While the outflow of Damariscotta Lake isn't a particularly large stream, it hosts one of the largest runs of anadromous herring—known through much of New England as alewives and as buckies farther south. Every year, about the third week in May, around a million alewives run up this stream and into the lake. The heart of the run lasts about three weeks, but there are stragglers arriving until around the Fourth of July. Most alewives make their only spawning run as four-year-olds, and they are about nine inches long, but some live and spawn repeatedly and can be as much as nine years old and fourteen inches or so in size. All of these fish are too large for a five-pound striped bass to feed on, but stripers larger than nine or ten pounds simply love them. Of all the forage available to striped bass, large, oily baitfish, such as herring and menhaden, are probably their favorite food. Every one of these baitfish packs a lot of vital nutrients. In 1963, we only understood that in Damariscotta because we had read about it. We simply hadn't had stripers around big enough to feed on alewives.

I had read about anglers on the Saco River, about sixty miles south, in Biddeford, who caught much larger bass than we did in Damariscotta, and one of the places they caught these fish was where the freshwater portion of the river came over a dam at the man-made head of the tide. The alewives there circled in the current beneath the dam and could be readily snagged by throwing in a large weighted treble hook and jerking it back. If there was a big striper there, it would readily find the wounded alewife from among the multitudes of healthy ones in the confused circles there.

After Jimmy Campbell caught that big fish, we should have put the pieces together and checked out the alewife run, but we didn't. What did reportedly happen was that Spencer Gay knew someone who lived by Great Salt Bay in Damariscotta

Mills. That person, while walking along the railroad trestle at the point it crossed the bay, just offshore from where the stream from the lake ran out, saw big striped bass chasing alewives. Knowing that Spencer was a fisherman, he told Spencer about it, and for a period of time Spencer had some great fishing that no one else was in on.

Striped bass fishermen are notoriously tight-lipped about their fishing spots, but Spencer was not a tight-lipped kind of guy. That early summer, Spencer, it was said, could be heard talking loudly to himself and the fish as he paced back and forth on the trestle while fishing for bass. No one took him serious enough to wonder what he was doing, but when the next season rolled around, a lot of people were in on it.

The fish at Damariscotta Mills weren't forty and fifty pounders, but there were a lot of midteens- to low-twenty-pound specimens, which were gigantic by our experience. In no time a whole new fishery sprang up. Access to the stream where the alewives ran up into the lake was tightly controlled by the town. The alewife fishery was ancient and historically important. The fishermen who got the harvest were tightly regulated. Above all, the town wanted to make sure a high percentage of these fish made it up through the hand-made pools to the lake where they would spawn. You couldn't just walk in there with a net and catch fish—at least you weren't supposed to. Nighttime created other opportunities. Also, there was a fishery across the road from the stream mouth, where alewives were caught and smoked. To some degree the new demand for bait was filled by the folks who caught them for smoking.

The trestle soon became a busy place. The preferred method of fishing was to put a single large hook in the tough tissue, where the front of the dorsal fin connected to the body, then tie a balloon about six feet up the line from the hook.

Great Salt Bay is shallow and has lots of weeds. Without the balloon, your alewife was soon fouled in the bottom. The good part of this was that most strikes occurred right on the surface. The alewife would try to evade the striper in the surface film. There would be a little frantic swimming, then a big boil, and your balloon would be off on a wild Nantucket sleigh ride. You let this happen with the reel in free spool, or the bail of your spinning reel open, and when the balloon took off, you would set the hook with a mighty sweep of the rod. Some anglers caught several large stripers in a single evening.

Back to the Bridge

The clock was ticking along, and I can date the next big striper revelation for me because I was taking driver's education at my old high school in the early summer of 1965. It started fairly early in the morning, and I was walking through town, across the bridge, and up Academy Hill to the school for classes. Parked in the Page Memorial parking lot by the bridge was Kensell Krah, and he motioned for me to come over.

Kensell was the older brother of Dean Krah. Both of them had been brought up in a rural part of Newcastle and were terrific fishermen and hunters. Kensell was the quieter of the two, but I had gotten to know him while I was fishing off the bridge during the last couple of seasons. I learned a lot from both men, as they were inventive and aggressive fishermen, always trying something new, whether it was different places at various stages of the tide, new ways to arrange the hooks, or trying new lures retrieved in some unusual way. Kensell was straight and serious, but Dean was a card. He talked a mile a minute and valued everything in terms of the number of marine worms it required to pay for it.

As we were fishing from the bridge, he might say, "Gee, Brad, do you know how much a new reel like Kensell's costs? I guess you'd have to dig two good tides to pay for that."

Actually I think the world might be a lot better off if people compared values like that more often rather than seeing if the purchase would fit on their credit card.

As a marine worm digger, Dean always had worms to burn, and he saved some impressive specimens to fish the Damariscotta bridge with. I had been fishing the bridge for four or five years before I first met Dean, who was from Sheepscot and did a lot of his fishing over there. When he started fishing the bridge, though, he was there all the time, and he soon became very good at it.

One thing Dean would do was to let his line downriver much farther than we had been used to doing. He would reach an eddy that, at the latter stage of the dropping time, came in from the main flow just outside of the old schooner I mentioned earlier. I don't know if I ever understood what it was exactly about that spot, but it was clearly something, because it produced consistently.

Dean was always baited with not one but two particularly long and thick sandworms. I could never do that. The worms were too expensive, and the culls I got from Truhl never contained such specimens. Usually, at least once or twice during the tide, Dean managed to hook a big fish, and I'd watch with envy as he repeatedly went over the railing by the Cheney Realty sign and walked down the embankment to the shore to land another large striper. At other times, when Dean wasn't there, that became my spot, and I scraped together the best worms in my stockpile and occasionally got a nice fish myself.

"Take a look at this, Brad," said Kensell, and he opened the trunk to his car, beaming a broad smile.

There, laying on some fresh seaweed that Kensell had just picked up down on the shore below the bridge, were not one but a half dozen stripers, all between twelve and twenty pounds. There was no size or bag limit for striped bass in Maine during the 1960s. I was stunned with disbelief at what I was seeing.

"Have you been to Cape Cod?" I asked him with dead seriousness.

"No, Brad. Don't tell anybody, but I got them right here."

"You did? My god! When?"

"Last night during the dropping tide. Don't tell anybody, but just come down around midnight tonight, and I'll show you what I've learned."

The bridge was only about a ten-minute walk from my house, so getting there was easy for me. I don't remember now, but I'm sure I never slept that night while I waited for the time to meet Kensell at the bridge.

When I got there, Kensell was standing on the wrong side of the bridge, peering down into the water. I stepped up to the rail beside him and looked down into water that was illuminated by the lit sign from Sproul Furniture that was hanging from the side of their building. The foundation of their building actually formed the upstream shoreline on the Newcastle side of the river.

"Look in the shadow line of the bridge," said Kensell.

The tide was running out, and the side of the bridge we were standing on was the upstream side. The shadow line of the bridge was very distinct, and with their noses up against the leading edge were a half dozen large torpedo shapes facing upstream. Perhaps twenty feet beyond them, gathered in a room-sized ball, was a big school of much smaller fish.

The ball shifted back and forth in the current. Sometimes a fish would break the surface with a small splash, and sometimes a fish would turn on its side, making a flash in the light, and the whole mass would drop down in the water column almost out of sight.

After dropping out of sight one time, the ball emerged closer to the shadow, and downstream most individuals were perilously close to the large, dark figures in the shadow line. In the blink of an eye, one of the big stripers bolted out of the darkness and into the pod of baitfish. It was followed a split second later by the rest of the wolf pack. The herring jumped into the air, bolted for the bottom, or generally swam off in all directions as quickly as possible.

The bass, meanwhile, rocketed back and forth through the same area, making big swirls on the surface. Then, the water again became calm, but there were no sinister figures in the shadow line, and no pod of herring in the lights. Less than a minute later, the herring started to collect again in the light, and one by one, the bass reappeared in the shadow line.

"Now, watch this," said Kensell.

With a rugged spinning rod, he tossed a large treble hook into the river just upstream of the herring. The hook sank quickly beneath the school of baitfish, and Kensell came up with a powerful sweep of the rod. The hook sank into an unlucky fish, and he pulled it to the surface, turned the reel's handle a couple of times, and swung the herring up onto the bridge. The fish was about five inches long, locally called a kayak by commercial fishermen. The shiny scales of the herring are impossible to exaggerate. The fish looked like a thin slice from a silver mirror. The scales of these fish are very easy to simply wipe right off the fish, and it is impossible to handle them without being covered with the shiny scales as well as acquiring a strange, sweet, fishy odor.

Kensell wasted no time in inserting one of three hooks of another treble hook that was tied to a more powerful conventional rod with a large baitcasting reel, and then he ran across the road to the other side of the bridge. He then flipped the herring into the V where the current poured downstream from under the bridge and met a back eddy running slowly in the other direction, until they met in a tumultuous pocket just off the bridge abutment. Almost instantly the herring was taken in a big splash by a husky striper.

I wasn't the only person Kensell told about his discovery, and before long one or two people were peering at that shadow line, with their hands shading their face every time the tide was running out at night. Some anglers even tried fishing that pocket; Jimmy Campbell was one of them. His technique was to snag a herring and let it drift down into the shadows. If a bass came up and grabbed it, Jimmy grabbed the reel with both hands and locked the spool in place with his thumbs and lifted. Using thirty-pound-test mono, Jimmy could hold a bass up to about fifteen pounds from getting back underwater. They would pound away for about thirty seconds or so, and then lie quietly on the surface of the water with their head elevated a little and the current sliding along underneath them. Jimmy then walked them to the edge of the bridge and slowly played out the line until the fish reached the other side, where a friend could grab it.

If the fish was much bigger than that, though, it would usually manage to get back under the water and head downriver in the strong flow. Finally, after breaking a rod tip against the bridge, Jimmy gave up on that technique.

The Beginnings of the 1970s Crash

We were now in the throes of big bass fever, and large stripers were being caught in both the Damariscotta and the Sheepscot, along with all the locations farther south of us. Gene Letourneau frequently wrote for the Portland newspaper about the successes of Bob Boilard of Biddeford who fished the Saco River and the Old Orchard Beach area.

I now had my driver's license, and while I thought about driving down to try these areas, I was more inclined to spend my nights and gas money chasing girls and not stripers. Besides that, the fishing was becoming less consistent. We did have some large bass around, and every year they seemed to get a little larger.

Dean Krah figured it out when he said they were the same fish we had been catching when they were small. The same exact ones were coming back every year, but they were bigger. The flip side of this was that there were fewer of them, and we started to get used to putting in a fair amount of time to catch a single fish.

In Chesapeake Bay, the late 1950s and early 1960s produced what was called a dominant year class of stripers—officially larger than the normal number of baby stripers—every couple or three years. Most striped bass don't migrate up the coast from Chesapeake Bay until their fourth spring of life. The repeat dominant year classes provided a lot of these three-year-old sixteen-inch-long fish to migrate to New England.

Beginning in the mid 1960s, though, except for the record year class of 1970, that pattern began to falter. Year class production started to decline, and the larger, dominant year classes were absent from the mix. The numbers of small stripers we were catching began to decline markedly. We didn't complain about it much. We still had our big fish, and occasionally now some of these were topping thirty pounds. We didn't realize why we weren't catching more small fish, and we expected every year that it could change.

The 1970 class was the largest on record, but since it was to be almost twenty years until the next one, it amounted to a dead cat bounce. There were tons of tiny two-year-old twelve-inch bass in 1972, though surprisingly not as many three-year-old or sixteen-inch fish as you would have expected in 1973. I think we now know that was because this was all happening at the time when more and more people were fishing for stripers, the commercial fishery was largely unregulated, and fishing had become deadly efficient. The commercial catch hit record numbers in 1973 with a reported catch of 14.7 million pounds, a number that has never been equaled since.

Bearing the brunt of this fishery was the 1970 class. Surrounded by other much smaller classes, 1970 stood alone as a target, and was mowed down before its members really got a chance to populate the coastal fishery.

I came home from college after my freshmen year, turned over the old aluminum boat in the backyard, drove up to Damariscotta Mills, poached a dozen alewives from the stream, carried them home in the trunk in a small garbage pail with a couple of buckets of water to sustain them, and went fishing. I took the boat upriver of the Damariscotta bridge in back of Page Memorial, and live lined one of the alewives.

The next day I was showing off my thirty-four-pound fish at Strong Chevrolet, where I had worked summers in high school. George McCloon grabbed the fish, threw it in the back of his pickup truck, took me to the *Lincoln County News*, and suddenly I was a fishing celebrity. But it wasn't long before someone beat that fish.

It was around that time, 1969 or 1970, that I first met Clem Walton, who worked for the Department of Marine

Resources in Boothbay Harbor. Clem was one of the best talkers I ever met. In almost any crowd of people that I saw him in, he ended up holding court.

I was fishing on the bridge at Damariscotta one night, when a Jeep Wagoneer decked out with rod holders on the front bumper—a very unusual touch in Damariscotta in 1970—pulled into a spot near the bridge, and Clem got out. He pulled a fishing rod from a rack on top and walked onto the bridge and started fishing. He was close enough that we could talk, and there were just the two of us on the bridge. Clem always seemed to have a pipe in his teeth, and he fished with only the very best equipment. I recall he had a pair of Garcia Ambassador reels. They were much more stylish than the Penn equipment most local fishermen, including me, used.

"I always fish all night on Saturday nights," said Clem, staring intently ahead at the water with his pipe clenched between his teeth.

He was a spellbinder, that's for sure, and one story after another came out, each one with a little more fantastic twist than the one before. A lot of what he talked about was from fishing on Martha's Vineyard. In one story he hooked a herring through the nose with a big treble hook, and then a large striper took the herring and ran between his legs, burying the hook through his waders and into his leg, missing his scrotum by the smallest of margins. In another story, he and a friend wrestled a garbage barrel half full of water and containing a couple of dozen live alewives from the back of his Wagoneer and out to the tip of the Sheepscot Reversing Falls, and then they proceeded to catch a number of large stripers.

I knew both of these stories were far less than likely and that Clem was a storyteller on a scale I had never encountered before. Nonetheless, Clem was very entertaining, and from a lot of other things he said, I knew he knew a lot about striped bass and striped bass fishing.

It was very early in the dropping tide, and not much was going on yet when Clem announced that the tide would just be getting right at a place he knew of for us to be fishing. Clem suggested I jump in with him—I had walked to the bridge—and we could try a couple of his secret spots.

On the way, Clem kept up a constant dialogue about all the great places he fished for striped bass, especially Martha's Vineyard, and the high caliber of his circle of fishing friends. The monologue was intensely egocentric but anything but boring to someone like me, who was just starting to fish in places other than his own backyard.

After about twenty minutes, we ended up in Sheepscot village, parking in the same tiny grange hall lot, just before the bridge, that my father had often parked in when he took me fishing there years before.

"Here we are," said Clem. "After tonight, let's just keep this spot between you and me."

"I know this place very well, Clem," I told him.

He seemed quite surprised, which in turn surprised me, since just about everyone within twenty-five or thirty miles knew about this spot.

As we got out of the vehicle, he said, "You'll see. It's a different world at night."

Clem sent me to the bottom of the abutment for the smaller of the two bridge spans. I had walked over this spot many times on my way out to the outer bridge, but I had never fished it, because there was very little water flow through this small span. Even the current coming toward the larger bridge from the Dyer River went around this area on its way out to the main channel.

I had a swimming plug on my line that Clem wanted me to use. He said that he was a product tester for the manufacturer. I fished for about a half hour without a strike and without hearing a fish slap on the surface, something I would have expected to hear from time to time if there was anything around. Finally I reeled up, hiked up over the banking, and walked down the bridge to the main channel, where Clem was fishing.

I watched Clem for a while and listened to the silence, then I finally asked if he had done anything. I was very suspicious of the whole idea of our coming here there this evening. I knew this to be a small bass spot, and while it was possible that things were different at night, I didn't think it very likely that the kind of large baitfish that attracted the big stripers back in Damariscotta would be found this far up the Sheepscot, which didn't have the Damariscotta's massive alewife run. I was beginning to wonder just how much pure bullshit was mixed with Clem's bravado.

"No," said Clem. "Just had one good strike."

He said he was considering our next move, and I said I thought the tide would be getting good down at Cod Cove. Clem appeared not to hear me and continued talking about the various factors we needed to consider, including where the right kind of bait for bigger striped bass could be found etc.

We got back into Clem's vehicle and headed across the bridge toward the Wiscasset side of the river. As we drove up to the top of the hill, leaving the river valley, Clem said very emphatically that he knew just where we needed to go right now.

"Cod Cove," he said.

It took me a second to realize this comment was serious and that he had to just be pretending he had not heard me say it ten minutes earlier.

We arrived at Cod Cove, and Clem chose for himself the shoreline on the west side of the bridge and told me to head over and fish the east side. I was fine with this, because I had fished this spot at night dozens of times, and my experience was that the best spot was just out from some rotted pilings on the east side.

"Use this plug," Clem said and handed me one of his field-test swimmers.

I took it but decided I'd look the situation over and make a final selection as I got down to the shore and saw what was going on. As I picked my way down to the beach, I realized it was starting to get gray out. Sunrise in late June in Maine starts around 3:45 a.m., and it must have been close to that.

When I got to the edge of the shore, I could see stripers chasing bait in the current flowing from under the bridge. The bass were also slapping the water with their tails to stun the baitfish they may have missed with their mouths as they darted through the prey, trying to evade them by jumping in the surface film.

I felt that under these conditions a popping plug like the Atom Striper Swiper would work better than the subsurface swimmer Clem had handed me, as long as I didn't move it too rapidly. After a moderately long cast, a turn or two of the handle, with a gentle pull on the upper rod hand, and a yank, a bass was on my line. For the next half hour or so, until it started to get really light, I had a strike or a fish on every cast. When they stopped, it was almost like shutting off a light switch.

When the action came to an end, I carried my catch up to the bridge and walked across. Clem was still down on the rocks on the other side.

"Goddamned things," he bellowed. "They've been busting all around me, but they won't take anything."

Clem was a far better angler than he seemed that night, and I had a chance to see that for myself ten years later on Martha's Vineyard. I would occasionally see Clem on summer evenings in Damariscotta over the next couple of years. That night at Cod Cove never came up in conversation, and I'm sure Clem would have remembered it very differently.

We never fished together again in Maine. He haunted the old yacht club pier, where he fished on the bottom with bait hoping for a big striper. Catching big ones, that was Clem's game, and he focused on it.

For most of that summer I worked down at Coveside Inn at Christmas Cove, waiting tables, tending bar, and partying with my coworkers after hours. Fishing for striped bass went further and further from my mind.

Chapter Two

Reawakening, the Portland Surfcasters, Old Orchard Beach, and the Graveyard

I had graduated from college just before Christmas 1972 and married a girl I met while walking back to my dorm after macroeconomics class. I had told June about my earlier addiction to fishing for stripers, and one day, while shopping at the Star Market in Wellesley Hills, Massachusetts, she saw a special for fresh Chesapeake Bay striped bass. These fish were about fifteen inches long and came from the dominant 1970 class. I remember this was early in our marriage, probably late March 1973, and June brought two of the fish home, along with a can of crab meat, and bake-stuffed them as a surprise for me. They were really tasty, but I quickly forgot again about striped bass.

I had a lousy job, working for an alcoholic single-practitioner CPA, and an uncomfortable living situation in a single bedroom of a large mansion in Wellesley Hills. I wanted to

get back to Maine, and in the late summer a job came along that sounded good to me.

We started out with a winter rental apartment by the ocean in Yarmouth. Every day on the ride in and out of Portland, we crossed the Route 1 bridge over the Presumpscot River, and we frequently saw someone fishing for stripers. My fishing equipment was up at my parents in Damariscotta, and there was no time that fall to get it, but just seeing the people fishing from this beautiful Casco Bay overlook made me feel comfortable and happy to be back in Maine and near striped bass.

June and I bought a house that winter in North Windham, and one early summer morning I got up before light and drove down to Camp Ellis, in Saco, where the Saco River flows into the ocean through two long jetties at Old Orchard Beach. I had only a vague memory of what I was doing. I knew this was a famous area for stripers and that inlets and outlets, whether they be in lakes or the ocean, are potentially good fishing spots, because baitfish must pass through the narrow space and can be more easily caught by predators.

I walked along the top of the jetty not long after first light, and perhaps a hundred yards out from the beach I saw a bass roll on the surface and scatter a small pod of baitfish. The fish was only about fifty feet from the jetty. I made an easy cast, started my retrieve with a Rebel swimming plug, and hooked the fish. This little bass of about eighteen inches or so was the first for me in a couple of years, and it went home with me for dinner. I didn't see any others that morning. I can't tell you that was the spark that rekindled my interests, but it at least helped to keep them alive.

During a few years, from the very late 1960s until the summer of 1974, I had another hobby with a strong hold on me: drag racing. I had a 1970 Chevelle that we ran in Super Stock D. My brother Jason built the engines and did the things that required a solid knowledge of auto mechanics, and I did the brainless tasks, such as changing tires and driving. Oh, yes, I paid the bills too.

I've always loved the sport. It amazed me then as it does now that you're allowed to go as fast as you can down that quarter-mile track without being hassled by some authority. I loved the sheer horsepower, the acceleration, and the competition with the other cars and drivers. It was, though, a totally insane hobby. In addition to the possibility of getting killed, you were constantly broke from buying new gizmos and replacing broken parts.

At one point, we carried an entire new engine short block to the dump. Hundreds of hours and thousands of 1970s dollars went into this engine that lasted for about four runs before a connecting rod and piston flew out through the oil pan and shut down the New England Dragway for a half hour while they cleaned up the mess.

Doing engine work became so common that, when I was making sales calls as a copy machine salesman, I tried to hide my hands so the deeply embedded grease in the creases of my fingers wasn't obvious.

Finally, one night I came home from the Oxford Plains Dragway to find June waiting up. She had been crying and was madder than the proverbial wet hen.

"I've been going through the checkbook," she said. "I'm not in this marriage to support your car. It is either that thing out there on the trailer or me!"

It was an easy decision. I didn't tell her until sometime later, but I had felt something go wrong in the drivetrain during the last run that night. My car was geared for the quarter mile, not the eighth, and there was always a point when running in the eighth where I had to decide whether to shift into fourth or overwind a little in third as we crossed the finish line. The elapsed times were about the same, but if it was a really close race, I usually opted to let it wind in third. That was when I felt something. I don't know what it was for sure. I never did find out. When I got back to the pits, I pulled the dipstick, and the oil was a little cream colored. There was water in it. It could have been as simple as a blown head gasket, and it could have been a cracked head. As I said, I never found out.

On the ride home I had come to the decision to get out of the sport, and June's emotional outpouring just reinforced it.

I swapped the damaged race engine for a street-ready Chevy big block and sold the car to Willy Hornberger from Heath Road in Bremen. (His father, Dr. Richard Hornberger, wrote a book about his wartime experiences as an army surgeon and titled it *MASH*.) It still amazes me that I was able to walk away from racing without ever looking back at a hobby that had been so absorbing. I'm very glad of that to this day.

The Portland Surfcasters

I got out of racing and jumped right back to striper fishing. I guess I have always been like that. I'm just not happy without some sort of pursuit I feel passionate about. I found, though, that I was surprisingly unfamiliar with what was happening in the Portland area with a sport I had felt quite competent at just a few years earlier. The truth was, my expertise was in river fishing for stripers, and ocean fishing from a boat, along with all forms of surfcasting, were largely unexplored by me.

I bought an aluminum boat and trailer, and later that summer, I took it up to Damariscotta for a few weekends of fishing. I also took it out on the Saco. I found the striped bass that had been so abundant and easy to catch a few years back were now quite elusive, and I caught almost nothing.

Somehow, the exact source is now lost to my memory, I heard about the tri-state striped bass tournaments being carried on by fishing clubs in Maine, Massachusetts, and Rhode Island. The 1950s and 1960s were a very active time for striped bass clubs, which were mostly surfcasting organizations, and Maine had two, one of which was called the Portland Surfcasters. There was another one out of Biddeford that Bob Boilard was involved with. My path crossed with Boilard's many times over the years, as you will read more about later. Boilard was a well-known authority on all aspects of Saco River–area fishing and generally anything to do with striped bass. Writers such as Nelson Bryant included reports from Boilard in his *New York Times* outdoor columns, and he eventually became the tackle master for George H. W. Bush at his nearby Walker's Point summer home.

I found that the Rhode Island leg of the tournament was coming up in October. The Maine fishing season pretty much came to an end in September, but with my renewed enthusiasm for striped bass fishing, I was eager to expand my horizons. I looked up Boilard and called him. Bob told me that he thought their Saco Bay team for Rhode Island was pretty well set, but he thought the Portland Surfcasters might be looking for some people to fill out their team.

I received a call from Paul O'Donnell, a Massachusetts man who owned a cottage at Ocean Park on Old Orchard Beach. He invited me to join the Portland Surfcasters and fish for their team on the Rhode Island leg of the tri-state tournament in 1974. This was the start of the next phase of my striped bass fishing education.

I only sketchily remember that first tri-state tournament. Actually the tournaments themselves were never very important to me. I've never really cared for turning fishing into a competitive event. I always thought there was something silly about a man crowing about how many fish he had released or, even worse, how large a one he had killed. It's not that I'm not competitive, I could never deny that. If you aren't catching fish, but the guy next to you regularly is, then you're doing something wrong. In that sense, measuring your success against that of others can be important so that you can learn better angling techniques. On the other hand, you may not give a damn how many fish you are catching as long as you catch enough to make you happy.

Personally, I like to be competent at fishing. Simply fighting fish has never been the biggest part of it for me. I do like to hook a good fish and to successfully bring it to hand. But doing that over and over again gets boring very fast. If fishing is really good, I'll usually catch a couple and then move on, trying another location to see what I can learn about another place. The time to try new places and techniques is when the fishing is good, not when it is bad. When there are no fish around and you can't catch them anywhere, it is impossible to know if you're doing things right or wrong.

The tournament was held in Rhode Island, and the headquarters was in an off-season motel near Point Judith. There was a big meeting room where the anglers assembled before and after fishing and where the catch results were reported. Team leaders were selected from anglers who were familiar with the area, and these teams had members from a variety of fishing clubs. It was a fair enough system designed to put everyone on an equal footing, though, of course, the team leaders were by no means equal in their knowledge of the area. It turned out not to matter much anyway at this particular event.

We arrived in Rhode Island on a Friday evening at the start of a vicious nor'easter storm. The next morning, when we looked out at the water, we saw a really angry sea. It was white caps as far as you could see, with wind-driven rain and a heavy pounding surf. But everyone went fishing anyway for that first session.

My group went to a well-known striper spot that I would visit a few more times over the years. The area was in Narragansett, and it was known as the Avenues. Here, small streets lined with threatening signs warning against trespassing and parking ran by large shingle-style homes—many reportedly owned by members of the Rhode Island Mafia—and ended with tiny areas stuffed with a car or two owned by fishermen who walked from there to the impressive rocky shoreline. These ledges presented a moderate danger on good days. One of the streets, in fact, was appropriately named Hazard Avenue.

In six-foot seas, thirty-knot winds, on surfaces slick with sea spray and rain, this rocky shoreline was absolutely treacherous. I had never fished in anything like these conditions. After my casting plug was blown far of course and thrown high up on the rocks long before the intended end of my retrieve, I switched to a brand-new Hopkins No=EQL metal lure. This cast like a bullet into the wind, but before I could get it back to the shore, it hung up securely on the rocky bottom. Since I had carefully crawled into a somewhat protected perch above the pounding waves—which could smash me into the rocks or kill me in a second if I fell in—I couldn't change my angle of pull, and I finally had to snap off my brand-new lure. I couldn't wait for this morning to end.

Back at the hotel, many people were canceling the rest of their reservations, moving out of their rooms and heading home. A handful of fishermen, though, were determined to find a way to catch fish in spite of the conditions, and, indeed, a couple of anglers had actually caught fish.

Ritchie Schlagenhaff of New Jersey, and his son, both members of the Portland Surfcasters, had tied themselves together with a heavy rope and crawled out onto one of the jetties near the Harbor of Refuge in Point Judith. (At least that was the story I was told.) Using live eels, they had a striped bass of around forty pounds and another of around twenty, which were now lying in some grass on the edge of the parking lot. Those fish generated a lot of envy from the rest of us.

In the afternoon, my group went up the shoreline to the remains of the old bridge out to Jamestown. There was a little corner in the shoreline there, and you could cast your plug up into the wind and it went on forever. There was a tiny lee from the waves, and you could actually fish in some comfort. None of us caught anything, but on one cast, using a big Creek Chub popper, a sizeable striper came up and slapped at my plug. I had a brief but clear look at the broom-sized tail, which I still can see in detail forty-five years later.

I could count the active members of the Portland Surfcasters on my fingers. Paul O'Donnell and his friend Tony Fagnoli were close friends from Upstate New York. They always stayed and fished together at any club outings. Pete Mathews was from South Portland, and he was one of the best fishermen in the group. Lou Zglobicki was an optometrist from Falmouth, and we became friends. Lou loved fishing of all kinds at least as much as anyone I've ever known. George Irving owned a lumber mill in Tamworth, New Hampshire, and Wes Eayers was a professor of marine biology at the local technical college. These were the ones that did any of the work that needed to be done and regularly attended meetings, but there were others who fished for the club during the tournaments and attended some of the other fishing events that came up from time to time.

An example of one of these events was the Plum Island cod trip, which took place every April. In the mid-1970s, there were still a fair number of codfish in the Gulf of Maine, and the waters off Plum Island were one of their big spawning grounds. Primarily at night, a fair number of these fish, some of them of considerable size, came into the surf to feed.

The Portland Surfcasters set up a camp with a couple of RVs on the beach and fished. It was a great way to start the season. But this fishery came to an end around the time I joined the club. In the 1960s they had often bailed the codfish on the spring outings. By the mid-1970s, getting even one cod was a big event. Today, in 2021, there are only two weeks during the season that it's legal for a recreational angler to keep even one codfish from the Gulf of Maine. Commercial fishing destroyed the fishery, but recreational anglers are shut completely out of the harvest, even though their effects are inconsequential. Our marine resources management is full of many such examples of poor public policy.

When I joined the Portland Surfcasters, a man named Jack—I forgot his last name a long time ago—lived in Scarboro and hosted the monthly meetings at his home. He worked for Fairchild Semiconductor and was transferred shortly after I joined. So the club needed a new place to meet, and I volunteered the basement of my new home in North Windham.

Wes Eayers was a marine biologist, and he was very interested in striped bass tagging. For years, at Wes's urging, members of the club had been tagging striped bass with American Littoral Society spaghetti tags. Wes developed a tagging station, which was a board with an inlaid ruler, a series of holes to hold the tagging needles loaded with tags, a pen to fill out the tag, a flat place on which to write the catch information, and attached boxes to hold both filled-out tags and blank ones.

The club's prized possession was a huge chart of the upper half of the East Coast that had pins stuck in it to show every location that striped bass tagged in Maine had been recaptured. That chart was moved to the new meeting place in my basement, where it was proudly displayed.

Wes died of cancer only a couple of years after I first met him, and his widow took back the chart. I don't know whatever happened to the chart or the data from the tagging and recaptures, but I distinctly remember a considerable number of pins being placed, not only in Chesapeake Bay tributaries, but more unusually in the sounds of North Carolina, indicating there was a considerable striper interchange with that area that is believed now to no longer take place.

The monthly meetings of the Portland Surfcasters became a lot of fun for me. June always made refreshments for us, and after a little bit of business—which centered on getting more active members—the conversation would all be about striped bass fishing.

I was all ears. I was now living in the Portland area and had the Saco River and Old Orchard Beach nearby. For Maine, this was big bass country. Some of these men, such as Pete Mathews, had grown up in South Portland, and they clearly knew a lot about fishing the area. Pete was always very friendly and relatively generous with his information. Others, such as Paul O'Donnell and George Irving (who was originally from New Jersey), had fished up and down the East Coast for striped bass. I learned a lot about equipment, fishing techniques, fishing places, and the striped bass fishing culture of not only southern Maine but also of New England in general.

The only dampener on all of this was that my new friends confirmed what I had observed myself: there were very few young striped bass entering the coastal migratory fishery. Did my hobby have a future? My knowledge of striped bass biology was not great, but my education was about to begin.

Wes Eayers, in particular, knew a lot about the creatures, and it was he who first introduced me to the Chesapeake Bay Young-of-the-Year Index. The index is an average of the number of striped bass born that year in Chesapeake Bay that were caught by sweeping a net through the same places several times each summer. The last really good year class had been spawned in 1970.

I remember one meeting in November 1975. The previous month, George Irving had been invited to the Piscataqua River in Portsmouth, New Hampshire, to fish for striped bass using live menhaden as bait. George told the group about the big stripers he had caught, and at one point said excitedly, "They were all huge fish, nothing smaller than thirty pounds among them."

With that, Wes launched into a tirade, not just at George, but really directed at all of us.

"George," he said, "don't you understand, that's not good, that's terrible. What that means is that when those big old females—virtually all the large bass in the coastal migratory fishery are females—are gone, there won't be any striped bass at all."

When fishing in the 1970s, the nearly total lack of small or "schoolie" stripers created a backdrop of dread, we were never really able to fully escape. It was the elephant in the room in every conversation about striped bass fishing.

It might be good at this point to gather a frame of reference on striped bass by considering my summary of parts of a paper written by Mitchell Tarnowski of the Maryland Department of Natural Resources Fisheries Service (DNR), "A Historical Background for Striped Bass Landings in Maryland, 1928–1998." In this fifty-page article, Tarnowski lays out in chronological order the annual commercial harvest of striped bass in Maryland as well as outlines the emergence and growth of the recreational fishery. He also discusses recorded observations made during the subject years by individuals close to the fishery, and he notes important changes in regulations. While the Maryland waters of Chesapeake Bay aren't the only nursery for striped bass on the East Coast, they are the most important one, and trends there speak for all of Chesapeake Bay. The Delaware and Hudson Rivers are huge rivers, and their contributions are regionally important, but the Chesapeake has been shown to be the critical supplier of East Coast stripers, especially for the upper New England states.

From the 1920s until 1990, when the fishery reopened after the moratorium of 1985, Maryland stuck with the same basic management philosophy. They had a twelve-inch minimum-size limit on striped bass for most of that time, and a fifteen-pound maximum. Given that a fifteen-pound striper is probably around thirty-two inches, Maryland, in effect, had a slot limit of twelve to thirty-two inches. This system seemed to work fairly well for Maryland, which definitely had its ups and downs in their annual catch, which Tarnowski relates were caused by a variety of things that ranged from weather to all the unemployed men during the Great Depression turning to netting stripers to feed their families and make some income. At different times, Maryland fishermen used just about every imaginable netting technique to catch striped bass. This included dragging trawls normally associated with open-ocean fishing around the inside of the bay. Gradually, fishery managers learned more about how much effort they could get away with, but it was slow in coming.

According to Tarnowski, early catches inside the bay were smaller than commercial harvests of later years, because the population was so heavily harvested that adult fish were often in short supply. They frequently talked about strong year classes, but with nets harvesting the fish down to ten inches in size during the early years of the fishery, not many survived to become large specimens.

In the 1930s, the commercial harvest was calculated to average around 1.05 million pounds a year.

In the 1940s, that number doubled to 2.2 million.

In the 1950s, it grew further to 2.8 million.

In the 1960s, they hit their peak with an average annual commercial harvest of 4.1 million pounds during the decade.

The 1960s, according to Tarnowski, were the golden years. There were big year classes in 1958, 1961, 1964, and 1966, and these kept the catches high. Poaching was a factor in Chesapeake Bay during all of these periods, just as it still is today. Officials in Maryland estimated that the catch from unlicensed netters was at least as high as the reported average catch of 4.1 million pounds during the 1960s.

This level of harvest could not be sustained. The numbers declined slightly to an average of 3.46 million pounds per year in the first half of the 1970s, but then they dropped to 1.62 million during the second half. In the early 1980s, the numbers slumped to well under a million, and then, in 1985, fearing federal intervention, a moratorium on harvesting was enacted inside Chesapeake Bay.

In 1975, when Wes laid into George, we were on the way down. There were virtually no small stripers to be found along the New England coast, only the remnants of the great 1950s and 1960s year classes. These had been beaten up badly by the Chesapeake Bay commercial fishery, but those four big year classes occurring over eight years put out enough fish so the numbers of large stripers in the ocean in 1975 were still very substantial. You just had to know where to find them and how to catch them.

Old Orchard Beach

Pete Mathews loved to fish for striped bass, and his specialty was an area that was comprised of Old Orchard Beach, the Nonesuch River (which Pete referred to as the marsh), and Scarborough Beach, including the Graveyard and the mouth of the Spurwink River. You could catch fish at all of these places fishing from the shore, and that is how Pete fished the area most of the time. He had places like the Hot Dog Stand over by Camp Ellis, Ocean Park at the mouth of Goosefare Brook, the areas in front of several Old Orchard Beach hotels, the Pink Stucco House, the trestle up in the Nonesuch, and the Flagpole and the shipwreck at Scarborough Beach.

I remember reading John Cole's book *Striper* and his take on surfcasting as a way of catching fish: "In addition to being the least comfortable of any fishing form, surfcasting is also one of the least productive. Restricted to the arc of his casts, the beach fisherman has a most limited range. To be caught, the fish must first swim within the small quadrant the caster can cover, then it must decide whether to strike the lure. The combined variables generally guarantee the surfcaster a relatively small catch."

Surfcasting was never John's thing, but he left a key element out of his analysis, namely, that the small quadrant the surfcaster will cover is the choice of the fisherman. It is also true that most fish in the ocean are housed in a very small percentage of the ocean habitat. Being a savvy fisherman is knowing where these fruitful locations are. Actually, along the beach, they can often be found surprisingly easily.

Stripers love shallow water, not necessarily all the time, but often, because everything about their design allows them to prosper in that environment. Bass have some amount of the dark muscle found in tunas that provides the ability to swim long distances at high speed, but they have more of the white muscle found on fish that are able to accelerate instantly from low speed to flat-out attack speed. Along with their muscle structure, they have large fins for high maneuverability and a huge tail for quick thrust. In a short burst, they are very quick, and they look for environments where they can capitalize on their design.

Surf lines are wonderful environments for bass. In the tumult of breaking waves, stripers launch themselves at disadvantaged prey species and enjoy the further advantage of the shallow waters that provide prey with only a limited area in which to try to escape. A break in the bars along the beach that force water to flow rapidly through a comparatively narrow slot is invariably a good spot, as are almost any rocky areas.

Stripers are called rockfish (or simply rock in Chesapeake Bay) because of the creature's affinity for rocks. Rocks are not only habitat for the stripers' prey, but water crashing into or bending around rocks provides additional ambush places for the strong swimming stripers to hang out. Inlets and outlets are also important, since baitfish moving through these narrowed openings with the tides or freshwater outflows are at a disadvantage compared to the robust stripers due to the current speed and the tumultuous swimming conditions.

While Pete knew many of the spots along Old Orchard and Scarborough Beaches that were likely to hold stripers, and he could get to all of them on foot. A boat, he said, allowed you to check out all or many of them in the course of a relatively short time, whereas on foot you were limited in your ability to move around.

One thing that I remembered from my summers at Christmas Cove and then heard about fairly frequently from my fellow saltwater anglers, was the fishability of the open, center-console boats. Aquasport and Mako were two brands that stuck out in the 1970s. I developed an itch to replace my leaky aluminum boat with something better, and I found a 22-2 Aquasport for sale in Freeport. The boat was a brand-new 1974 model, but it had been sitting on the lot for a bit, so, toward the end of the 1976 season, I got what I thought was a good deal and ended up with a new boat and a fat payment book.

The next June, Pete Mathews, Lou Zglobicki, and I, along with my brother Jason (who cared nothing about fishing but loved boats) launched the *Sea Beagle* at Ferry Beach in Scarboro and motored through the mouth of the Nonesuch River. The first order of the morning was to catch mackerel for live bait, and I was prepared by setting out two rods with long rigs of mackerel flies tipped with heavy metal lures. Sometimes catching mackerel is the toughest task. If you can only get a couple of mackerel, and the day is wearing on, you give up mackerel fishing and cut the mackerel you have into pieces for bottom fishing bait. If, on the other hand, the mackerel fishing is good, you put the badly hooked bleeders or overly large specimens into a bucket to cut up for bait or even chum, and you put the live ones into a live well.

I had bought a big Rubbermaid garbage can and rigged an overboard hose to a fitting three-quarters of the way up the side of the garbage can. I had not hooked up an incoming hose to keep up a circulation of fresh water (I did do that later), but initially we just poured in a bucket of salt water every now and then. Once the water level reached a certain height, it drained out of the garbage can. It actually worked just fine.

As I remember that morning, we worked fairly hard for our mackerel, but after a while we had a couple of casualties and a dozen beauties swimming round and round in the large garbage can.

"Now," said Pete, "I'll show you how to catch stripers."

We were not too far off the rocky shore of Prouts Neck, and Pete pointed to a distant speck to the west at Old Orchard Beach.

"Head for that pink stucco house over on the beach," he said.

Once we were near the shore and just outside the breaking surf line, Pete yelled to Jason to keep the boat right there, just beyond the breakers. He said to run along at a little slower speed than a real planing speed, what my brother termed a "lumbering plane."

Running along an ocean beach like this was new to me, but I had loved looking into the water my whole life. When I was growing up in Friendship, we used to lift out a hatch in the bait house on the dock that my grandfather lobstered from. The hatch was inside the bait shed, where the lobstermen kept barrels carved with their initials. The bait truck came to the wharf once a week, and the man running the truck would climb into the open back, then stand on top of the mountain of redfish racks that filled the bed and pitchfork them into the waiting barrels that had been rolled out to meet the truck. The racks were then heavily salted down, and each day the lobstermen would fill a few tubs with them to rebait their traps as they hauled them. As the barrel started to empty of redfish racks, the remaining ones were covered in a foul fluid called bait brim. To be able to see the remaining bait, the barrels were rolled over to an opening in the floor of the shed, and the content was poured off. This made a huge cloud in the water below. But after a few seconds, it started to clear, and the area was descended upon by hundreds of harbor pollock, the biggest of which were about eighteen inches long. I could have spent hours peering down into those fish and watching the crabs crawling around the bottom for the pieces the pollock missed.

Looking down into the four or five feet of water in back of the surf line was similarly fascinating. We saw crabs shuttling along the bottom, skates laying nearly motionless as we passed over them, and schools of small fish (probably herring). Then, suddenly thirty feet or so in front of the boat, a half dozen large shapes appeared. Almost invariably, and I'm sure instinctively, the twenty-five- to forty-pound striped bass avoided the boat by darting in toward the breakers and not out into the deeper but calmer water.

Pete Mathews came completely unglued.

"See 'em, see 'em," he roared, pointing at the fish that were as visible as the finger at the end of his arm. "Shut off the engine now! Put the boat in neutral and turn the bow toward offshore."

Jason instantly complied. The Aquasport dropped off its lumbering plane, and Pete and I came perilously close to launching ourselves over the bow rail.

Pete tossed over the anchor, and we went back into the boat to fish. On most summer days an onshore breeze swung the boat around and tried to push it onto the beach. The boat, anchored by the bow, hung nicely, bow into the surf. If a wave a bit larger than expected happened along, as they occasionally did, we rode up and over it quite safely.

Occasionally in the late summer, we would have dazzling clear days with an offshore northwest breeze and almost flat surf. On these days, we set the anchor off the stern to keep the bow into the surf, and sometimes were close enough to the beach to piss off the life guards.

It was not unusual to stand up on the seats in the Aquasport and see the bass swimming like sharks among the bathers who were only wading up to their waists. Old Orchard Beach was often crowded with French Canadian tourists from Quebec City, some of them young and very good-looking in their tiny two-piece suits, and the strong smell of suntan lotion was sometimes almost overpowering.

Our fishing rods mostly held revolving spool conventional reels, which were definitely best for live baitfishing. We'd reach into the garbage can and grab a mackerel, then stick the hook through the tough area, where the dorsal fin attached to the body of the fish. Then we'd put the mackerel in the water, the reel in free spool, and let the fish swim away from the boat.

It was important, especially with three of us fishing, to keep track of our mackerel. If someone failed to do that, the mackerel would invariably cross paths with each other, circle the anchor line, and soon everything was tangled up.

If you needed to set the rod down for a minute to light a smoke or take a whiz, you put on the clicker. You did not want the reel left in gear. For one thing, you didn't want it to suddenly disappear over the side, though more likely, if a bass hit the mackerel, it would not get it far enough into its mouth quickly enough to get hooked before it felt the unnatural pressure of the line holding the mackerel and spit it out. Instead, when a fish hit, we would let the bass swim off for a short distance without tension, and then, hoping the bass had the mackerel solidly inside its mouth, we'd flip the reel into gear and lift up sharply on the rod to set the hook. That was called getting a run, and most of the time it resulted in a hookup.

Sometimes, though, the bass would start out with the bait and drop it, sometimes coming back again and picking it up and sometimes not. On occasion, the mackerel were strong and fast enough to keep the bass at bay for a little while. Often they would use the ancient technique of swimming into the surface film to try to evade the bass. Sometimes this resulted in a race across the surface, with the bass lunging at the mackerel. Finally there would be a loud pop as the broom-sized tail of the bass literally knocked the mackerel into the air, and then a big swirl as the bass grabbed its prey. When that happened, the reel started spinning like crazy, and we simply flipped it into gear and hung on.

A lot of how any fish fights once on the line is determined by where it is swimming when its hooked. A codfish hooked in two hundred feet of water will try to stay down on the bottom, where it is comfortable. There will be no long drag-blistering runs. A bonefish, hooked in inches of water on the flats, will head for the horizon to get away from whatever it is that has grabbed it by the lip. A bonefish, though, caught on deep mud will fight much more in the style of codfish and try to remain deep in the dark, protective water.

The big bass that we hooked at Old Orchard did everything within their power to get out of the surf line and back to the sanctuary of deep water. It was a great place to fight a large fish, because no matter how capable the bass was, it wasn't going to clean out two hundred yards of thirty-pound-test monofilament protected by a stiff drag. The best of them might get a little over half that line off the reel, but the end is never in doubt, and eventually they are finning weakly on the surface beside the boat.

By this time we all knew enough to realize that the striped bass population was in trouble, and we released all of these fish. We found great pleasure in seeing them swim away and back to Chesapeake Bay, we hoped, to spawn the next spring.

The Graveyard

If you launched your boat at Ferry Beach as we did to fish Old Orchard Beach but turned left on coming out of the Nonesuch River, you went around Prouts Neck, once home of the famous artist Winslow Homer, and then came to another sandy stretch called Scarborough Beach. This didn't have the miles of open expanse that Old Orchard did, but it nonetheless could hold a lot of stripers, and the very best spot was in front of the flagpole of the old Atlantic House (long since redone into a massive condominium project). At the far end of the sandy beach is a treacherous, ledge-covered stretch called the Graveyard, followed by another sand stretch, Higgins Beach, which ended with the outlet of the Spurwink River. This entire area is a terrific striper habitat.

In September 1970, Wes Eayers was fishing at the Graveyard and could see pods of striped bass breaking on the surface of the ocean in front of him. At one point the pods became so thick and were attended by so many gulls that they covered the whole area from near the mouth of the Spurwink

River south to a ledge called Old Proprietor, a mile and a half distant. That was one helluva school of striped bass.

Generally we preferred fishing from the boat at Old Orchard. This was mostly because we could spot the bass and knew we were fishing over fish. But we couldn't see the bass at the Graveyard because of the dark, rocky bottom. The Graveyard, though, was for many reasons a superior surf-casting location. Not the least of these were the aesthetics. Old Orchard Beach was and is covered with a solid line of hotels and condominiums from one end to the other, and there is a real honky-tonk atmosphere that didn't necessarily completely ruin it as a fishing venue, but it didn't compare favorably to the essentially undeveloped rockbound Maine coast beauty of the Graveyard as it was in the 1970s.

The Portland Surfcasters were always trying to recruit the king of Graveyard surfcasters, Al Emmons. One night the members were talking about sending Al a letter to invite him to join the club. I didn't know Al, but I volunteered to call him and see if we could sit down and talk.

"Come fish with me at the Graveyard," Al said.

And I did.

Your ability and willingness to fish the slippery, rocky ledges of the Graveyard was Al's way to measure your mettle as a surfcaster. We became fast friends and we fished there together many times over a span of years, but the Portland Surfcasters Club was never Al's thing.

Al was a big, rugged man who ran a paper machine at S. D. Warren in Westbrook. He had chosen his home in Scarboro so he would be near the fishing at the Graveyard. Al was a frustrated artist, and he had done a stint of brokering artwork to dealers in Boston and New York. The current manifestation of his creative talents was a side business of manufacturing his own line of plugs, which he called Striker

Lures. These plugs were custom tailored to the kind of striper fishing that Al did, the only style of fishing he was truly interested in.

To fish the Graveyard, Al and I parked at the Higgins Beach Inn. Al knew the owner and gave him a few bucks a year to park there. We then walked down the main street of this cottage community until we came to Higgins Beach. At the sand swimming beach, we took a right along the shoreline path designated for access by the private property owners, whose homes we walked by, and carried on a couple of hundred yards to the Graveyard. The Graveyard ran from the end of this private stretch just under a half mile to Scarborough Beach. This area was all rock, both on the shore and stretching out into the water, with a complex array of ledges that were submerged completely at high tide, but at low tide it stretched more than a hundred yards offshore with many finger ledges, rock islands, and gullies scoured out between them. If you waded through some of these rocky tidal pools early in the morning of a low tide, you could simply pick up lobsters (which was illegal, of course).

The lobster fishing industry in Maine has long since seen to it that the only way to legally catch lobsters is in the same traps the commercial fishermen use, but only hauled in at very specific times that are again designed to make it inconvenient for recreational harvesting. For instance, Sunday hauling of your traps is not allowed from June 1 to August 31. This makes sure that people visiting their summer house for the weekend can't bait and set their traps on Saturday and then haul them in on Sunday.

There are really two times to fish the Graveyard. First, at high tide, when you can walk along the rocky shoreline and cast out over the submerged ledges, hoping to find bass feeding there. This was really Al's specialty. His equipment was totally geared for this operation. Al used a surf spinning rod of about twelve feet, and the largest spinning reel he could buy. When we fished together, Japanese reels such as Shimano were just gaining traction over U.S. brands like Penn or Mitchell. Al used twenty-five-pound test or thereabouts, and he set the drag just tight enough so that squeezing the line between his very strong thumb and forefinger could not pull the line out of the reel against the drag. I can tell you that with the increased drag from the friction with the fishing guides that you needed a strong fish to pull out any line against Al's drag. The final item of custom outfitting was the plug itself. Naturally, Al liked to use his own plugs, although in our time surfcasting together, he also became fond of the Atom P-40, a big plastic "bottle plug" swimmer with three sets of trebles and a metal lip. Striker Lures were typically surface plugs in basic design concept. What Al called his chugger was about six inches long and made of a dense wood. It must have weighed four ounces, complete with a pair of oversized, ultrastrong treble hooks. The front of the plug featured a slanted surface that plowed into the water, lifted the plug, and splashed a lot of water around. A lot of big bass were caught on that plug.

Al would rear back from his perch on a ledge overlooking the Graveyard, cock the big surf rod as if it was going to break right in half, and send his Striker Chugger hurtling into space with a roar of the stiff mono rushing out through the big stainless spinning guides. Al had turned a handicap to his advantage when it came to making these casts. Somewhere along the line, the last digit of his right index finger had been lost to machinery. Sticking out of the end was a small polished nub of bone, and it was between this bone and the thick tissue at the end of his finger that the line rested on the cast. Casting such a heavy plug this hard would tear apart the skin on a normal index fingertip, but Al's bone was up to the task. In any case the big plug would land with a resounding plop even at the end of a hundred-yard cast.

After the plug hit the water, Al immediately began to rapidly pump the long rod back and forth while slowly turning the handle of the reel. The massive chugger would splash and dart back and forth over the surface, and on its long way back to shore, it trolled by some mighty good striper habitat.

Other people came over to the Graveyard by boat and fished live mackerel or trolled a rig called a tube and worm (a length of rubber hose with a hook in the end baited with a sea worm). And still others fished various pockets in the rocks with dead mackerel on the bottom.

Al was the king of the Graveyard, though, a purist to his plug fishing, and he definitely caught some big fish. He even hooked a couple over the years that despite his massive equipment kept pulling out line to the point where Al put his thick hand over the spool to stop it before he was cleaned out. The result was always that the 3/0 trebles were bent out straight and the barbs lost their grip on the fish.

I never fished the Graveyard with anything like Al's passion. I knew it was a good place for big fish, but it was a hassle to get there. Parking at the store and walking down the public street and across the narrow path by the waterfront homes was not something I enjoyed. Once you got there, the rocks were absolutely treacherous, as my friend Kent Mohnkern experienced when he fell and broke his ribs fishing there with me one day. Most of the time that I went there, I was either alone or with Al. With Al, you felt like you were fishing with the Zen master of the Graveyard and hoped some of it would rub off.

When the tide dropped, Al unhesitatingly waded up and down over the weed-covered rocks, through tidal pools with deep crevices between the ledges, often stumbling into unseen rocks, even though he knew essentially every inch of the Graveyard.

One September day, I made a solo trip to the Graveyard on a tip that the bass fishing had been pretty good. Al must have been working. The tide was especially low that day, and I set my eye on a ledge named Fowler's that was a little farther out than I was normally able to get to. Fowler (whose first name I have forgotten) was a Higgins Beach surfcaster who worked at Fairchild Semiconductor, and he was about seven feet tall. His time at the Graveyard was slightly before mine, and he was famous for wading out to his namesake ledge and fishing from a point that others just couldn't get to.

I got out there on this big tide, though, wet wading to my waist, and began casting. I was standing on the highest point of the ledge, maybe four feet above the water. After casting for a while, I looked seaward and saw a veritable wall of water coming toward me. The surf was generally high that day, but this was the proverbial rogue wave that is often talked about.

I had encountered one when I was a kid, fishing on the bow of my grandfather's lobster boat off the Eastern Egg Rock in Muscongus Bay.

"Look there off the bow," hollered my grandfather. "Hang on tight, boy!"

The bow of the thirty-six-foot *Riptail* stood high in the air and then plunged so far down I was afraid I'd be thrown off into the water. But I wasn't, and that was that.

This situation, though, was another story altogether. There was no question this wave was going to sweep effortlessly over the top of my ledge, submerging it in several feet of rapidly moving green water. In the seconds I had to make a plan, I decided to climb down from the highest rock, lay flat in one of the shallow crevices of the ledge below me, and hold on tight, hoping the wave would simply pass over me. I'd be wet but hopefully unhurt. There was no fear. There wasn't time for that.

I remember the roar of the leading edge of the wave breaking over the ledge, and then I felt the ledge ripped from my grip by a force I simply couldn't resist. I remember a tremendous impact, and I was underwater for a few seconds, and then I came to my feet in waist-deep water about fifteen feet in back of the ledge from which I had just been separated. The wave had ripped me off the ledge and pounded me against the jagged surface of the rocky bottom. My head and chest were both throbbing, and my right knee would barely move. Both hands were bleeding from being scraped over the barnacle-covered ledge, and I had cracked several ribs. My thought was that certainly I was going to die. There was no way to

survive that blow, but I wanted to get closer back to shore so I would easily be found, and at least June would know what had happened to me. They would have a body to bury.

I started stumbling shoreward. After a few steps, I realized my plug was snagged back on the ledge. The plug was a valuable P-40 Atom, but I just kept walking and snapped it off. I tried to wind in the broken line, but I realized the handle of my reel had been broken off when I was swept from the ledge. I continued to slowly head for the shore, one painful step at a time. Soon, though, I found the steps came a little easier, and I realized I might very well live. I haven't thought about that moment in many years, but it actually may have been my last trip to the Graveyard.

Chapter Three

The Kennebec River, Part I

All fishermen know a few people like Paul O'Donnell. If Paul had to give up either fishing or talking about fishing, there would be no contest. As a result, Paul was always picking up information about where the bass fishing was good, what the hot lures or baits were, and gathering details about how to access difficult-to-get-to locations.

At a Portland Surfcaster's meeting, probably during the winter of 1976/77, he told me in a low, confidential tone that a guy named Norm, a Boston firefighter, was catching a lot of big bass in the Kennebec River in Maine. A large number of hard-core striped bass surfcasters are firefighters. The reason probably is that the occupation and the hobby both have crazy hours that to some degree enable each other.

"You know the Kennebec has got to be good," added Paul, "because Norm has access to a cottage on Martha's Vineyard,

and he has fished out there for years, but now he is going up to the Kennebec instead, because the fishing is better than on the Vineyard!"

To me, the Kennebec River was a bit of a mystery. It wasn't all that far from where I grew up in Damariscotta, but I knew nearly nothing about it as a fishing spot. The Kennebec is quite a bit larger than most of Maine's coastal rivers. Rivers such as the Sheepscot, Damariscotta, Medomak, and St. George all represent substantial saltwater wedges that cut ten or fifteen miles inland before reaching the head of tide, where they are all met by a modest-sized freshwater stream or small river. The Kennebec, however, is on an entirely different scale. The Kennebec is tidal for about forty-five miles to Augusta, where it is met by a much larger freshwater source originating in Moosehead Lake, deep within Maine's highlands. It was the Kennebec that Benedict Arnold traveled on the way to besiege Quebec. Twenty miles inland from the mouth, you run into Merrymeeting Bay, a sizable inland tidal freshwater lake. In addition to the Kennebec, which it is really a part of, the Merrymeeting is fed by the Eastern, Cathance, Abagadasset, Muddy, and the larger Androscoggin, which has roots in far northern New Hampshire. The upshot of all this is that the Kennebec, throughout much of its tidal course, is purely fresh water. The fresh water runs as far seaward as a stretch in Bath called Long Reach, where the mixing begins. The river is then brackish for another ten miles or so downriver. Saltwater clams aren't found until just a couple of miles before the mouth.

The Kennebec's great size and its abundance of fresh and brackish water habitat create a large and diverse food chain and a historically abundant variety of all anadromous fish found in Maine. These include rainbow smelts, tomcod, white perch, Atlantic sturgeon, short-nosed sturgeon, Atlantic salmon, alewives, blue back herring, and shad. The river is also a favorite of seasonally visiting filter feeders, such as menhaden and sea herring. Sea herring in particular are abundant in all sizes, and during striper season there is simply not a time when one or another species or several bite-sized oily baitfish isn't present in large numbers. On top of this, the river has historically been a major eel fishery.

Not only do all of these fish and prey species enter the Kennebec to feed and spawn in late spring and summer, but from late August on, the young-of-the-year of many of these species, alewives especially, head down the Kennebec to the sea. The alewife run alone is upwards of three million adult fish coming to spawn. It is hard to estimate the number of the one- to three-inch young alewives that travel down the Kennebec in the early fall on their way to the sea, but it could easily be one hundred million fish or more. The number is simply mind boggling, and there are times when stripers will corner the alewife schools as they head back to the sea and leave the shoreline on a falling tide coated with the silver of their dead bodies.

The Kennebec is also a spawning river for striped bass, and it once was a significant one. By the nineteenth century, the Kennebec had already been severely altered by dams and industrial pollution, C. G. Atkins in 1887 described in *The Fisheries and Fishery Industries of the United States* the extensive under-the-ice fisheries for striped bass that occurred in the Kennebec and Sheepscot Rivers. Atkins observed: "In the winter great numbers of young, 2 or 3 inches long, are found in the rivers, and many of them fall into the bag-nets and are captured along with smelts and tomcods." Interviews with local fishermen cite that striped bass ripe with roe were found in Merrymeeting Bay in early June. Another account tells of a fisherman discovering stripers overwintering in Winnegance Creek, which is at the downriver end of Bath's Long Reach, and taking "tonnes and tonnes" with nets. M. B. Spinney was the area's leading commercial striped bass fisherman, and he reported catching a striped bass that weighed eighty-nine pounds, another that, after dressing, weighed sixty-two and a half pounds, and "hundreds" that weighed over fifty pounds.

In 1976, June and I befriended Kent and Anne Mohnkern from Yarmouth. We vacationed with the Mohnkerns to visit Friendship Sloop Days. While we were there, Kent mentioned an old friend from his days at Bowdoin, Erle Kelly, who was a guide on the Kennebec. Over the last few days, a good run of big stripers had come into the river.

Erle was a semi-local man in that his mother was a Brown from Browns Point, which is in the middle of Merrymeeting

Bay, and she had married a larger-than-life character, Ransom Kelly, who had come to Maine from Massachusetts. Ransom owned and operated the Magnum Tour boat line (which included a converted PT boat) out of Boothbay. In the fall, Ransom outfitted for sea duck hunting on the ocean as well as puddle ducks and geese on Merrymeeting Bay, where he came to own extensive farm fields. Erle had grown up working in his father's businesses, and in the summer he ran the Magnum line's head boat for ground fishing. He really loved fishing.

Unfortunately Erle had a bad heart, and we lost him shortly after Thanksgiving 1978. I went to the funeral at Bowdoin College and his interment ceremony at Bay View Cemetery in Bowdoinham on a miserable cold day, with wind-driven rain from the northeast sweeping in dark sheets across the bay. As rough as it may sound to say, it was a perfect day for Erle's funeral. People were standing by the grave, bundled up against the cold rain, and the bare black limbs of the trees, the ancient stone walls, and the dead brown grass combined with the gloomy gray sky to make the dreariest of scenes. It was the kind of day a Maine duck hunter and fisherman like Erle relished, and it was not an unfitting one on which to say goodbye to him.

I had met Erle in the fall of 1976 at a party at the Mohnkerns, and Erle and I had to really work at not monopolizing each other's time with striper talk. Erle was three or four years older than I, and he had spent the years that I fished Damariscotta and the Sheepscot fishing Merrymeeting Bay, the Kennebec, and the Sasanoa, which connects the Kennebec and the Sheepscot Rivers. Erle was one of a number of Mainers I've met over the years who caught their first striper at the ledges near Averill's cottage across from the Reversing Falls.

I kept track of Erle's fishing on the Kennebec that summer through Kent, and Erle was landing a good number of large fish. The next spring I received a call from Erle, who was a schoolteacher in Wiscasset during the offseason. He had a cancelation just before Labor Day and asked if I would like to book it. In 1977, Erle's fee for a day of guided fishing was seventy-five dollars, which I saw as an incredible bargain. I still have one of Erle's business cards, maybe from that year. Erle's sports caught 37 tackle buster fish in 1977. A Maine tackle buster striped bass is at least twenty-five pounds or forty-two inches long.

We fished our way down the Kennebec that morning, beginning at Fisher's Eddy, then the Flat Top Cottage, the Hump, Green Point, and Ram Island, including Lower Unit City. Anglers would anchor near the tip of a long ledge leading out from Ram Island, and they were sometimes treated to spectacular boat crashes of partiers recklessly trying to cut between the anglers at the tip of the ledge and the island, some two hundred feet distant. Some boats might make it, but sometimes an outboard just didn't clear the ledge.

We then dropped down to the twin ledges of Goat Island and on to Bald Head Flats and the Crow Islands. We either made a quick cast or two at each spot or Erle gave me a verbal tutorial as we idled by. Eventually we reached Pond Island, set on the west side of the mouth of the river. We trolled Gibbs Trolling Swimmers on rods and reels Erle had set up with lead-core line. The best spot, according to Erle, was fairly high up, near the top of the rip. He was absolutely right, and later on I learned that place so well that I could call a strike about to happen within seconds.

"Hold on tight," I'd tell whoever was with me, and while they were laughing, the rod would almost come out of their hands.

Pond Island tide rip was to be the site of my catching two sixty-two-pound stripers, one in 1979 and the other in 1982.

But we didn't catch a fish on the day Erle showed me the spot, but I must have liked the Kennebec a lot, because it became the focus of a great deal of my fishing activity for the next twenty years.

The time when I fished the Kennebec can be divided into two distinct periods. The first was from 1978 to about 1990, and the second was from this 1990 until 2002. The first period was dominated by a large but declining number of really big stripers and the beginnings of the eventual recovery of the Chesapeake Bay striper population that was characterized by steadily increasing numbers of small fish. In the second period there were very few really large bass in the Kennebec, but a rapidly increasing number of bass of all sizes was created by the tremendous conservation measures invoked up and down the coast.

The second period is the one that the Kennebec became famous for, and we'll talk about it in considerable depth a little later. The first period was the aftermath of individual fish from the consistently producing Chesapeake Bay striped bass year classes of the 1950s and 1960s eventually reaching large sizes and then dying off. Some of those fish were undoubtedly the brethren of the fish I had pursued around the Damariscotta and Sheepscot during my schoolboy days.

Stripers grow to different maximum sizes and have different growth rates, but generally speaking a five-year-old is about twenty-four inches and five or six pounds. A ten-year old fish is about thirty-six inches and twenty pounds, and a fifteen-year-old fish is about fifty inches and fifty pounds. Stripers do, though, live to be well over twenty years old, and it was very likely that many of the big bass I caught in the Kennebec during the late 1970s and early 1980s had first migrated to Maine when I began to fish for striped bass in the 1960s.

My first trips to the Kennebec were in a 22-2 Aquasport. I even used it for that first trip with Erle. What a boat that was! In many ways, it was the perfect striped bass fishing machine. I kept it on a trailer and used it to fish Old Orchard, the Kennebec, and also took it out of Portland on some ground fishing trips. Boats, when you're young, though, create their own disease. You are always looking for one that is a little better or a little bigger. You know the fish don't care if you are in a row boat or a Bertram, but deep down you think you will catch more fish in an upgraded boat or at least look better in it while trying.

I sold that Aquasport in the fall of 1978 to George Watson, my closest longtime fishing friend. We scheduled a day on the Kennebec in September for me to give George some instruction and to try a little fishing. As luck would have it, that was the best day I ever had on the river, which I was just getting to know, and we landed four or five twenty- to thirty-pound class stripers. I began looking for a new boat right away.

I've forgotten how I heard about the used 240 Aquasport Sea Hunter model, but it was in winter storage over at Hancock Marine on the New Meadows. It was love at first sight, and I bought it on the day I saw it.

The Sea Hunter had a long spray hood that I kept up all the time, and molded-in lockers on each side of the boat that doubled as cushioned bunks. The small console was on the starboard side of the boat, and it was powered by a 165 MerCruiser inboard/outboard. The Sea Hunter was heavier and better riding than the 22-2, and the four-cycle engine was miserly with fuel. You couldn't just walk around the boat in a circle like you could the 22-2, but this was before my fly-fishing days, and I didn't mind being restricted to the back of the boat.

I bought a trailer for the boat, but the whole setup was too much for me to enjoy dragging it all. I was able to get a mooring at Burgess Marine on the south end of Long Reach for seventy-five dollars per year. You needed to supply your own dinghy, which was kept at the dock and rowed out to where the boat was moored.

I had met John Cole, the author of *Striper* and several other excellent fishing books published by Nick Lyons. On John's first fishing trip with me, we walked onto that dock and stopped in front of the dinghy. John looked warily at me.

"Is this your boat?" he asked with some trepidation as he scanned the seven-foot rowboat.

I laughed and pointed out at the twenty-four-foot Aquasport. "No, this is just for me to row out to that boat."

"Thank God!" he muttered and wiped his face nervously with the red bandana he always kept in his pocket.

As a newbie to Burgess, I was low on the totem pole, and my boat *The Sea Beagle III* was moored about a hundred feet off the dock and another hundred feet or so upriver. This was a really rough mooring spot. The Kennebec is a fast-running river, and at larger tides the water is full of floating grass and even trees coming down from its huge freshwater drainage. It was by no means unusual to arrive at your boat and find a big limb and a ton of grass on your anchor line. If the tide was running hard, it was very difficult to pull up enough slack on the anchor line to unhook it from the boat.

On top of that, the row out to the boat was itself often quite an adventure. I would row out alone, leaving any guests on the dock, because rowing the dinghy with a second person was almost impossible going into the current. To get there even alone required that I row up-current through the back eddy close to the shoreline until I was parallel to the *Sea Beagle*. Then I angled rapidly out into the flow, still rowing upstream at about forty-five degrees. Once I got to the boat, I had a split second to ship the oars and grab the coaming on the side of the boat before I was swept downstream and had to do it all over again. Some days it was very easy, and some it was a bit of an adventure, but it all worked out okay for a few seasons. And then a piece of land came up for sale across the river, and I bought it and built my own dock and float.

Starting at a time of great scarcity for striped bass had its benefits. As good a fisherman as Erle was, he was seldom or never on the river when he wasn't guiding. For one thing, he came down to the big striper grounds in the lower river every day from his house on the tip of Browns Point, upriver in Merrymeeting Bay. This was a run of about twelve miles each way, and if he needed to run to the mouth to fish there, it amounted to more like twenty miles. So Earle really only fished when he had a charter, and he took his charters to his proven spots so they had the highest likelihood of catching a fish.

When it comes to fishing of all sorts, I have always had a bit of wanderlust. I'm always curious as to how the fishing is down the shoreline a little farther. If the fishing is hot, I see it as an opportunity to find some new fishing spots. If you only look around when the best spots aren't producing, you aren't very likely to find anything biting anywhere. When I started to seriously fish the Kennebec, the fishing wasn't that good, but I had the energy of youth, curiosity, and a burning desire to learn the river. It wasn't unusual for me to leave my office early Friday afternoon, drive to Bath, fish the Kennebec well into the night, anchor up in a quiet spot for a few hours of sleep, and get back into action before light the next morning. I loved to lay there on one of the *Sea Beagle*'s bunks, listening to the wind blowing and the waves lapping against the hull, always hoping to hear fish jumping.

I'd get home on Saturday, a little sleep-deprived and windburned, but I was just thirty years old. I mowed the grass, took June to the Clambake for dinner, and collapsed early in bed. I was up again, though, at two in the morning and on my way back to the Kennebec for another morning of fishing.

In those first years on the Kennebec, the late 1970s and early 1980s, there were few others on the water. There were some old-timers, though those who were left were very disgruntled with the small numbers of remaining fish and didn't put in a lot of time. Still, there were a few, and I took careful note of the spots they regularly fished. Even Erle didn't know all the good spots. I would study the charts and try to understand why an angler had picked a particular spot to fish and at what point in the tide. I'd check back on the angler from time to time, and eventually I learned what it was that made that spot productive.

One of my old business mentors, Charlie Locke, used to say, "There is a season for all investments, but no investment for all seasons." Striped bass fishing in a river is like that. There is a place for all stages of the tide, but no one place that is good at all stages. There are some places, though, that regularly produce over a much longer time frame than others. The Hump is one of those places.

Erle didn't really have a name for the Hump that I can recall, though he was the one who showed it to me. He just said that there was a shoal spot here that often produced fish. Erle fished it by anchoring up there as the upstream current of the flood tide began to come to a stop. He then fished the place for an hour or so, until the current started to firmly move downriver. At that time, he would pick up anchor and move over to the end of Ram Island's Lower Unit City and anchor up again.

I think Erle anchored mostly because of the difficulty many anglers had handling their tackle in the hard-running Kennebec River, where current speeds are frequently in excess of three knots, and because you could only lift your anchor off the bottom during the strongest flow of the tide with Herculean effort. The huge size of the Kennebec, which in many places is nearly a mile across, combined with the large amount of fresh water entering the river from the different sources, and the fact that, while the tides are not in a class with the Bay of Fundy rivers, they are still substantial. This also meant the tide changes direction at different times and in different places all over the river. And this meant that Erle could move from one place to another through most of his time on the river and put his sport in a place where the current was still running gently and the fishing was comfortable.

In my early days on the Kennebec, I frequently anchored up near the Hump at the same time Erle and his sports were there. I was always very careful to give them all the room in the world. There just weren't a lot of fish present in the late 1970s and early 1980s, and as you sat there at anchor, it often seemed as if there wasn't a fish anywhere in the system—except for sturgeon.

The Kennebec had a good population of both short-nosed and Atlantic sturgeon, and for whatever reason, these fish love to breach, just launching themselves several feet out of the water and then falling back like a big log. Locals called this "spanking." It wasn't unusual to be anchored on the Hump during a foggy, completely silent morning when, all of a sudden, a ten-foot-long Atlantic sturgeon would rise out of the river twenty-five feet away. The sturgeon were so close you could see every aspect of their bony, prehistoric face and eyes. They had a completely blank expression as they hung in midair for a second before landing on the surface. The big ones made a terrific wallop when they landed that scared the crap out of me more than once.

Even though there were none of the surface schooling stripers that so characterized the Kennebec striper fishery by the late 1980s, as the incoming tide came to an end and the currents began to slack, we would usually have some contact with striped bass. At the top of the flood tide, the surface of the Kennebec begins to change. With the decreasing current speed, the areas of rip tide occurring near points of land or narrow areas of the river calm down. Long, meandering tide lines snake across the surface here and there. These lines are formed by the current flowing in one direction and meeting current flowing in the other.

Anchored at the hump as the beginning of the ebb tide approaches, you can see the tide line downriver from the boat gradually moving in your direction. If you were to look at the water level on the shoreline, you would see it has already begun to drop. As the line approaches the boat, you can see the line itself is the intersection of two broad sheets of water, one headed downriver to fill the dropping water level caused by the tide that has now been pouring out for two hours at Fort Popham, and the other in the final momentum of the current that has been pushed inland for the past five hours or so.

That's right! About five hours, not six, since while the ocean in the area rises and falls in six-hour intervals, that is not so with the Kennebec. Here the millions of gallons of fresh water pouring in from the upper Kennebec and Androscoggin Rivers have to get out to sea, along with the normal dropping tidal salt waters, and the pressure is enough to change the amount of time the river must flow in each direction.

It is at this time, when the tide is slowing up to change direction, that the stripers are most likely to leave the river bottom where they have been waiting for prey in a layer of water slowed by the friction of its rubbing against the riverbed, and they swim freely until the new direction picks up sufficient speed to motivate them to take up a new lie facing in the opposite direction. During this period, shoals of baitfish will attempt to hide in the surface film of the water, and the bass will rise up and try to catch them, leaving big swirls and splashes and revealing their fins and big striped sides as they chase the herring and menhaden.

Eventually the tide line reaches the boat and passes it. If there is no wind, the boat will swing around on the anchor line and trail downriver. For a short while, just before that, though, the current underneath the surface will continue to flow upriver before giving up its futile push and joining forces with the outgoing tide that is already flowing downriver along the bottom.

It was at this period of upheaval that Erle and his clients were most likely to catch a bass. Sometimes the strike would come on a plug being cast by one of the sports, generally a large surface popping plug. A Rebel Windcheater was a favorite of the day, but more often a bass would pick up one of the eels being fished at the bottom on the end of a three-way rig.

Erle always had a tightly tied burlap bag floating in the water beside his boat. It was the perfect live well for eels that, unlike menhaden and even more so mackerel, require very little water circulation to live. When you wanted to go fast, you just picked up the burlap bag and set it inside the boat. As long as they are damp, the eels can breathe out of water for a long time, and the wet burlap kept them both cool and damp. One just had to remember to pick up the bag when you started to move. Burlap bags won't hold up long when they're dragged across the surface of the water at twenty knots, and eels can find even the tiniest hole and quickly escape. I lost my eel supply that way more than once.

It was on just such a tide change that I had my first good striped bass fishing on the *Sea Beagle III*. After we bought the boat, I spent late April and early May weekends at the New Meadows Marina getting the boat into shape. As I recall, it hadn't been used during the last year when Gordon Hentz from Harpswell, Maine, had owned it. The boat just needed to be cleaned and waxed, the teak oiled, and all the running gear to be sorted out a bit. I've kept a fair fishing log for many years, but 1979 was the beginning of that log, though I didn't write anything about our first trip down the New Meadows and around Cape Small to the Kennebec—but I remember it as if it were yesterday.

It was around the third week in May, which in midcoastal Maine can still mean almost wintery conditions if the weather isn't in your favor and you have a little easterly direction in the wind. It was too early for stripers, especially since there were essentially no schoolie bass in those years, and they are the ones that arrive first. In all my years on the Kennebec, I only landed large stripers before June 10 on a couple of occasions. We had heard, though, that the lower New Meadows River had some good winter flounder fishing, and Lou Zglobicki was with me that day, and he could never get enough of any kind of sinker bouncing. He brought along some sea worms, but we were so intent on navigating out of the unfamiliar New Meadows that we never wet a line.

The mouth of the river was rough, with a cold, easterly wind, and we decided to keep moving and get inside the Kennebec. Once there we decided to try flounder fishing in Stage Island Bay. I had no idea if the fishing would be any good there or not. Even though it was just on the other side of a small island from the mouth of the Kennebec, I had never been there or fished it, but on the charts it had all the right attributes, according to Lou, who, in his formative years of fishing in New Jersey, had been well educated in Barnegat Bay flounders.

We had scheduled our trip out of the New Meadows and into the Kennebec to coincide with high tide because this gave us the biggest safety margin from rocks in unfamiliar waters and because the mouth of the Kennebec can be downright treacherous if a wind from the east or south meets a falling tide. We got through that just fine, though, and then we motored around the east side of Stage Island and into Stage Island Bay. The bay is a little more than a quarter mile across, separating Stage Island from Salter Island. The places are named after their part in the historic salt cod industry on the coast of Maine where cod were dried on platforms (called flakes or stages) and salted for preservation. At its inshore end, Stage Island Bay continues a fair distance inland, gradually shallowing until it becomes mudflats at low tide.

We chose a spot roughly parallel with the middle of the island, and at this very early point in the dropping tide, the depth was about twenty-five feet. Over went the *Sea Beagle*'s anchor, down went a chum pot full of cracked clams, and down went our hooks baited with bits of Lou's sea worms.

The short of it is that the action was simply fantastic. We were fishing with a couple of Lou's New Jersey flounder specials that featured snelled-on Chestertown hooks dressed up with a couple of corn-colored plastic beads. If you waited for a second or two after feeling the first bump, you inevitably had a double, and these were fat, thick flounders the size of a large dinner plate. My God, they were lovely!

After we brought in the first few flounders, something much heavier grabbed onto one of the rigs and started pulling line out against the drag. A few minutes later I gaffed a codfish of about fifteen pounds and swung it into the boat. It was about ten flounders to the codfish, but that was still very good cod fishing. Everything went into a big garbage barrel that became my live well when the herring, menhaden, and mackerel showed up later in the summer.

We hadn't been fishing forty-five minutes when I told Lou the live well was half full. As it was, we would be cleaning fish for a long time once we got home.

"We'd better knock it off," I suggested.

There was real pain on Lou's face as he pulled himself away from the fishing.

We went another time or two that May or early June, and the results were the same. The next season, though, the fishing was about half as good, and the year after that the flounder were all but gone. You could spend half a tide out there and maybe catch one or two or maybe get skunked. I haven't tried in twenty-five years, but I'm told it has never recovered. No one can tell you with any certainty how they disappeared in such a short time, but it happened more or less simultaneously all along the New England coast.

1979: Aboard the *Sea Beagle*

On the evening of June 29, 1979, Al Emmons was fishing with me on the *Sea Beagle*, and at the beginning of the dropping tide, we motored into a big cove called Fisher's Eddy. On my first trip to the Kennebec, Erle had told me this was a good place on the early drop. A large creek entered a big marshy cove on the east side of the river. From where this creek came out, you could look downriver and see the Flat Top Cottage, the Hump, Green Point, Ram Island, and Lower Unit City. They were really all part of a large habitat that was perhaps a mile and a half long. I'm quite confident that when the water temperature and prey species (largely herring of all sizes) are present here in June and early July, the bass just moved around this area from one feeding station to the next with the rise and fall of the tide and the resulting changes in current flow.

There was a dock in Fisher's Eddy, and there was seldom a boat anywhere near it. When I'd finally get too tired at night to continue fishing, I'd sometimes pull into the float with my lights out and tie up for a couple of hours' sleep. There was an old farmhouse overlooking the eddy, but if the occupants saw me pull in, they never bothered me.

I had caught a striper or two at Fisher's Eddy by casting popping plugs into the creek mouth on the early drop, but I'd never done really well there. This day, though, as Al and I turned the corner around Bluff Head to pull into the cove, I could see the boils on the surface made by a whole school of big stripers. The fish were strung out here and there along a hundred yards or so of the marshy shoreline, so it was a pretty fair bunch of fish, and they were big. Really big! I know from my later education of seeing surface-feeding cow stripers that many of these were over forty pounds. It was also the first school of stripers I had yet seen on the Kennebec and probably the largest congregation of big bass I ever witnessed. For me, it was practically a religious experience.

These fish were feeding on the surface, and they let us get well within casting range. I shut the motor down (which may have been a mistake, as I learned later chasing bass in this same place), and Al and I began casting plugs into the feeding fish. We tried every conceivable plug type on these fish, along with varied retrieves and any tricks we could think of, but we never even had a follow.

Three days later, on July 2, I was anchored up at the Hump at the top of the incoming tide just after dawn. As the current slowed and the tide line began to approach the boat, I could hear the pop of feeding stripers knocking bait with their broad tails. There was a small group of fish, very likely an offshoot of the big school Al and I had seen at Fisher's Eddy. I considered picking up the anchor, starting the engine, and motoring over to them, but in a moment of uncommon patience I decided to wait, since I thought the tide line might bring them right to me. And it did. I landed and released two bass, both around twenty-eight pounds. After the last fish was landed, the tide was moving steadily downriver and the surface action was over. I put away the spinning rod, pulled up the anchor, and started trolling the underwater ridge of which the Hump was the shallowest part.

After you left the Hump, heading upriver, there was a comparatively deep section that went on for a couple of hundred yards, and you then came to an interesting little complex that we called the Flat Top Cottage after a little 1950s California-styled ranch house that sat just a few yards from the shore. In front of the cottage, running straight out into the river for about two hundred feet, was what I always believed were the remains of an old dock. It was a mystery to us as to why it was there. There was no natural resource area of any consequence—lumber, granite, and ice were the historical merchandise shipped out of the Kennebec, which had been a center of coastal commerce in the days of sail. And the flat top was well down on Arrowsic Island, nowhere near the commercial center of Bath. Nonetheless the dock was there. You could see the structure clearly on the fish finder, and once, when I tried to anchor there, I got my rope back fouled with creosote, which was commonly used to coat dock pilings. After many years underwater, there was still a strong and unmistakable smell. On the dropping tide you might catch a bass anywhere along the ridge of that dock, but the very outer end was the prime spot.

When I reached the top of the old dock out in front of the Flat Top, I turned the wheel over to port and let the *Sea Beagle* stem the tide, dragging the lures all along the ridge of the structure. I hadn't gone far when a bass of about thirty-five pounds nearly tore the rod from my hands. It was the last fish I was to get that morning, but I had landed three big stripers in that day on my new boat, and I was a very happy soul.

I'm looking at the fishing log I kept at that time, and though it was forty-one years ago, I can remember the day and my emotions very clearly, right down to the pen strokes I made to record the information. After I caught that last fish, I decided to quit on a winning note and headed back up along the shoreline in front of the Flat Top. It was 8:00 a.m., according to my log, and the morning was sunny and warm, with just a little breeze from the southwest. It was the beginning of high summer in Maine, birds were singing and flying around the little lawn in front of the camp, and the rip line just beginning to form sparkled in the sunshine. It was a perfect day, and I knew then, even though I was just twenty-nine years old, that there would never be enough days like this one. I leaned back in the seat of the *Sea Beagle* and tried to let it sink in. And thankfully I was reasonably successful.

I also noted in my old log that I was trolling a Danny plug behind an umbrella rig and fishing with lead-core line. All of this started with Erle, who used lead core for his trolling to get near the bottom. I had very little experience with umbrella rigs, but they were all the rage at that time. This particular rig just had four tubes, one at the end of each cross of wire. There were no hooks on the tubes, since I planned to use them as attractors. The plug was fastened to about four feet of fifty-pound test mono running out of the center of the rig. When I pulled this rig out and showed it to Erle, he thought it was terrific, and so it became my standard trolling rig. The first evolution, though, was to get rid of the umbrella part. It was just awkward and required too much work and worry to keep it from getting fouled up, especially if you were fishing alone. Besides this, I often trolled two rods, and I noticed I got just as many hits on the rod without the umbrella.

The second evolution my trolling rig began with a change in my preferred brand of trolling plug. The plug maker's name was Danny Pichney, and he was a machinist from New York City who lived with his mother. One of my fishing pals, Fred Thurber from Rhode Island, got to know Danny and made regular visits there to buy plugs from him. I placed my orders with Fred, and I still have some original Dannys new in their original wrappers; they have become a sort of striper fishing cult collectible. The funniest part of the story was that Fred told me that Danny made the wooden plugs for a hobby and to make a little extra money. This was in the mid-1990s, and Danny told Fred he did a lot of striper fishing, mostly in the East River, and that all he used anymore were rubber lures. Danny thought they were much more effective than plugs!

The trolling plug that Erle used was the Gibbs Trolling Swimmer. Erle had the modern design that is still made today. Prior to the mid-1970s, Stan Gibbs made the plug with a long, thin tail. Both of these designs worked fine being trolled out in Cape Cod Bay near Stan's home in Sagamore, but in fast water the plug would turn upside down and skate back and forth.

An article appeared in *The Fisherman Magazine* by Charley Soares about fishing the Danny Plug in the Elizabeth Islands, southwest of Cape Cod, and around that time Lupo Lures began making and selling the Danny Plug, I assume under license from Danny. These plugs had a long, flat, planed top that made them more stable in fast water. It isn't that the bass were to be found in fast water so much as that, when you are trolling, there are times during your pattern, such as when you're moving across a rip, when you may hit water that is much faster than at other times, and you don't want your plug to go swinging wildly around or flip over and rise to the surface.

In any case, I bought a couple of the Lupo Dannys, and it immediately became my plug of choice. Years later, at Martha's Vineyard and Block Island, we fished the flat-faced casting version of this plug, called the Casting Swimmer, along with another heavier version called the Conrad. We also used a special Danny-made stubby needlefish that produced very well when the bass were feeding on sand eels along the beaches.

The next evolution of my trolling kit was to replace the lead core with single-strand stainless wire. The lead core was fat and used a lot of space on the Penn Squidder reels that I trolled with. Also, from time to time, a big bass would get part of a ledge between the two of you, and this could instantly cut off the lead-core braided line. I replaced the lead core with 100 feet of fifty-pound test stainless wire, and I filled the rest of the reel with fifty-pound test Ande pink monofilament for backing. The total amount of line on that setup probably wasn't over 125 yards, but I never had a fish get to the bottom of the reel, and that included quite a few bass over fifty pounds. I put 15 feet of the same monofilament from the wire line out to a big snap swivel that attached to the plug. I replaced the leather drag washers every year in the Squidder, because the heat would burn them up. Then an aftermarket maker started to offer Teflon drag washers, and that was the end of the problem.

On July 5, 1979, I caught another thirty-five-pound striper on a pencil popper, and on July 7 I got one of the same size trolling a Danny a little farther downriver between the twin ledges at Goat Island. Those five fish, the smallest being twenty-eight pounds, were my entire catch for the first half of the Kennebec striper season, and I was over there most of the time for about three weeks.

The fall fishing, though, was a bit more productive. On September 8 I landed two stripers at Earle's old spot down at Pond Island on a minus 1.9-foot low tide. The current was really roaring around the corner on the north end of the island that day. The first one was thirty-five pounds, and the second was fifty-three inches long, and on our brass Chatillon scale it weighed sixty-two pounds. The thing I remember most about that fish was that it was pristine. Some of the larger fish, which have been swimming around for twenty years or so have beat-up fins, healed-over wounds, jaw hinges ripped by gill nets, etc. This creature, though, was absolutely perfect! The body had a classic filled-out shape, the eyes were huge, and the violet colors in its sides were striking. We never had a camera aboard in those days, and after ogling the fish for a second or two, back in it went.

The next day the tide was still a minus 1.6-foot tide, and we again caught two bass. One was thirty-five pounds, and the other was fifty inches long and weighed fifty pounds on the nose.

I caught my last Kennebec fish that fall on September 23. I ended my season that day by catching three large bass, the same as I had begun it on July 2. The first was trolled up down at Pond Island with a Danny Plug behind a red umbrella rig. The fish was weaker than any others I had on the line that summer, and I was relieved to see that instead of being sick or injured, it was relatively small at about fifteen pounds. The other two that day were thirty-five and thirty-eight pounds, and my catching them was a testament to what I had learned that summer.

I recorded every large striper I caught in my logbook by writing the number caught that day and circling it in the margins. This was nothing fancy, but it kept a clear record, and it was a total of seventeen large stripers for the season. That was five in July—the first on July 2—and twelve in September. And I put in a pile of hours to catch those fish.

For the last couple of weekends I had spent a lot of time three-waying eels at a place called Bald Head Flats. A three-way rig has a three-way swivel—a small ring with three places to tie on a line, all of which can swivel. This prevents the line from twisting. You attach your fishing line to one swivel, a sinker to the next, and then a short line and baited hook on the third. Bald Head Flats was another spot Erle had shown me. The flats were comprised of a long stretch of essentially level muddy bottom punctuated by an occasional patch of rocky bottom. Earle told me it was a good producer on the dropping tide, but I later learned the fish could show up there on any tide. When the bass established a pattern of showing up at a certain stage of the tide, they seemed to repeat it for a period of time, and then that pattern would end.

On September 16, I fished the flats by three-waying a live eel and a three-ounce lead sinker. At 8:30 that morning, after a small eight-foot-high tide an hour earlier, the current on the flats turned to go out on the surface while it was still slowly flowing upstream, low in the water column. In the space of a half hour, I landed a forty-eight- and a forty-six-inch bass. These fish were fat from a summer of feeding without a lot of competition, and they both had to weigh well over forty pounds. The thirty-five and thirty-eight pounders I caught the next weekend were taken in the same area at the exact same stage in the tide. I was the only boat in sight. There is simply no substitute for putting in your time.

My notes for the 1979 season in review said that some small bass were said to have been taken in the Saco and the Androscoggin early in June, but they were few and irregular in their appearance. Nineteen seventy-nine would prove for me to be the lowest point in the curve for the population of small striped bass. For all practical purposes there were none. Even a fifteen pounder, the smallest I caught all year, was not much more than half the weight of the next smallest one I caught. Not only were there no small bass on the horizon, but the ones we were catching were all big, old fish that were ten years or more in age. It was apparent that if the current trend continued, bass fishing was going to end within a very few years.

Also, a pattern emerged that I learned repeated itself again and again over the years. Even in their reduced state, bass were evident in the Phippsburg area of the Kennebec up until the middle of July. After that, they seemed to disappear, but then they returned again with the cooler nights and shortening days of late August and early September. During the warmest part of the summer, the bass spent most of their time on the beaches, and in later years I learned some of the places where they regularly hung out.

Chapter Four

The Kennebec River, Part II

1980: A Flicker of Hope

What many of us weren't aware of, because we just weren't following those things yet, was that the 1978 class of striped bass in Chesapeake Bay, while not a dominant year class, was nearly average by historical standards. It's bay-wide geometric mean count of 3.75 had broken a chain of declining years that began in 1971, and it would be eleven years before it was matched or beaten—though 1982 came close at 3.57.

    I spent the weekend of May 30, 1980, on Martha's Vineyard with my fishing pal Phil Perrino. I'll get back to that trip in a couple of paragraphs. I was relatively new to fishing the Vineyard, but I had a friend, Coop Gilkes, who became an important part of my bass fishing life for many years. Coop would be a good candidate for the world's friendliest man, and like a lot of commercial fishermen, Coop was just plain fish savvy.

I remember going bonito fishing with Coop in the mid-1980s. He was running a tackle shop by that time, and he had sold out of sand eels.

"Let's go try for some bonito," he said, "and we'll get some bait for the shop while we're at it."

Every move Coop made when it came to fishing was efficient. Every activity was a well-rehearsed and, in his own way, well-organized routine. He needed his beach seine and a fish box to put the sand eels in. These were right outside the back door to the shop, where he had dropped them the last time he used them. Rods and reels were permanently sitting, regardless of the weather, outdoors in some console-mounted rod holders in the seventeen-foot Boston Whaler that Coop had won in a bass tournament a few years before. Absolutely nothing was maintained well or neatly organized in a conventional sense, but unlike the anal-retentive types who had every little thing properly marked, organized in little plastic bags, and cleaned and oiled to the manufacturer's specifications, Coop's gear was used a lot, and it caught lots of fish. That is what he concentrated on.

Coop didn't live vicariously through expensive fishing tackle, even though he had expensive tackle. He knew what good stuff was, but he didn't waste a second fawning over it. He focused on the fishing and grabbed his tackle from the last place he left it, which was usually somewhere along the path to his boat or truck.

When you fished with Coop, he was always a step or two ahead of your thinking when it came to observe a situation and fine-tune his technique. On this day we jumped into his unkempt truck, dragged the whaler down to the launching spot, and within no more than fifteen minutes from when he said, "Let's go fishing," we had launched the whaler in Edgartown harbor and were running south along the outside of Cape Poge. Without talking about it back in the shop, Coop's mind had already calculated the wind, tide, and visibility for this moment.

A minute or so south of the lighthouse, we pulled in close to the beach, and Coop ran the boat right on top of the curl of the wave closest to the beach. East Beach is a back beach in most winds, and the waves are normally very small. The visibility was terrific, and suddenly we were in a dense school of what appeared in the bright September sunlight to be long, thin shards from a broken mirror. In a second we passed the school, and Coop softly said they were sand eels as he hauled back the throttle and turned the boat in toward the beach. A split second later, Coop jumped out of the boat in his hip boots and held the boat in the wash of the gentle East Beach surf.

"Get out here, Brad, and hold this end of the net," he said.

Coop hopped back into the low-sided whaler and payed out the net, then he ran back outside the wash and into the tide, running along the beach for a short distance. A few seconds later the boat was back on the beach, bobbing in the wash, and Coop was walking it down the beach while hauling in the net. As Coop got close to me, I could see the cloud of fish gathering frantically ahead of him as their swim area became smaller with every step.

"Grab that fish box," said Coop, who had taken my end of the net along with his end. "Hold it right there."

With a truly rugged heave, the net, complete with leads and a good many pounds of sand eels, stuffed itself into the fish box. Coop then lifted the box, with water pouring out its drain holes, and placed the whole thing into the boat. I occasionally tried over the years to guess what that box must have weighed. Whatever it was, it was a lot.

A minute or so later we were anchored in the strong current flowing down East Beach with a couple of sand eels dangling off the back for bait. The Whaler had a little semi-self-bailing well with a plug in the back. Coop pulled the plug and water washed in and out as the boat went up and down in the swell. He placed a handful of dead sand eels in the well, and every time some water washed through the well (which it did regularly), it also washed some sand eels out the back, chumming the water.

Coop flashed a smile at me and said, "That's my secret weapon."

It worked like a dream, and we caught more fish than anybody out there that day.

In 1980, after we got off the ferry from Woods Hole, Phil Perrino and I checked into an Edgartown motel, and after unloading the few things that weren't fishing gear, we drove over to Coop's tackle shop for the latest word on the fishing.

There were some big bass being taken out at Wasque Rip, according to Coop, but the exciting news was that for the last couple of mornings, guys had been taking a few school bass at the big bridge over Sengekontacket Pond, from the shore on the inside. Coop was excited because he knew there was no future for striped bass fishing and his whole way of life without small fish, and just as we hadn't seen any in Maine for the last few years, neither had he. Phil and I managed to get a couple of great bass during that trip from the mussel bar at Squibnocket Beach, but we didn't get any schoolies.

Before the next weekend I had word that school bass had shown up in the Kennebec around Sasanoa Point and in plain sight of the old Bath Bridge. I was up there early on a Saturday morning, June 7, with Phil and Wes Eayers of the Portland Surfcasters. Wes was sick with cancer, but his symptoms at the time were largely contained to low energy, as long as he was getting regular blood dialysis. Wes was by strong preference a shore fisherman, and he spent most of his fishing time either on the Saco River or at the Graveyard. He was excited, though, to be fishing the Kennebec on that day and to be in the relative comfort of a twenty-four-foot boat. It was also possible he'd have a chance at tagging some school stripers, and that was something he hadn't had much opportunity to do in recent years.

We had a bonanza. On the dropping tide, the small bass pinned pods of young sea herring against the rocky shoreline of Sasanoa Point, directly across the river from the mammoth destroyers moored in front of the Bath Iron Works. The point divides the Kennebec from the Sasanoa, and the area where the current piles directly onto the rocky shoreline makes a perfect killing ground for the predatory stripers. There were small pods of bass chasing herring on the surface here and there over a quarter mile stretch of shoreline. The silver bodies of dead sardine-sized herring littered the rocks as the tide dropped. Later on, as Hanson Bay and the flats on both sides of the Sasanoa began to drain, the action moved into the center of the channel. Wes was regularly tagging striped bass for close to three hours, and he was overjoyed with it all.

I never got to fish with Wes again, though. His cancer progressed beyond being manageable, and soon after that he dropped everything he was involved in, including his work as the state chairman of a new government organization, the Citizens Advisory Committee for Striped Bass (CACSB). The group was funded by Senator John Chafee from Rhode Island's striped bass amendment to the Migratory Fish Act, and it required some reporting, meetings, and occasional out-of-state meetings. Chafee had been motivated to add the special funding for striped bass work because an old classmate from Yale, author John Cole, convinced him that striped bass were in serious trouble.

When he saw my intense interest in the fish, Wes asked me to take over for him, and later that fall he passed away. The CACSB started me on a path into volunteer fishery advocacy work that consumed a measurable percentage of my time and energy for the next fifty years, and striped bass were always at the center of it. The battle to see striped bass managed as game fish—meaning no commercial fishing—is an old tale and it is a fascinating one.

Many of the best, worst, and most interesting people I have met in my life came from what another old comrade-in-arms, Dick Russell, called the Striper Wars (also the title of his 2005 book). I have letters from Dick dating back to the early 1980s, and he came to visit and interview me when he was writing that book.

After many lean years, 1980 presented us with the first fishing for small stripers in a long time. The schoolies had always arrived in the lower Kennebec two to three weeks ahead of the larger fish. That, too, was the case in 1980, even though the schoolies had been essentially absent for the last five or six years, and I got my first large fish of the season on June 21, three weeks after the small bass had arrived in the Kennebec.

On that day I caught three big stripers; one of which weighed forty-nine pounds. I remember that fish well, so let me digress with a little story about it. It was hooked in a similar way to many others I caught on swimming plugs. Frequently the bass turn on the baitfish and take them head-first. I assume this allows large baits with large spiny fins to easily slide down their throats. The line attached to the plug, though, keeps the plug from going inside their mouth. That means the bass are often hooked in the corner of the mouth, the jaw hinge, by the most forward treble hook on the plug. Not infrequently, though, that will mean that, during the fight, the other hooks on the plug will thrash around as the plug changes direction and snags the fish in the side of the head. When the bass again changes direction, this can turn the angle of the pull 180 degrees, and the poorly set hooks on the plug come under a lot of strain.

I've seen big stripers landed that were hooked on just one hook of a three-hook plug and the other two were simply gone, ripped right off the plug. I've also seen them still attached to the plug—without the fish—and twisted beyond recognition as a fishing hook. After all these years, I still have the big treble hook from a deep-diving Danny plug that was stuck in the gill plate of that forty-nine-pounder when I landed it. I hand it to people and challenge them to try to bend it back into shape. I don't believe that the human being lives who can straighten out the thick, rugged wire of that treble with his bare hands.

My friend, the late Tom Lazor, owned the Eel Skin Inn in Nantucket, a collection of nailed-together scallop-shucking shacks on a sandy finger of land at Madaket Point. He had an old-design Stan Gibbs trolling swimmer, with the long, thin tail pinned to the wall of the inn as a testimony to the strength of a big cow bass. That plug had been used by one of the guides on Nantucket back in the 1960s. One night, out in Miacomet Rip, a huge bass had struck the plug. Since the rip was running against a stiff wind, there was no backing down into the steep waves, and the standard practice was simply to lock the reel up and engage in a tug-of-war. The striper's attempts to get away had twisted the plug with so much force that it simply ripped the heavy stainless wire, which ran the length of the inside of the lure and connected all the hooks, right out of the wood at the tail end, and rolled it right up the length of the plug as one would roll back the lid on an old-fashioned can of sardines. The bass then straightened out the hooks and was free. Later, using pliers, the guide unrolled the wire and stuffed it back into the groove the bass had cut open with the wire. He held it in place by closing off the gap in the tail of the plug with a heavy piece of copper fuse wire. According to Tom, he fished the plug successfully for several years after that.

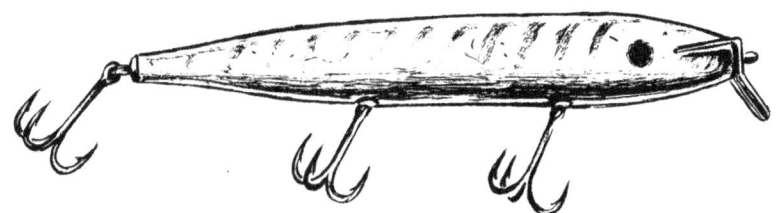

Unlike the late 1970s, when there were essentially no school stripers along the Maine coast, fishing during the early 1980s started to include occasional catches of smaller bass. After that early run in June 1980 dispersed, though, there weren't many of those small bass to be found. Meanwhile, the large, old fish that had comprised the late 1970s fishing became increasingly rare. But I was rapidly gaining experience on the Kennebec, and I was able to catch a few more fish just because I knew the river a lot better than when I started.

When those schools of stripers arrived in 1980 off Sasanoa Point, word got around quickly, and many local anglers got in on the action. Some of those anglers were grateful to see the small fish and treated them accordingly. But another element of the local angling fraternity had learned nothing from the collapse of the striper population during the 1970s and welcomed the return of the small bass with the same wasteful, insensitive treatment they had given them before.

To be fair, in those days, not a lot was known by average fishermen about striped bass biology. Most of them had no idea the small bass hadn't been around in recent years because recreational anglers and commercial fishermen up and down the coast had killed so many during the late 1960s and early 1970s that spawning success had failed. That may oversimplify it a bit, but even today most experts believe it to be accurate. Up until 1984, Maine had no regulations on the minimum size or maximum number of striped bass that anyone could keep. Fishermen routinely kept every one they caught, and if they no longer felt like cleaning them, they just threw them in their garden or in the trash. Whenever there was a good run of stripers in Maine's Saco River that ran between the old mill towns of Biddeford and Saco, there were always plenty of whole dead stripers to be found at the town dump.

Other people, such as the proprietor of the tiny marina in North Bath where I kept a boat for a couple of summers, used to cut small stripers in half to bait his eel traps. Half of a twelve-inch schoolie, he told me, fit perfectly as bait in one of his pots. Other people used them as fertilizer, claiming they were a perfect dressing for heavy feeding plants, such as roses.

That spurt of small bass in 1980 also introduced me to Steve Wilson, who would go on to be one of my closest comrades in the striper wars to come, until October 16, 2020, when he passed away from Alzheimer's. Steve lived in Bath, where he had grown up not far from the Bath Iron Works, the shipyard that during World War II produced more destroyers than the Empire of Japan. Steve spent his working career in BIW's management, negotiating for the privately owned company with the unions that represented the thousands of workers it took to manufacture the six-hundred-foot-long military ships. It was a tough job, but Steve was up to the task. He was one of the smartest and best organized men I ever met in any avenue of my life.

During his time with the Maine chapter of the Coastal Conservation Association, Steve's banquets were legendary for their organization and profitability. He could accurately forecast, from analyzing the data in his incredible self-designed record-keeping system, the gross and net for his upcoming dinners. Every seat was filled because Steve gave every board member a certain number of tickets to sell, and starting about four months before the dinner, he would call each of them on Sunday nights to find out exactly what ticket sales had been made for the week, and then he'd either heap praise or chew on their ass, depending on the results. He was relentless, but in the end, every seat was filled.

Steve also did a little writing for the local newspaper. Upon seeing a couple of local fishermen walk away from the shore with a plastic bucket full of tiny stripers, Steve wrote an article titled "Bucket Slaughter" for the *Coastal Journal*. I read it and contacted Steve, and for the next forty years we worked on striped bass conservation issues together.

Even though the general trend in the number of large striped bass was definitely down, if you added up all the large old stripers still surviving from some good year classes between the mid-1960s and the early 1970s, there were still a lot of them. It was a tiny number of fish, though, compared to what we found once the recovery began in the late 1980s. Until 1989, the Atlantic States Marine Fisheries Commission (the political body that governs striped bass fishing on the East Coast) was still holding the line on fishing mortality.

Some years the fishing in the Kennebec for large stripers was much better than others. It just depended on where that body of remaining large fish went. Sometimes they came to the Kennebec in great numbers, sometimes there just weren't very many. I have often compared the distribution of striped bass along the coast to the relative fullness of a glass of water. No matter how full of water the glass is, there is always the same amount of water at the bottom of the glass. The same is true with striped bass. The population overall may be drastically down, but the best places on the coast, spots such as Plum Island, the target ship in Cape Cod Bay, the Nantucket rips, Sow and Pigs Reef off Cuttyhunk Island, and North Rip of Block Island always seem to have decent fishing, at least some of the time during the season.

Other places that can be good some years can be poor in other years if the population is dwindling. The Kennebec, with its huge amounts of herring, combination of beach and river habitat, and endless feeding stations created by outsized tides and ledged constrictions, was terrific striper habitat, but it was also near the far end of the Chesapeake striper's migratory range, and it was by no means immune to downturns in the striped bass population.

Nineteen eighty was the very beginning of the turnaround in small striped bass, and it was also the best year in a long while for large bass. Those two occurrences are probably related in some way I don't understand: bait, water temperature, etc. But one thing is certain: there weren't more large stripers alive coast-wide in 1980 than there had been in 1979, even though we sure caught a lot more of them in the Kennebec. I ended up catching thirty-nine cow bass, more than double my 1979 catch.

Six of those fish and possibly more weighed greater than forty-five pounds each. The first one was on June 21, and it was the first of seven in June, twelve in July, seven in August, and thirteen in September. A pattern was clearly developing. I caught all my early fish prior to July 12, though my notes show I lost some big stripers during each of the next two weekends. But after that, my next Kennebec River large striper was caught on August 26. I ended my striper famine in style that day with four cow bass, and the bite continued more or less up until the last one was brought in on September 28.

The bass arrived in the river in mid-June, fed in the river up until the end of the first week in July, when the river became too warm for their liking, and then they moved out to the ocean until things cooled down in fall. That's the way it worked, a few days one way or another, year after year.

I was very ready for the 1981 season. I now had a lot of hard-earned knowledge—I say hard-earned because when there aren't a lot of fish around, you have to spend a lot of time trying to figure out things. You may be in the right spot at the right time in the tide, and you may be presenting your lure or bait perfectly, but if there are no fish there to validate all this, you'll never know if you're doing it right or not.

1981: Expanding Horizons

I began my 1981 season on Martha's Vineyard with Phil Perrino. We fished at the mussel bar at Squibnocket, where, between us, we caught three large bass casting white P-40 Atom plugs. The season was underway.

My first trip to the Kennebec was on May 30. Tymer Savage owned the little dock in North Bath where I kept my boat for a couple of years, and he liked small stripers to bait his eel traps. Tymer told me he had been hearing good reports about stripers for a week. We fished the mouth of Hanson Bay in the Sasanoa River, which connects the Kennebec and the Sheepscot, and landed five stripers (eighteen, seventeen, seventeen, sixteen, and fifteen inches). These were all three-year-old bass that came from the 1978 class that had produced the previous year's bonanza of twelve-inch bass.

The next weekend, June 7, was particularly notable in my records. Again Phil and I had good fishing down at Green Point on the Arrowsic Island shore for small bass, with each of us landing a half dozen on popping plugs. The big story, though, was that we caught two high thirty- to low forty-pound bass from more or less the same area while trolling Danny plugs. They were the only big fish we hooked, and we tried all the nearby structures for them. Those June 7 cow bass were the earliest I ever caught in my years on the Kennebec.

The fishing continued to build through the rest of the month, and on the next weekend, June 15, I landed six bass that each weighed between twenty-five and thirty-six pounds. My notes say it was the best day I had ever had while fishing the Kennebec, but that record didn't last long. On June 21 I hooked eighteen and landed nine. One of those fish was fifty-six pounds and another was forty-four pounds and forty-eight inches. The next day the we landed ten more of these leviathans.

The next weekend was slower, but still we had five huge bass, and the following weekend, July 4–5, we had seventeen, with twelve of them coming on the Fourth. I hadn't read this page in my old fishing logs for probably close to forty years, but I remember it quite well, especially the feel of the air on those mornings. I had John Cole with me, and it was warm and overcast, moist like before a rain, which came the next day. We used to meet at what was once a twenty-four-hour Howard Johnson's restaurant in Brunswick, close to where John lived. At that time of the year, we met at around 3:00 a.m., which got us on the river by a little after 4:00, which was very first light.

John was always waiting in a booth when I got there. He'd shake his head and complain about how crazy I was to go fishing that early and how he was even crazier to be there. But he loved the fishing as much as I did.

My normal trolling pattern on the favored outgoing tide was to start about fifty feet off Green Point. We trolled into the tide and angled the boat along a roughly twenty-five-foot drop-off that ran gradually in toward the shoreline, and then after about a hundred yards turned straight up the river, toward an old farmhouse in Fisher's Eddy. That was our range. There was a deep trough that went down to about fifty feet perhaps another hundred yards up from the little ledge off Green Point, and then we came up a long rise over the course of another hundred yards or so to an area called the Hump, which was an underwater plateau that got as shallow as about seven feet in one spot at low tide. I tried many times at dead low water to see the bottom there, but due to the murky color of the Kennebec, I never could quite do it. Usually the deep area was void of fish, and normally we'd find a pod or two somewhere along this large structure, with the Hump being the premier spot.

This morning, though, the strikes came as soon as we got the lines out. I would love to have known how many of what Cole called "slammers" were situated along that ledge that morning. We hooked them everywhere, including the fifty-foot-deep spots and on top of the Hump. When we started, it was so dark in the warm misty morning under the dense cloud cover that we couldn't see the shore except in occasional glimpses. We trolled by my knowledge of that bottom. I could tell where we were by the depth of the water and the direction of the flow.

The strikes on the heavy trolling rods were actually arm jolting. Some of the hits weren't accurate enough to result in a fish on the line, but you could feel the power of the bass's missed strike right down to the soles of your shoes. I used to leave my rod in the holder most of the time while I steered the boat. John, on the other hand, usually held his rod and jigged the tip. It was a habit from his years mating on a charter boat at Montauk, when it was vital to make the bucktail jig they used jump along like a nervous squid. You didn't really need that added action with the Danny's. The large metal lip and planed head of the plug caused it to dive and swim vigorously from side to side. The bass sure seemed to like it.

You didn't have to worry about feeling the strike either. When a bass hit, the rod would go down hard in the holder, and line would scream out against the drag, making the clicker screech like crazy. After a while you could more or less tell the size of what you had on by how aggressively the line left the reel. I used Penn Squidders and changed the drag washers every winter. The old leather washers (later replaced with Teflon) were almost worn completely through after a season's use. The only problem with this setup was that the trolling rods of that day had wooden butt sections. There was no question in my mind after hearing one crack that if we used too much drag pressure we would be left with only part of the handle in the rod holder, so I backed off the drags a little when the rods were left in the holders.

That same summer, Pat Abate, who I'll introduce you to in a couple of paragraphs, gave me an Ugly Stik bottle blank that was made of rugged fiberglass right down through the handle. After that, I never worried about breaking the rods off in the holder. We wrapped the Ugly Stiks ourselves and used silicon carbide guides. I still have the rods; they are indestructible.

The fishing had slowed a little, but it was still very good when I decided we had spent enough time at the Hump. I knew there were hundreds of huge stripers (if not more) there that morning, and I was curious to see if they were all clustered in that area or if our other favorite fishing ledges had fish. I see from my notes that we didn't go all that far, but we caught more bass at nearby Ram Island and a little farther downriver at Goat Island. That is as far as I went. We released twelve that morning, the largest was about forty pounds, and while I experienced some other great mornings on the Kennebec, I don't think I ever saw any action to equal what we had at the Hump that day in 1981.

Nineteen eighty-one was also an exceptional year, in that, other than a few weeks from mid-July to mid-August, when the bass followed their normal pattern of moving out of the river onto the beaches, there were bass in the river all summer long. I noted that on the morning of August 8 I found bass feeding on the surface where the Sprague River entered the beach a couple of miles west of the Kennebec's mouth, and then a little later that same morning I caught a twenty-two-pound striper at Green Point in a completely freshwater environment. I thought it was remarkable how these large bass were completely comfortable in two wholly different environments on exactly the same day in the middle of the summer. The salinity and water temperature couldn't have been more different.

The next weekend, August 15, I landed five, including a fifty-pounder, while fishing between Green Point and Crow Island Ledge.

Pat Abate

I met Pat Abate in 1981. I was working for Toshiba, managing the New England territory for the copy machine manufacturing division. One morning I was in the New Haven office of one of my dealers, Bill Palumbo, and I mentioned I had been fishing for striped bass the past weekend.

"I've got a friend who does that," said Bill. "He's crazy though, stays up all night, drives up to Cape Cod just to catch fish. You aren't that silly about it, are you?"

Abate sounded just like my kind of guy. Bill called Pat from his office and we started talking about bass. Before we hung up, we made tentative plans for Pat to come up to Maine and give our striper fishing a try. Pat later characterized Maine as the Alaska of the East Coast and for a while contemplated moving there.

Pat was originally from New York City, and he still had a circle of friends there that he rendezvoused with on the outer beaches of Cape Cod in the fall. It was hard-bitten stuff, and I loved their stories. They would get on the beach in their four-wheel trucks at the north end of Nauset Beach, then bounce and thrash back and forth the entire drive of more than fifteen miles to the point where the outer beach ended and the current from the vast expanse of Chatham harbor emptied into the Atlantic. The outgoing tide there created one of the world's great striped bass feeding stations. In 1987, a winter storm tore through the beach opposite the Chatham lighthouse, and that was the end of that fishery.

Pat was there for some good fishing, though. He had a fishing partner, Frank Bentrewick, another New York City man, who went to Brooklyn Tech, the school for those gifted in the sciences, but he loved fishing too much to get serious about a career. He was a Sears television technician, and he spent his summer nights commercial fishing for striped bass in Long Island Sound in his seventeen-foot Boston Whaler. This was in defiance of Connecticut's largely unenforced game fish laws. He wasn't alone. The night I went out with him, there were several other boats launching from the Niantic ramp that we used, and all the anglers knew each other. I remember one of the fishermen was trailering a twenty-two-foot Mako and referred to the bass as "hundred dollar bills."

Frank's approach was that of a scientist. Even his tackle was customized right down to the hand-made sinkers designed not to snag on the sound's rocky bottom as he three-wayed eels at various tide rips at just the right stage of the tide to provide the best fishing. You could hardly see the hand at the end of your arm on the night we went. We were drifting through the rip by Old Silas Rock when the hull of what turned out to be a SeaCraft 23, a big heavy boat compared to ours, came running up through the rip to get back to the top to start fishing. Everyone fished without lights, and with the SeaCraft lumbering up onto a plane, there was no way the men on board could see us. They went by about ten feet away.

"Oh, yeah," said Frank, "every now and then someone gets rammed. But it's rare."

After a night of beach fishing at Chatham, Pat and his partner drove back the length of the beach, which could easily take two hours, and drove into town to the Fisherman's Co-op and sold their bass. They'd get the only hot meal they would have for a while at a nearby diner, and then they'd head back onto the beach. Once they got back to the vicinity of their fishing area, they'd drive the truck partway up the side of a sand dune, crawl under it, and sleep for the day. Pat said it was really quite comfortable.

Pat came up to Maine to fish with me for the first time in 1981, the weekend of August 29. This was long before anyone had portable GPS units and cell phones. After seeing a nice school of bass off the mouth of the Sprague River from the boat on Saturday, August 30, we went out that night to find a way to drive to that point on the beach. Some kids had built a teepee-like structure on the beach out of long, dry driftwood branches, and as we drove without lights down a private cottage road, Pat saw it silhouetted against the night sky. It became a spot that for many years afterward I made some terrific catches of big stripers.

I would drive into the back parking lot of a closed store in Small Point, open the back of my car, change into my waders, and then organize my gear for the beach. I didn't take much, just my rod, plug bag, and a flashlight to hang around my neck. Then I'd get back in my vehicle, drive without lights down the cottage road we found that weekend in 1981, and park in the private association's parking area right at the beach. We'd leap out, grab the handily arranged bags from the back and our rods from the holders on the top, and head down to the beach.

In the many times I've fished the Sprague River, I often had people stop and look my vehicle over with lights, and then shine them around the bushes near where the car was parked.

But they never came out on the beach to look for us. When we were done fishing, we'd make sure no one was coming, and then do everything quickly in reverse. Since this was often on the backside of midnight, we were never interrupted. After Labor Day, we had the place pretty much to ourselves.

A trickier spot was Bald Head Cove, which could be reached off this same road. We never fished it until after Labor Day with the hope that the summer residents had all left. The property owners put a cable across the road when they left, and since the walk from there was a few hundred yards, almost no one bothered to fish this spot. Bald Head Cove was very much hit-or-miss, but there were times when it yielded some awesome catches.

I had a K-car station wagon, and it was a relatively low vehicle. I did a little measuring and discovered if I could hold the considerable belly in the cable up in the air, I could drive under it. I measured a couple of small poles and ground a groove in their top. I would arrive at the gate, drive the nose of the car under the cable, get out and place the poles to hold up the cable on either side of the car, and drive through. Once

inside and down by the beach, I found a great spot to park behind a big spruce tree. A few times cars went by while I was on the beach, but they had no idea anyone had violated their private ocean preserve. As the saying goes, I left nothing but footprints.

More New Spots

In mid-September of that year, my favorite spots up inside the Kennebec just weren't providing much action. John Cole and I worked the dropping tide down the river on the morning of September 19 without much success. We went by Perkins Island, where a small defunct lighthouse stood. This was the last of the river's navigational lights before you reached Fort Popham at the mouth, which was visible just a couple of miles in the distance. I caught a glimpse of a few gulls wheeling in the air over the water on the other side of the island. I'd never been on the backside of Perkins. It was out of the river's main flow, and I never expected to find anything there as good as the other locations I already knew about, but I was about to further my education.

When I turned the corner of the island and could see over to the Georgetown shore—actually a very long island, Marr Island, was between us and the Georgetown Island shore—we found a typical Kennebec scene of busting fish and diving birds. Gulls and terns were all through the air, and a dozen or more great blue herons were arranged along the shoreline. Young-of-the-year alewives were dropping back down the Kennebec, and a school of stripers was pinning pods of the two- to three-inch baitfish against the rock-and-seaweed bank. In an hour or so we landed a couple of thirty-pound class bass as well as quite a few nice schoolies.

We also found three or four particularly good spots, where I found feeding stripers many times over the next few years. One of those spots was right at the top of the run along the island. Above that spot was a stretch of quite deep and lazy water. A ledge came out from Perkins Island and reached toward a point of land on Marr. As the two structures approached each other, the bottom came up quite shallow, and all the baitfish coming downriver with the tide were funneled into the gap. This is where the greatest action was situated, so we nicknamed it the Funnel. For whatever reason, the Funnel was only good to me in the fall. On many occasions I caught fish there well into October, when they seemed to have gone from almost everywhere else inside the river.

In fact, 1981 was one of those years. Unless you knew about that spot or one just like it, you would have thought the season was over and all the fish were gone. But in the late afternoon of October 1, John and I made a trip to the Kennebec and ran right down to the Funnel. There was a school of big striped bass hanging out there, and since they might be gone any day, we were haunting the place.

There was something special about that school of bass. I'd say that, for their size, they were a little shorter than I would have expected. Not a lot, but they were visibly stocky, especially in the shoulders. The most defining feature, though, was the slope of their heads. The heads on this group of bass were about 30 percent shorter from the gill plates forward to their snout than I was used to seeing on stripers, and combined with the thick shoulders, this gave a very steep angle to the tops of their heads. There was no mistaking the look. I occasionally found other fish that looked like this in the Kennebec over the years, but this was the only real school of these fish that I ever found.

There wasn't a big body of fish present, but there were enough so that we would get a strike every pass or two along the productive part of the island's shoreline. It was late that overcast and gloomy fall afternoon. The weather was cool but not really all that uncomfortable in what was about the last hour of light. In fact, it was dark before I got home that evening. We had caught several nice bass, and given the late date, each one of them was a real bonus for the season.

Suddenly one of the wire-line rods trolling a Danny was hit and started bucking in the holder and making a racket. I remember noting, though, that it wasn't the sustained screech that one of Cole's forty-pound slammers makes when the drag is overcome; instead, the line was going out in spurts and rod was jumping up and down in the holder.

"I'll take it," said John. "This one is my turn."

After a spirited but relatively short fight against the heavy trolling gear, the fish was alongside the boat, and I got ready to reach over the side and grab it by its big bottom jaw.

"Jeezus, Brad!" said Cole. "Don't put your hand near that fish. That's a bluefish, an enormous bluefish. Gaff it, we won't see another one of those this year. I'll take it home and eat it."

I gaffed the bluefish and put it on the deck of the boat, where it stretched out alongside the engine cover. John stood looking at it and shaking his head.

"Brad, in all my years at Montauk, I saw thousands upon thousands of bluefish. But this is almost a head bigger than any one that I ever saw before."

We had good-sized towel in the boat that we soaked down with water and placed over the eyes of the big bass while we tagged them. It really helped to calm them down. John wrapped the blue in the towel, and at the marina he put it in the back of his car and drove it to his wife, Jean, who I'm sure was thrilled to see this monster bluefish arrive.

Later that evening, John called and very excitedly stammered that he had been standing on the scales, and Jean handed him the bluefish for the third time. And each time it weighed twenty-six pounds!

Later that fall, John and Jean stopped by our house on a Sunday ride. I remember that the leaves were off the trees and the *Sea Beagle* and its trailer were covered with canvas and up on blocks for the winter. John got out of the car with the fish towel all washed and carefully folded.

"This towel," John said with reverence, "has been wrapped around the heads of more huge bass than I can count. It deserves special care."

He looked wistfully at the boat and gazed around at the stark November landscape.

"Man," he said, "it really hits home that the summer is over when I see this boat under its winter canvas."

1982: The *Providence Journal* and Disappearing Stripers

In any given month during a fishing season the weather can be very different one day to the next, and only through observing subtle changes, such as the length of the day, color of the foliage, and angle of the light does one notice the season changing. It is the same way with entire years of a lifetime of fishing. The late 1970s right up through the mid-1980s really showed no discernible pattern as far as the number of large stripers available. Some years they seemed more abundant than others, but that was very likely due to the bait or the weather in those outlier years. There was no clear trend. The really large stripers I'm talking about are fish longer than thirty-six inches. After 1986 or so, the number of these fish seemed to more or less fall off a cliff. But not until then was the trend in their population really clear.

The definite and readily observable change during the 1980s was in the number of smaller bass, though. By 1982 that number was clearly growing every year, at least in Maine. Looking back on it, it was odd, because in Chesapeake Bay, where most of these fish were coming from, they were really struggling to find enough small bass to keep their commercial gill-net fishery going. In 1985, Maryland put a moratorium on anyone keeping any striped bass that were taken by any means. They were afraid the fish were going to become extinct.

The media got on the story as most states perceived their population was crashing. In July 1982, I received a call from Bob Pond of Stripers Unlimited, a conservation organization he founded and ran. Bob was also the owner of Atom striped bass fishing plugs. He called me to help out a reporter from the *Providence Journal* in Rhode Island who (at Bob's urging) was doing a story on the disappearing striped bass.

"They're having a problem finding any fish to write about and photograph," said Bob. "They're getting discouraged and don't want to waste much more energy on this if they can't find any fish."

Apparently they had been fishing with Bob's contacts all the way from Chesapeake Bay up to Cape Cod and had yet to photograph a bass. A few days later one of the reporters called me and laid it all on the line.

"We'd like to come up and go fishing with you in Maine," she said. "But to justify the trip, we really need to be almost guaranteed that we will see a striped bass. Can you do that?"

"No," I said. "I can't guarantee anything, but I will tell you that my track record is pretty much a hundred percent and fishing recently has been very good."

They decided to come up, and I met them at the HoJos where John Cole and I met for breakfast. Three a.m. on July 24 was no problem.

I realized I had been talking with a woman when I made that appointment, but when I walked up to a booth with two very attractive twentysomething females, you could have knocked me over with a feather.

One of them hopped up with a huge smile and stuck out her hand and said, "You must be Brad."

There is a little gut that runs between Goat Island, right off the famous church in Phippsburg, and a long, thin ledge on the outside of the island. At the upriver end of that gut is a relatively shallow area of broken bottom that the bass like to lie in and wait for herring or menhaden on their way downriver. The current absolutely pours through this area, and it is one of the few places in the Kennebec that I can think of where you can actually see the current running downhill. That morning we trolled up through the gut, and as I always did, I swung the *Sea Beagle* over to the right, pulling the plugs across the top of some very productive structure.

My two passengers were struggling a little to stay awake. They had driven up from Rhode Island the night before and were a bit groggy. The photographer was taking an occasional picture of me and various things around the boat. We were about a half hour into the fishing and had not yet connected with a fish.

"What do you think our chances are this morning," the reporter asked, clearly prepared for another disappointment.

"Oh, they're pretty good," I replied. "I was just going to ask you to stand over there and be ready to pick up that rod. A fish is going to strike it in about fifteen seconds."

I knew that in about that time the plugs would pass over a spot that had been almost no-fail for a bass the first pass over it in several successive recent trips. The tide was perfect, and everything felt just right. *Besides*, I thought, *if we don't get anything, they'll just think I was joking anyway.*

When the boat was in the exact spot I wanted, I held it for a few seconds before turning the wheel to make one more sweep across the area. This gave the plugs a few seconds to hang straight downstream and behind the boat.

As soon as I started that turn of the wheel, what turned out to be a forty-three-inch striper that we had tagged with American Littoral Society tag number 138702 grabbed the Danny plug and took off for the deep water in the middle of the river.

That happened four more times that morning, and the gals from the *Providence Journal* were ecstatic to finally have some material for their story. I still have three of the black-and-white photos on the wall in my office.

Another Sixty

On the morning of August 21, the Kennebec River water in Bath was 70 degrees Fahrenheit. The air temperature was only 50 degrees, and there was a strong northwesterly breeze. We had an outgoing tide, and the end of summer or early in the fall was the perfect time to fish Pond Island Rip. We ran straight down the river early that morning and began trolling the rip. As luck would have it on this day, I had my brother Jason with me, the same crew I had back in September 1979 when I landed a sixty-three-pound striper. My notes say that the rip was full of both bass and blues that morning. We landed and tagged five large bass, one of which was a forty-four-inch fish that swam away wearing ALS tag number 138700. This fish was recaptured the next fall, on November 5, 1983, at

White Horse Beach in Plymouth, Massachusetts—about ten miles from the entrance to the Cape Cod Canal. Clearly that was the path the fish intended to take south. I have also had bass recaptured on the outside of Cape Cod, which proves to me that the fish migrate both north and south by a variety of routes.

Another of the bass we landed that morning was fifty-three inches long and weighed sixty-three pounds on our Chatillon scale. I had now caught two sixty-pound-plus stripers in Maine. There have been other sixties caught, but not many. My childhood friend Dougie Dodge caught one at Reid State Park a year or two before, and I remember one being caught in the mouth of the York River, but there sure haven't been very many.

One thing I remember clearly about those fish was that they were absolutely perfect specimens. There wasn't a visible scar, missing scale, broken stripe, or split fin anywhere on them. Perhaps it was just circumstance, but I think it's quite likely that only the finest genetic specimens live to such a ripe old age.

Of the other three fish released that morning, one was forty-nine inches. I estimated it was around fifty pounds.

The Missing Teaser

On the weekend of September 10, 1982, Pat Abate was up from Connecticut to fish. The tide was right that evening to try a spot I had wanted to fish for some time. At the mouth of the Kennebec a long bar runs off the west side of the river mouth to a small spruce-covered, ledge-shored island, Wood Island. This bar bares completely at low tide, and I often saw summer beachgoers mixing with the fishermen and walking along the bar to the island. The tides run very hard into and out of the Kennebec due largely to the considerable size of the local tides, but also to the fact that all that fresh water coming downstream from the Kennebec and its tributaries has to get out of the river along with the ocean water that came in with the last high tide. An outgoing tide runs more or less straight out into the ocean. The incoming tide, though, stuffs water into the river, instead of being supplied by a narrow chute, the river presents to the ocean on a dropping tide. The water comes in from the ocean on both sides and the middle, and on the incoming tide, the water runs along Popham Beach, up over the bar at the mouth of the river, and then into the river itself at a considerable velocity. The current sweeping across this sandy bar looked to me like a perfect feeding station for striped bass, and given the shallow water and clean sandy beach, those bass would be most comfortable there at night.

On the night of September 10 the weather was perfect, and a decent onshore breeze kicked up some surf. Turbulence is always good in striper fishing, as well as a dark night, which we also had.

A great feature when Pat and I fish together is that he is left-handed. This allowed us to fish practically next to each other without fear of hooking the other while casting. This evening, though, we were separated, searching this new spot and trying to find fish. About a half hour into our trip, Pat appeared out of the murky night and shined the light hanging around his neck onto a very substantial striped bass.

"He took the teaser," said Pat, and he slid the mid-thirty-pounder back into the surf.

We were both casting the hot lures of the day for sand-beach fishing. This was just a few years before the needlefish ascended to legendary status on Block Island, and its deadly reputation spread up and down the striper coast.

We were using moderately thin plastic swimmers, typified by the Cotton Cordell Red Fin. Sophisticated Cape Cod bass fishermen drilled holes in the heads of their Red Fins and added measured amounts of mineral oil or even just plain water, then sealed the holes with epoxy. This was called "loading the plug." It gave more weight for better casting and provided for a little deeper retrieve. For smaller plugs, we used either a very thin plug called a Hellcat (these were never loaded) or the popular Rebel plug.

I was using a weighted Red Fin that night, and I had not had a touch. I decided to follow Pat's lead and add a teaser to my outfit. I had twenty-pound mono line coming off my spinning reel, and this ran to a small swivel, then five feet of forty-pound test shock leader, then a big Berkley cross snap was used to attach the lure.

I had been using teasers for bass for years, sometimes even ahead of the trolling plugs I used on my boat. The teaser could simply be a saltwater streamer fly or a rubber lure. The Red Gill teaser, which looked like a sand eel, was very popular on the Cape Cod beach scene.

I remember an article in *Fisherman Magazine* by Frank Daignault, who was a Massachusetts surf fishing luminary and one of the first to fish the surf with a fly rod for big stripers. Frank said that people tied all kinds of flies for striped bass, but he had never found anything to be an improvement on simply strapping a half dozen saddle hackles to a good hook. By my own experience, he was probably right.

The way I rigged the teaser was to tie a simple clinch knot with the heavy leader shock leader material to the small swivel used to connect the shock leader to the casting line. I tied my knot purposely using more mono than necessary for the knot, leaving an eight- to twelve-inch tag end on the knot. I tied my teaser directly to that tag end.

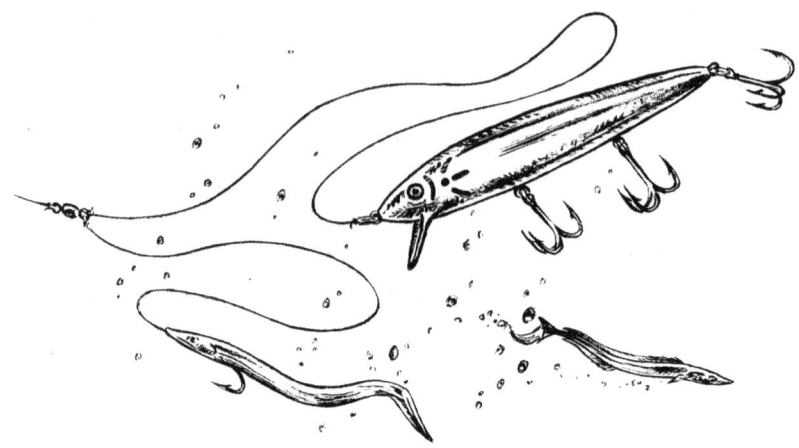

Pat disappeared down the beach where he had hooked his fish, and I tied on a feathered streamer fly, probably six inches long, as a teaser. The thinly profiled teasers were popular on the theory they mimicked sand eels, a long, thin, baitfish that were often present in good numbers along Popham Beach. I decided to work a short distance to my left, moving closer to where the beach came to a point and turned in toward the river mouth.

After a short while I felt the solid strike of a heavy striped bass and the fight was on. The fish was running with the current, and I thought ahead to where it might go and what could possibly be in the way for it to get caught on. Everything was clear for the rest of the bar and for a little distance beyond, but just a little farther out there was a big green can that marked the port side of the channel for boats entering the river. That can was less than a hundred yards off the beach. I determined to keep the fish as close to me as I could, hoping that if I did run out of beach and had to move into the river, I could keep the fish well inside of that can and land it in the back eddy that I knew existed for a distance after I made the turn into the river.

The bass was strong, though, and with the increased current flow as we approached the river, it was constantly pulling out line and moving farther away. Then, suddenly, everything changed. The fight of the bass took on an entirely different feel, becoming very erratic. I could feel a lot of gyrations taking place on the end of my line, and the weight I was pulling against suddenly became too much for the rod to make any progress against. Luckily there was no real direction to the new energy or I would quickly have been spooled. Instead this heavy, undulating mass, slowly moved along with the current toward the top of the bar and the river beyond.

I imagined that perhaps a shark had grabbed my bass, and I imagined myself fighting with it in the surf with my flashlight and a pair of Sargent's pliers. This probably all lasted about thirty seconds, and then everything suddenly changed again. The situation was back to normal, but most of the fight was now out of the bass, and I quickly gained ground. In a few minutes the bass was rolling in the wash in front of me. I slid it up with an incoming wave and held enough pressure on it so the wave receded and left the bass laying on its side. I could see in the moonlight that the plug was where it should be, in the corner of the fish's mouth. I slid the fish up a few feet, knelt down, unhooked, and released it.

I examined my rig as I walked back along the beach to tell Pat about my catch. I slid my hands carefully up the shock leader to check the condition of the teaser, and to my surprise it wasn't there at all. I started to think about the possibilities. I suppose it could have been a monster bluefish that inhaled the fly and nicked the leader just enough so that it held for a while. Bass have no such teeth. But there were very few bluefish around, so I doubt the shock tippet was bitten through. The length of mono from the knot to where the fly had been was not perceptibly changed from its original length. I guess my knot could have failed, and that is exactly what I think happened, but not because there was anything wrong with it. My guess, nearly forty years later, is that a second big bass grabbed that feathered sand eel, and a violent tug-of-war ensued between the two big fish. Just the right combination of simultaneous head shakes or twists in opposite directions and the leader parted at the weakest knot, even though that knot was freshly tied with forty-pound-test Ande monofilament.

I ended the 1982 season by catching an estimated forty-pound bass and losing another similar fish using live eels at the Sprague River at daybreak on October 7. That was my eightieth large striper for the season. After the big bass were gone, we did catch small stripers that year near the Route 1 bridge in Falmouth, until almost the very end of October.

Two of the small stripers I tagged in the Kennebec, numbers 90037 and 138721, sixteen and twenty-two inches, respectively, were captured by a commercial netter named McIntosh in Rhode Island on November 5 that fall. I remembered his name from the Citizen's Advisory Council meetings. He seemed like a really nice guy, and at least he turned in the tags. It wasn't very happy news for me. One of those fish I had tagged on June 5 and the other on September 9, both in 1982. Clearly those fish had joined a big school migrating south along the New England shoreline that fall. The deadly efficiency of the fish traps and the gill nets used in Rhode Island is obvious. The fish trap might well have taken a large percentage of the school they had been a part of.

Rhode Island has kept that net fishery open through the worst years of the striped bass population crash, and in 2020, as we appear to be heading toward another crash, it is still open. It is a prime example of what is wrong with fishery management in our country. Every fisherman in Rhode Island—and everywhere else in New England—had traditionally been able to take home school-sized stripers to eat, but that right was soon to disappear. For the netters, though, the state's fishery managers refused to cut out this wholesale slaughter of small bass, and Rhode Island netters were to have the only exemption from the conservation regulations that applied to everyone else.

Important Bits of Striper News

October of every year is when the Maryland Department of Natural Resources releases the final striped bass young-of-the-year count. This important statistic is probably the most reliable indicator of what the numbers of striped bass along the East Coast may look like in a few years. The number is the average catch of baby striped bass caught in the sweep of a certain-sized net deployed in the same locations within Chesapeake Bay three times during the summer growing season. Throughout the 1970s, abysmal numbers such as 2, 4, or even 1 were the rule rather than the exception. In 1978 the count was 8.45, and though still slightly below the long-term average of about 10, it was a huge improvement and provided the small bass we found in 1980 in the Kennebec. Those fish were beaten up early in the game as we discussed in the last chapter. In October 1982, though, another 8.45 count was announced, and this time the Atlantic States Marine Fisheries Commission (ASMFC) was ready to do something to protect them.

In 1984, before the 1982 class was large enough to harvest, Congress passed the Atlantic Striped Bass Conservation Act, which required under federal law that states adopt the conservation measures prescribed by the ASMFC. A twenty-four-inch minimum size and four-fish bag limit became the coastal benchmark for the 1985 season. Even though four fish with a minimum of twenty-four inches sounds very liberal by today's standards, there were practically no schoolies to be found as large as twenty-four inches, and the large, old fish that would measure a foot or two longer than that were always very hard to find in any quantity. To protect the 1982 class, a chart was produced by the ASMFC that projected the minimum size each year. It indicated thirty-four inches by 1989. The states stuck with that mandate, updating their minimums annually. Many of them finally got as large as thirty-six inches.

1982: Reintroducing Striped Bass to the Kennebec River

Through my involvement with the Striped Bass Citizens Advisory Council, I met Lew Flagg, who was in charge of anadromous fish for the state of Maine, and we shared the bond of coming from the same neck of the woods near the town of Waldoboro. The department needed a point man from the public to testify and organize support among anglers and conservationists for the initiatives the Atlantic States Marine Fisheries Commission was putting in place to help the stripers. I became that person and often worked closely with Lew. He educated me to the Kennebec's formerly having had its own resident spawning population of striped bass.

I asked him why the river no longer had such a spawning population and if anything could be done to bring them back. Lew explained that wood products, dumped into the river by the many mills along the waterway, decomposed during the warm months, and this deprived the nearby sections of the river of oxygen, which killed not only the young stripers but also the adults that had come in to spawn.

During the 1960s new pollution laws had more or less fixed the anoxia problem, and in Lew's opinion, the river could probably now support a population of stripers. How to get some wild stripers to stock or the money to undertake the project was another story. I was hooked on the idea, though, and determined to find some solutions. Sometimes a little ignorance of the complexities and difficulties involved is a blessing, and it was in this case.

John Cole, the founder and owner of the *Maine Times* newspaper, knew an awful lot of people and especially everyone who was running for political office in Maine. John was a very lively person, full of ideas, and even more oblivious than I to the roadblocks of prudent behavior. John immediately started calling senators Bill Cohen from Maine and Rhode Island's John Chafee (his Yale classmate) to get the air force to use transports to fly millions of baby striped bass grown at federal hatcheries to Maine. He nearly got everything he asked for to, but it took a little while.

Lew and I had lunch with then Marine Resources commissioner Spencer Apollonio in the late spring in Hallowell to talk over some ideas about putting stripers back in the Kennebec. Spencer thought it was a grand idea and enthusiastically envisioned Maine's becoming a mecca for striped bass angling without having to depend on the Chesapeake Bay. Lew was the conservative member of our group, and he worried about introducing striped bass from the mid-Atlantic that might have trouble adjusting to the Kennebec's big tides and colder temperatures. Stock from the Hudson was Lew's preference.

I took the results of my meeting back to the irrepressible John Cole, who immediately thought of his friend Bob Boyle, who was with *Sports Illustrated*. Boyle loved striped bass as much as John and I, and in fact he had a long, elaborate tank in his home that replicated the flow of a river. He entertained himself by dropping minnows and other small forage into the upstream end of the tank and watching his pet bass rocket out from behind rocks to eat them.

Bob was very plugged in with everything to do with the Hudson, and he offered to net or get his friends in the New York State Department of Environmental Conservation to net some wild striper fingerlings from the Hudson to put into the Kennebec. This solution sounded good to everyone—until Lew came up with the next roadblock of concern about introducing a Hudson pathogen of some kind to the Kennebec. The New York officials solved that by holding the fish in a government facility for a few days while the fish were tested.

When it was determined the fish were clear, in the fall of 1982 the state of Maine sent a hatchery truck to the Hudson and picked up 317 wild striped bass fingerlings of between two and four inches in length. They were driven back to Maine and unloaded into the Androscoggin at the public boat launch just below the falls in Brunswick. These were probably the first young-of-the-year striped bass to swim in the Kennebec system for a century or so.

1983

After rereading my notes from the 1980s a few times now, I see that 1982 had really been a pivotal year. That year probably saw more forty-inch-plus striped bass swimming in the Kennebec than in any year since. Every year the number of fish in that size bracket coastwide probably shrunk, though the tendency of the fish to clump together in schools and to follow prevailing baitfish species still made for some great days of fishing in the Kennebec on that age class of fish. The fish that were already forty inches or more in length were being reduced each year by natural mortality as well as fishing, both recreational and commercial. Actually during those years the distinction between recreational and commercial groups wasn't all that great. There has been a long-standing culture in parts of the recreational striped bass angling community of some fishermen selling part of their catch.

There are a number of reasons why that fishery—which some of us called the recre-mercial fishery—came to be. First, stripers are only available seasonally through much of their range. Second, stripers are a relatively inshore fish and not historically caught by dragging or gill netting the open ocean bottom, though midwater trawls fished for herring have killed lots of big stripers over the years. For these reasons the traditional commercial fishing industry didn't really bother with striped bass. What stood for an actual commercial fishery for stripers was a low-capitalized, small-scale fishery of independent operators who fished inshore with small nets or even rod and reel.

Striped bass are considered tasty by many consumers, and so the demand is there when they are available. Restaurants and fish markets have never had a stable or consistent supply of the fish, so they got into the habit of buying them whenever someone comes along with any to sell. In many cases this provides cash or "under the table" compensation that the anglers can get away without reporting. This is not as true of the Chesapeake Bay fishery, where striped bass along with crabs and oysters have historically been a staple of the "waterman" culture. Even in the bay, though, some estimates by officials as far back as the 1960s put the illegal commercial effort as being roughly equal to the aboveboard one.

That sort of recre-mercial fishing went on in the Kennebec too, but I believe it was on a very small scale. Nonetheless, the pressure the large stripers were under from this shadow fishery up and down the coast was quite great in the aggregate, and if it was ever reported at all, it was charged off as recreational fishing.

On the other end of the fish supply chain is the supply of smaller fish that were growing to replace the older ones being removed in any given year. The reality was that in 1983 there was a relatively small number of striped bass smaller than twenty-two inches or so in size and very, very few between twenty-two and forty inches. That is because the last great year class of striped bass, the 1970 dominant class, had now reached forty inches or more in size, and the years of 1970 through 1979 were very weak on average. On top of this, the regulations designed to protect those fish were minimal. What few young fish that were produced were being netted to death in Chesapeake Bay, and the survivors were being hunted along the coast.

That isn't to say that all the big stripers were gone. That is not the case at all, but they were greatly diminished, and stripers don't spread themselves evenly along the coast. They are a school fish, and if you found a school of striped bass, it was good times all over again. But with the large fish especially, it was getting harder and harder to find those schools.

On June 18, 1983, I found schools of small striped bass breaking the surface at all of my good Kennebec spots, from Goat Island to Jones's Eddy. My notes say that we tagged fifteen fish between twelve and twenty inches and released at least as many more again. We hooked and lost one large bass at the north of Goat Island on June 18, but it was June 24 before I could put my first big fish in the book. And that was really the story of the Kennebec fishery that year. By July

1, I had only six large bass, and I noted in my record book: "Nothing like '81 and '82." It got a little better right after that, and I had some excellent fish, including one weighing forty-eight pounds on July 30 and another of fifty pounds on August 28.

September 1983 was poor in the Kennebec River itself. The month was exceptionally warm, and the bass seemed to stay outside. I caught most of my fish by surfcasting at the Sprague River, and that continued to be decent through the first week of October. I also landed seven large bass on the Danny and wire during the first nine days of October inside the Kennebec, which was unusually good for that late in the season. On my last day in the boat, I tagged a forty-two-inch and a forty-five-inch fish at Green Point to wrap up my season. The total was only thirty-five large fish, 56 percent less than the previous year, and not for lack of effort. Much of that had been due to the very slow fishing in June.

1983: Kennebec Stocking

Running on the track established in 1982, we again received 572 wild baby stripers from the Hudson in the fall of 1983 and stocked these into the main stem of the Kennebec. I can't find any record of exactly where these fish were placed in the Kennebec, but I think it was in Augusta.

1984: A Tough Year, but My First Trip to Block Island

By Labor Day 1984, I had landed only eleven large bass in the Kennebec, and my first one was not taken until July 3. Just two years earlier, by July 3, 1982, I had landed thirty-seven!

My notes for the summer are full of accounts of catching schoolies near the Route 1 bridge in Falmouth. The fishing was quite good, and while the fish were small, it was a lot more fun than catching nothing.

On the Falmouth side of the river, and on the upriver side of the bridge, right where the land ends and the bridge starts out over the water, is a terrific spot on the incoming tide. I caught schoolies at this abutment on a variety of lures, but without a doubt the most productive was a little lead-head jig with a rubber tail called the Blue Fox Vibrotail. Probably others would work just as well, but this lure was deadly. I see the name Vibrotail is still being used, but the look of the rubber body is different. The problem with the original lure was that the hook was terribly thin, and after releasing a few stripers, it would simply break off.

An interesting Maine character, Pete Wescott, showed me the land's end spot at the end of the Falmouth abutment. Pete had just retired from the phone company when I met him, and being around the river and fishing was his first love. It wasn't his only talent, though. Pete frequented the same greasy spoon for breakfast every day, and when he left his table, the back of his place mat was a piece of art worth framing. Most of the drawings were caricatures of other diners, and they were impressively good.

One night I miscalculated the tide and, shortly after midnight on a foggy Maine summer evening, I walked the quarter mile or so from my house to the abutment to catch the incoming tide. When I got to the point, I realized the tide was far too low to start fishing. There, out on the huge mussel bar that we normally were fishing over, I could see someone moving around. It turned out to be Pete, and he shortly came ashore.

"My god, Pete, what were you doing roaming around out there in the middle of the night," I asked.

"Replenishing my lure supply," he said.

And while I couldn't see his face, I'm sure he was grinning from ear to ear. He shined a light down into the plastic bucket he was carrying, and there were at least a dozen striped bass lures of various kinds on the bottom. Without another word, he was up over the bank and off down the road.

A few days later that tide got around to daylight, and I thought I'd take a stroll out on the mussel bar to see if Pete had missed any. What I found, neatly built into the ups and downs of the bar, was a length of old, thick rope held in place by some well-driven-in wooden stakes.

Probably to try to make catching twenty-inch fish more interesting, I started tagging these fish. Tagging is a lot more difficult from the shore than from a boat. I would slide two or three of the American Littoral Society spaghetti tags into their needles, and then stick the needle through the card we had to fill out and send back to the ALS office. You had to get down on your knees on the rocks by the water's edge in order to stick the needle just under the skin, pull the tag through, and then tie it in a knot. The bank there is very steep, and it was easy to lose your balance and fall into the river. I was in my mid-thirties and didn't fall in, but it wasn't fun. Meanwhile, the fish was trying to get away, and you had your rod and reel to deal with as well. It wasn't easy, plus it was at night, and by taking just a small number of tags with me, I limited the aggravation. I'm sure I spent as much time with this as I did because there were very few large fish around to catch, and tagging made catching the relatively small fish more interesting.

On September 9, a Friday night, I ran into an old acquaintance, Dean Krah, who was fishing live eels at Reid State Park. Dean was the guy who had taken Dougie Dodge fishing the night he caught the sixty-odd-pounder at the very spot where Dean and I were now standing and talking.

"He got it right here," Dean reminded me. "I baited the hook, cast it out, and set it in the sand spike. 'You watch that while I take a piss.'"

No sooner was Dean unzipped than the bass took the bait. Anyway, the point of this story is to tell you that Dean said that night that he had been fishing the beach all summer long and had landed only five for the entire season.

On a brighter note, 1984 was also my first trip to Block Island. I'll write more about Block in a later chapter, but I did get a couple of nice fish on this trip, and I got an introduction to the island. There were a lot more bass around than I had been used to seeing on the Kennebec or along the Maine beaches.

1984: Kennebec Stocking

On September 28, 1984, the state of Maine stocked 2,306 four- to five-inch striped bass fingerlings into the Kennebec River from the state launching facility in Richmond. These fish were purchased with funds raised by John Cole and me from a group of largely Maine folks who were interested in seeing wild striped bass in the Kennebec again. One notable exception to being Maine folk among the donors was Robert Redford, whom John had met as a director of the National Audubon Society.

We purchased the striped bass fingerlings from Robert J. Valenti, a PhD who raised brood stock on New York's Long Island for striped bass aquaculture. The parents of those fish had been netted wild in Long Island Sound the year before. Those fish could have been from the Hudson River, which is the source the state of Maine preferred, but by the timing of the captures and other information, including tag returns,

Valenti thought they were more likely to have been from Chesapeake stock.

Regardless, we picked up the fry on an early summer day at the ferry terminal in New London, Connecticut, and then drove them to a U.S. Fish and Wildlife (USF&W) hatchery in North Attleboro, Massachusetts, where they were grown to fall fingerling size. With the well-known problems stripers faced, John's work with Senators Cohen and Chaffee, and with the state of Maine now being onboard, the feds were very willing to help.

In September, a Maine Department of Marine Resources hatchery truck drove down to Attleboro to pick them up and take them right to the Kennebec for stocking. That same fall we also stocked an additional 200 wild fingerlings that had been netted from the Hudson.

I watched those 2,306 fish go into the waters of the Kennebec in Richmond. There was just me, Lew Flagg of the Maine Department of Marine Resources, and Andy Hyde, a member of Lew's staff who drove the truck. The truck was backed down the boat launch ramp, and once in position, the big pipe that drains the tank was opened. The water poured from the tank, and in it you could see little specks of silver that were the four- to five-inch stripers. They had grown nicely over the summer in the warm ponds at Attleboro.

The wild Hudson fish were put in on another day in Augusta. They were smaller, at two to four inches in length.

I hung around for a while to look for the fish. Most of them were gone in an instant, but a few swam up against the shoreline and hung there for a little while in the shelter of the rocks. Within maybe fifteen minutes, though, I no longer saw any. Never had the Kennebec seemed so vast to me. *How in the world*, I thought, *if by some miracle they survive, would these fish ever find each other again when the first females matured in about four years? How would they know where in the river to be at spawning time?*

History now tells us, though, at least some of them were able to best all of those challenges.

1985: Tough One in Maine, but Better in Southern New England

In 1985, Maryland thought the roof was falling in on striped bass. They were getting poor results from their annual young-of-the-year survey of spawning success, but in New England, including Maine, the number of small bass migrating to our coast each summer, while still relatively small, was definitely growing all the time. Not only were we running into stripers consistently in most of the known places, but some of these schoolies were now getting to be twenty-five inches or better.

I've looked back through the changes in the Chesapeake Bay regulations that could have led to this reappearance of small stripers in Maine rivers:

1978: Spawning area closures were expanded in both the river tributaries and in Chesapeake Bay proper. Gill nets are required to be spaced a minimum of 1,000 feet apart, and no gill nets allowed within 1,000 feet of the Chesapeake Bay Bridge.

1979: The Maryland commercial catch drops to 950,000 pounds, the lowest since the 1930s. The minimum size is raised in the spawning areas to fourteen inches from twelve.

1980: Gill nets are prohibited in the middle and upper bay during the summer and early fall, and hook-and-line commercial fishing is closed within 1,200 feet of the Bay Bridge—same as gill nets.

1981: Government hatchery releases 1.2 million striped bass fry. I caught a hatchery-tagged Chesapeake striper in the Presumpscot in the mid-1990s.

1982: Maryland commercial landings drop to 518,000 pounds. Gill net mesh size is increased to three and a half inches.

1983: Minimum size is increased to fourteen inches throughout Maryland state waters.

1984: Designated spawning areas are again expanded, along with other various fine-tuning restrictions.

1985: The Atlantic States Marine Fisheries Commission (ASMFC) calls for a 55 percent reduction in harvest and now has the strength of federal backup due to the Studds Act. Maryland declares a harvest moratorium.

Looking back on those times, it was quite remarkable that while the situation was beyond critical in the minds of Maryland officials, in Maine we were seeing increasing numbers of school-sized bass every year. Actually, on many days, the fishing for them was quite good. In 1989, Maryland validated that viewpoint when their survey observed that the number of female stripers on the spawning grounds increased fivefold over those present in 1982.

It is difficult to say exactly which of the increased conservation measures was working, but the increased minimum size, spawning ground closures, and reduced commercial catches probably all helped. The number of small bass reaching northern New England was increasing during a time when the young-of-the-year counts in the Chesapeake were uniformly weak.

Large bass, though, were getting much more difficult to find. In 1985, I only landed one in June and only seven more for the whole month of July. In August we caught just two big stripers. It seemed the Kennebec River fishery I had enjoyed for really trophy-sized striped bass on most of my outings during the last few years was coming to an end.

While I'm sure that, taken in a coastwide macro sense, the numbers of large bass were falling, they weren't falling as fast as in some other areas. For a few more years in the mid- to late 1980s, there were some impressive schools of bass to be found in the Cape Cod-to-Montauk area during the fall. In many of those years there was some surprisingly good fishing to be had, even into December, and after that, the action moved down to the New Jersey beaches and finally on to the Chesapeake Bay Bridge-Tunnel area.

We'll spend more time talking about Martha's Vineyard in another chapter, but my notes show that, in contrast to 1985 being a difficult year in Maine, that one weekend in early October, Phil Perrino and I began fishing at Pilots Landing at Gay Head on Martha's Vineyard, then we followed the tide around to the mussel bar at Squibnocket. I was casting a new plug for me, the Gag's Grabber needlefish in a dark green color. That weekend we landed sixteen bass estimated at between fifteen and forty pounds each. I remember that well, and it was no big blitz for a few hours in one spot. We had a steady pick of fish that seemed to be well distributed all around the southwest tip of the island. In addition to the ones we landed, we had numerous other strikes and fish on the line. It was some of the best surfcasting of my life.

1985: Kennebec Stocking

In 1985, we settled on the final stocking program for the Kennebec. A Maryland company named Ecological Analysts with offices in New York had contracted with Con Edison to supply a large number of striped bass fingerlings to mitigate the wild fingerlings being lost as they were sucked into the filtering screens of the water intakes for a big hydroelectric facility on the Hudson at Storm King Mountain. Storm King was another famous conservation battle Bob Boyle was involved with.

They were netting wild brood stock near West Point, spawning the fish out in a temporary facility back on land, and growing the eggs and then fry in a series of plastic tanks beneath a big tent in the town of Verplanck, New York. The fry grew so fast they had to simply throw excess fry in the river at intervals to keep manageable numbers in the tanks. They agreed to simply give some of these fish to Maine.

We received a call just as one of the thinnings was being done, and we drove down to Verplanck to get the fish. They were netted from the tanks and placed in plastic bags set inside Styrofoam boxes partially filled with lightly salted water. The bags were then inflated with oxygen. We had a pickup truck that belonged to the Maine Department of Marine Resources as well my own pickup. After loading the boxes, we drove as rapidly as we dared for the USF&W facility in North Attleboro, where we put the fish in the ponds and allowed them to grow over the summer. (I managed to get a speeding ticket on the trip.)

The partnership with Verplanck really helped our numbers, and larger amounts were stocked annually for the rest of the program:

1985: 46,759

1986: 30,246

1987: 0. The pathogen screening sample was lost, and we missed our deadline to pick up the fish. They were released into the Hudson.

1988: 66,623

1989: 40,535

1990: 65,233

1986: A Few Surprises in the Catch

Just when we thought the previous generation of stripers was fading from existence (at least as far north as Maine), we were reminded that migration patterns can vary quite a bit from year to year. Nineteen eighty-six started out a little cold and slow, even with the schoolies, but by the end of the first week in June, the usual good spots in the lower Kennebec were full of stripers, and many of this new generation of fish were as large as twenty-five and twenty-six inches. They were becoming really fun to catch.

On June 20, I trolled up two jumbo bass at the tip of Ram Island at Lower Unit City, a bony piece of ledge that runs upstream quite a distance from Ram Island. When the incoming tide slacked up over at the Hump, Erle Kelly used to run the two or three hundred yards over to Ram and anchor just upriver of the tip of Lower Unit City. His sports would fish an eel on the bottom with one rod and cast plugs in toward the tip of the ledge with another. This ledge made the loveliest waves and eddies as the ebb tide started to pour over it. It runs a long way out from the island and is remarkably uniform in height. At high tide there is a good five or six feet of water covering the shallowest part, but on a real low drain tide you can land a boat there and walk up and down the exposed ledge for several hundred feet.

Every now and then, while Erle was quietly anchored there, a boat of partying yahoos decided to show off a bit and cut between Erle and the island. They were usually plastered on beer and waving their cans high in the air while they hollered as they roared by. This was all fine at the beginning of the ebb tide, but about halfway through, the drop parts of that ledge are only a couple of feet under the water, and they can be reached by the skeg of a big outboard, especially a boat that is overloaded and out of trim.

"Did you ever see anyone hit the ledge?" I asked Erle.

"Oh, yes," he said.

And I asked if anyone ever hit it hard enough to knock out their engine.

"Brad," said Erle, "I saw a couple of boats hit that ledge so hard that when the motor flipped up, the lower unit was completely gone, just the bolts were left where it had been connected."

The next day, on June 21, I had six more big fish, including two over forty pounds, and on June 22, Phil Perrino and I found them *in the morning* on all of our favorite Phippsburg ledges: the Flat Top, the Hump, Green Point, Lower Unit City, Ram Island, and Goat Island. We landed eight while losing many others.

In the afternoon of the same day, Lou Zglobicki and I caught another eight, with some again over forty pounds. The only difference was that the fishing was so good at Green Point during the afternoon that we never went anywhere else.

This went on for the rest of June, and we moved into July with forty-one jumbo bass landed and released. It was the best start for a season I had ever had.

I penned an important entry into my logbook on June 28: "High tide at 5:00 a.m. and schoolies everywhere—caught on fly rod." While I don't think these were the first striped bass I caught on a fly rod, it is the first page in my logbook where I noted it. I know I had been fly-fishing for a few years prior to this.

In 1985, I was invited to go to Iceland for some Atlantic salmon fishing with John Cole and his friend Pritham Singh. I remember that trip pretty well, and I was still struggling with my casting at that time; I couldn't seem to work my way around tailing loops. Fly casting really attracted me, but I was very much into catching big striped bass, and no one had yet shown me that a fly rod was an efficient way to do that. Fly fishing stayed on my periphery. If the fishing for schoolies was lights-out, and there was no wind to make my poor casting worse, then I'd try it. But when I was working the Kennebec's tide rips for jumbo bass or carousing a nighttime beach, I only had faith in the conventional tackle that I knew would work. That would all change over the next few years, not only for me, but for a huge number of fellow striper addicts who discovered the pleasure of the fly-fishing for stripers within a few years of each other as the stripers' comeback became official in the early 1990s.

At the end of the first week in July, the bass in the Kennebec started to thin out. They had just moved out to the beaches as the river water became too warm, and they were replaced by hordes of what John Cole called "Godzilla blues." The everyday fisherman's term for teen-sized and larger bluefish at the time was gorilla blues, but Cole had his own take, and it actually makes a better description. There is no wilder, meaner, never-say-die creature than a big bluefish. I never cared much for fishing for bluefish, but I certainly respect the creatures. I preferred jumbo striped bass, and time taken horsing in and unhooking unruly bluefish was not my favorite thing to do.

But it would be hard to exaggerate how prolific bluefish were along the coast of Maine at times during the mid-1980s. There seemed to be loads of them in every river along the coast, and there were even lots of them offshore. Bluefin tuna fishermen from well offshore complained that bluefish attacked their daisy chains and spreader bar rigs and bit their baits, even plastic squids, clean in half.

One day I was cod fishing with Fred Hinck, who I'd grown up with in Damariscotta. We were a couple of miles offshore and just south of Seguin Island. I was pulling up what would have been a seven- or eight-pound codfish. Suddenly, not far below the surface, there was a sharp yank on the line and my codfish stopped fighting. I turned the handle a couple of times and lifted the rod, pulling from the water a most grizzly sight. My jig hook was still stuck in the jaw of the codfish, but the body from just back of the dorsal fin was gone. There was a half-moon-shaped bite mark wide enough to cover the body of the fish from back to belly. The remains of the fish were just draining blood and guts into the water. That one bite must have weighed three or four pounds.

"Christ, look at that!" said Fred.

And very plainly visible now, directly under the carcass were several bluefish, all of which would have been around twenty pounds. I put the cod remains back out to catch them, but I didn't have any luck.

Nowadays I was spending most of my time fishing the beach at night. Here is my entry from Sunday, July 21, 1986: "Sunday, 3:00 a.m. fished the Sprague River. In one hour hooked five good bass. Beached three, one in teens, two in twenties. Gags Classic needlefish was the hot plug. No wind, dark and foggy, low tide. School was just east of the river mouth."

While the year had started out with a bang, and fishing for schoolies was better every year, the summer fishing for large fish along the beaches was just fair, and then in September it all fell off to almost nothing. By Labor Day, I had sixty jumbo bass, and when I ended my Kennebec season on September 24, I had just sixty-two. Trip after trip down through the Kennebec ledges with the Danny plugs was producing nothing.

Chris Knight from Cambridge, Massachusetts, had been hired by the state Audubon Society to produce a documentary on what was happening to the striped bass. He had heard of John's book *Striper* and had contacted him for an interview and perhaps do a little fishing with him. John and I took him aboard the *Sea Beagle* on a cool, drizzly, windless September 24. As I recall, we never saw another boat. When the tide turned to go out, school bass began surfacing along the tide lines all over the Phippsburg area. The fishing was incredible, and at the end of our session we moved over to the Hump, where I caught a couple of high-teen-sized fish on a sink tip fly line and an overly large deceiver that was to become the forerunner of a big fish fly we called the Groceries. What was special about these fish was that while they were too small to belong to the old 1960s- and 1970s-era fish, they were definitely big enough to be bass of note, and we had caught them on flies.

I quit fishing the Kennebec a little early in 1986. Part of this was because we simply weren't catching any of the really big fish we targeted, but part of it was also because we now had the knowledge to very productively fish on Martha's Vineyard.

I am going to spend more time talking specifically about the islands a little later, but for now I'll say that the fishing there in the fall was not only aesthetically attractive, but we caught a lot of fish there too. In fact, in 1986, we caught more than half as many large bass during a few October weekends as we did working the Kennebec the previous four months.

1987

This season started out with a brand-new engine and outdrive in my venerable old twenty-four-foot Aquasport. The original and now eleven-year-old 165 MerCruiser (a straight-six Chevrolet engine) was replaced with a 190 MerCruiser, which was a straight four-cylinder number. The new engine really made the *Sea Beagle* a fast boat and more fun to use.

Wanting to start using the new engine got me on the water a little early, and on May 17 we were fishing for cod at Seguin's southwest ledge in fifty feet of water. Using slab-sided jigs and red gill teasers, a friend and I had three dozen cod up to about fifteen pounds. Those days are sure gone, and I miss them. First, the codfish just aren't there in any numbers anymore, and second, it's illegal to keep them if you are lucky enough to find a few. Commercial overharvest cleaned out the inshore stocks of groundfish, and recreational anglers have been made to suffer for it right along with the commercial fishing industry that was really responsible for it. A small-bag limit of cod for private boat owners and head boat customers would make no material difference to the stocks. It is just a spite thing, and it has never set well with me. The next weekend, we caught four schoolies across from the Bath Iron Works, and the new striper season was under way.

While those days of multiple huge bass in the Kennebec were drawing to a close, there were still a few left, and with the strong conservation measures in place all up and down the coast—including a moratorium on commercial and recreational harvesting of striped bass—the number of schoolie stripers was going through the roof.

On the weekend of June 20, 1987, I wrote this account of the fishing: "This weekend one of best bass weekends ever. Massive schools all over lower Back River at the turn of the high tide. Caught nearly one hundred in two days, many on fly rod. Breaking fish everywhere, many gulls, osprey, and as many as twenty great blue herons at a time in the area. Fish were predominately of the '82, '83, '84 years classes, and some were twenty-eight to twenty-nine inches."

On June 25, I wrote: "Schoolies breaking from Fort Popham to my dock and probably upriver beyond Bath too. Everywhere! Trolled up a forty-five-pounder at Green Point. Also a thirty-five, twenty-five, and fifteen at Ram, and another fifteen at Goat."

The notes go on to say that we tagged four bass that day, and that one of them, a thirty-five-inch fish, was recaptured in Bath on September 4 of that same year. Clearly the new generation of stripers was now the backbone of the fishery, and we were looking at a level of abundance we had never seen before. At the same time, we were still catching some really big stripers too. Looking back on it, these were some of the best years ever to be a Maine striper fisherman.

On the morning of August 8 that summer, I was running the *Sea Beagle* back from the Sprague River toward the mouth of the Kennebec. I was about a half mile off the beach when we were suddenly in the midst of a school of breaking striped bass. They appeared to be of all sizes. I stopped the boat, grabbed a spinning rod, and began casting. After a few minutes we had released five schoolie bass. The school of bass sounded, and I decided to troll the Danny plugs over the spot. On my first pass I landed a beefy fifty-one-inch bass that certainly weighed over fifty pounds. We decided to call this spot the Cove, because it looked like an underwater cove on the charts, with a half-round rocky area surrounding a well-marked ledge, all set in an expanse of pure sandy bottom. Over the next five or six weeks of the summer we did very little up the Kennebec. All the action was out along the beaches, either with some live bait from the boat at first light or casting needlefish from the beach after dark. The only other place we regularly found bass was at the Cove.

Occasionally we saw them surface, but generally nothing there gave their presence away. When we drifted over the area, though, the bottom recorder showed fish just off the bottom, down about thirty-five feet, and all over the place. We just pulled in there in the boat and let out the Danny plugs and wire line and caught fish. The Cove was usually good for a jumbo bass or two every time we stopped by.

Since I was catching most of my fish from the beach, I decided to try a couple of other beach spots I hadn't fished before or at least not in a while. On September 19, Phil Perrino and I fished Scarborough Beach, just north of the state park. Using a new stubby version of the needlefish lure with a feathered single hook on the tail, we landed four bass, including one estimated at thirty-eight pounds and another at fifteen. On September 18, I fished alone at the mouth of the Mousam River at Parson's Beach in Kennebunk. This river, like the Morse River at Popham, has a meandering channel that cuts across a fairly flat beach. At night these places are a little unnerving to wade, because the edge of that channel can be a quick drop-off that takes you in over your waders and places you in some very fast-flowing water. I never actually went for a swim, but I came close on several occasions. That night at the Mousam, at about half tide down, fishing a Red Fin swimming plug, I landed a bass I estimated to be in the high thirty-pound range. With all the current from the river, this fish ran off a pile of mono before I was able to work it over to the south, out of the river's flow, and land it. On September 12, Phil and I fished some rocks south of parking lot five at Plum Island. Phil knew the spot, and he caught a mid-thirty-pound bass there along with some schoolies.

On September 15, Fred Thurber from Rhode Island rented the Spurwink House on the Sprague estate in Cape Elizabeth, and he invited me over to fish with him. We fished the mouth of the Spurwink River from the north side, near his rented house. I had fished this spot many times from the south side, which could be reached by walking down Higgins Beach, one of the most featureless beaches I've ever seen.

The beach is as flat as a pancake, and you have to wade a long distance from dry sand to find any water. That doesn't mean there aren't fish there, though, especially at the mouth of the Spurwink River, which drains a large, rich marsh system. A lot of bass go up that river on the flood tide and stop and feed here and there on their way out during the ebb. Often good numbers of bass congregate where the deeper water begins just below the low tide mark. But attempting to reach that area before low tide is really tough. Waves stand up and attain quite a velocity moving across that flat sand beach. If you are not looking for it—and often at night you can't see it anyway—these waves have a habit of hitting you right in the face or, at other times, in the groin, either scenario making for unpleasant fishing. As a result I didn't fish the Spurwink much, preferring instead the beaches around Popham.

The chance to fish it from the north side, though, was very compelling. Here, similar to the setup at the Sprague River, the Spurwink runs right along a small rock cliff before finally dumping into the Atlantic at a beautiful point of mixed sand and ledge. Not long into the ebb, a time when you couldn't have gotten within a hundred yards of where we were by fishing the sand beach side, a nice tide rip set up where the rapid outflow from the river hit the stationary ocean water. I made a long cast across the outflowing current with a Gags needlefish and hooked and later landed a bass we estimated (by measuring it against the rod) at about fifty inches. It must have weighed in the high forties or even fifty pounds.

I'm just reporting a few highlights of the 1987 fishing. My logbook records that I went fishing almost daily from mid-May until early October. When the tides weren't right at one of my favorite beaches, I fished the bridge abutment near my home in Falmouth for schoolies. Some of the bass I was getting there were nearly thirty inches long.

It was the chance for a really big fish that drove me, though, and when the tides were right at a place such as Reid State Park, the Morse or Sprague Rivers, or Popham Beach, I would go every night. The tides move forward by fifty minutes a night, and I set my alarm clock every day for the new day's trip. I'd sleep, usually fitfully, often waking up without the alarm, pull on some clothes, grab a coffee, get into my already loaded car, and drive the fifty minutes or so to get to the beach. After fishing a couple of hours, I'd drive home, crawl back into bed, usually infuriating my wife with my cold, damp body, and after a short but sound sleep, get up and go to work. Sometimes this would go on for five or six nights in a row. It is a wonder my career and my marriage survived it all.

The year just continued on and on for me. After the fishing in Maine slowed down toward the end of September, I started fishing on Martha's Vineyard. My notes for the season simply say, "Fished the Vineyard many weekends this year."

Phil and I made a deal with the manager of a hotel in Vineyard Haven, because we guaranteed him fifteen nights for the season. We only slept during the day. We'd shut the curtains, then use the extra towels to cover any cracks that might let in light. It was really never enough sleep, and we came off the island on Sunday dog-tired, but we loved it. Then, in November, we started going down to Block Island, and we ended the season there, fishing in snow squalls around Thanksgiving week. I guess I was too busy to write much more in the log. My notes on fishing Block Island that fall are quite sparse, though I know we were catching some big fish. I guess I was just too busy to write much more in my log.

There was also a surprising bit of good news in 1987. I found it penned in right after the August 16 entry: "Success in Kennebec—young-of-the-year stripers found near Abagadasset River mouth." The Abby, as it is locally known, is one of the Merrymeeting Bay tributaries of the Kennebec at the town of Bowdoinham. Like the rest of the small rivers that flow into the mini-version of upper Chesapeake Bay, which Merrymeeting amounts to, the Abby is a paradise for anadromous fish: shad, smelts, short-nosed and American sturgeon, alewives, river herring, tommy cod, and white perch. River herring get the most attention because they are prized as lobster bait, and so in Maine, the lobster capital of America, there is no shortage of interest in them. This means that Maine's Department of Marine Resources tracks the population levels in the Kennebec by doing an annual stream survey, whereby a seine of the same size is hauled in the same areas at set times each year, and the number of young-of-the-year fish of each species of interest are separated out and counted. While from the beginnings of European settlement up through the early years of the twentieth century, it was an established fact that baby striped bass were growing up in the river, none had been found in more than sixty years. But in 1987, the stream survey found twenty-six tiny striped bass that had clearly been spawned in the Kennebec earlier in the summer. It now seemed very possible that one day the Kennebec might again have its own self-sustaining population of striped bass and not need to depend on the struggling spawning and nursery areas south of us for the fish needed to sustain a recreational fishery.

Beginning in 1987, young-of-the-year striped bass have been found in the Kennebec in every year (except 2010) up to and including 2020. Unfortunately, while there have been some years where more young stripers have been found than others, it doesn't appear there are enough to make a real contribution to the Kennebec's recreational striper fishery. There are still essentially no stripers caught before the migratory fish arrive from the south, and fishing seems to grind to halt when the last of these fish returns south. Fish do hang in the Merrymeeting Bay area of the Kennebec as late as early November, but there is very little evidence of them regularly overwintering anywhere in the system. Why the local breeding population hasn't expanded as it has in some other northern rivers, such as the Shubenacadie and the Northwest Miramichi in the Canadian Maritime provinces of Nova Scotia and New Brunswick, is an ongoing mystery.

1988

A couple of my entries from the beginning of the 1988 season foreshadowed what were to become important developments in my saltwater fishing career. My first striper in 1988 came on May 1 from the mouth of Popponesset Bay on the south side of Cape Cod. I had bought a house on Cape Cod the year before (more on that later), and I remembered how we had caught stripers at the end of a long spit of land at the mouth of Popponesset Bay early in the season, while I was in college. My father-in-law and I went there on a damp, cool, very early May evening in a fourteen-foot aluminum boat that I had bought to keep in the new place on the cape. We found a school of small stripers in the same place I had the last time I fished there, twenty years before. We caught them on tiny broken-back Rebel swimming plugs. From then on the cape was to become an important part of my striped bass season, both in the early spring and in the late season.

A week later I made my first trip out to Platts Bank, a historic ground fishing area about thirty miles due south of the mouth of the Kennebec. The fishing for cod, cusk, and haddock was simply fantastic compared to what we were used to farther inshore, but what was really important about this trip was realizing you are very much alone when you are that far offshore, and so you need to be in a position to take care of yourself in every way and not rely on luck. My old Aquasport was a great boat, but the shallow semi-V hull, and stern-drive setup were not ideal equipment for spending time offshore in the Gulf of Maine. A desire to do more of this type of fishing motivated me to buy a twenty-five-foot deep-V Hydra-Sport with a two-hundred-horsepower outboard and, sitting beside it on the transom, a forty-horsepower for emergency power. The Hydra-Sport was a great hull for making time in rough water.

The next week, May 20, I flew to Key West to see John Cole, who was living there then and working with Pritam Singh. We planned to spend a few days fishing for tarpon in the Marquesas Islands. Over the next several years I did a little more tarpon fishing, though it never became a big part of my life. The main effect tarpon fishing did have was to motivate me to become serious about fly casting. I could cast well enough before that trip, though I had no idea how the mechanics of good fly-fishing really worked, to get a fly in front of a fish as long as there wasn't any real wind to contend with.

Our guide was Jeffrey Cardenas, whom Cole had befriended early in his guiding career. Jeffrey and I were both relatively young men then, and both of us were very interested in being strong, distance-capable fly-casters. Jeffrey was considerably closer to that goal than I, and I listened with great interest when he told me about guiding a tournament-caliber caster who could throw a twelve-weight line a hundred feet into a breeze. That, I thought, is something I want to learn to do. And I did learn it. Now, at seventy, I have the troubled shoulders that result from too much time wielding heavy fly rods, but I have no regrets. I've always believed that, to a very large extent, saltwater fly-fishing is fly casting. Being able to make a good cast in less-than-ideal conditions is required to consistently make good catches with a fly rod, especially in salt water, where distances are much greater and the wind is a nearly constant factor.

I see in my logbook that I only kept track of large bass on the Kennebec up through the first of July 1988, and that we had only nine. Fishing overall was quite good though. The change was that we were catching lots of bass now that were really quite large fish, but not of the thirty-or-so-pound fish that were the threshold of what we considered large bass a decade earlier. We still got some. On June 30, I landed one in the Kennebec down by the Funnel that was forty-six inches. Fish that size, though, just weren't common enough to be worth recording separately, as I had done in my earlier years. It wasn't even possible to target those fish, because all the good structures now held lots of stripers from twenty-five inches up to about thirty-six or maybe thirty-eight inches, and we were catching so many in that size range that the larger ones just showed up in the catch on rare occasions.

A September 11 note recorded our last trip of the season to Platts Bank in the Hydra-Sport. It seemed flat calm on the way out, but a northwesterly breeze gained intensity as the morning wore on. On the trip back, the new *Sea Beagle* ran comfortably at twenty-five knots through two- to three-foot seas. The Aquasport would have pounded so hard that you would have been forced to throttle back to half that speed.

More successful striped bass spawning was noted for 1988 with just four young-of-the-year bass being captured in both the Androscoggin and the Abagadasset Rivers. Two-year-olds were found ascending the fishway over the falls in Brunswick.

I fished most weekends on Martha's Vineyard that October and did quite well. Then I spent a few nights in November out on Block Island.

One day that November, out on Block Island, Fred Thurber, Phil Perrino, and I were hanging around the house we had rented, trying to get some rest before another night out on the beach. Fred had brought with him a large natural history book, and he was reading a story about the development of brains in animals. On the right side of an accompanying illustration was a drawing of a human, and the caption said something about the most advanced state of development of the brain. On the other side was a picture of a fish, and the caption said it was the most primitive example of anything that could be called a brain. The fish in the illustration was a striped bass, the creature we were spending all this time, money, and energy trying to figure out.

1989

The late 1980s were a good time in my life. I was in my late thirties, and I still had the energy of youth. This allowed me to fish several nights of good tides in a row and still put in a day's work. My copy machine sales and service business was doing very well, so I could take the time to travel a little, and I had the extra money to afford it. This allowed me to expand my fishing horizons with things like trips to Key West, weekends on Nantucket and Martha's Vineyard and Block Island and Cape Cod, and getting the new Hydra-Sport to fish offshore. Still, the heart of my fishing was in Maine.

I remember something my mentor Brock Apfel used to say: "As I get older, the fishing that I like best is the fishing right outside my back door." I'd go along with that today, as long as your backyard has at least the potential to provide good fishing. Even today, in the 2020s, the Gulf of Maine and the rivers that flow into it still provide such opportunities. Thirty years ago, though, I very much wanted to see and try different fishing places and experiences. The time required to take fishing trips away, however, reduces your focus on your home waters, and that in turn causes you to miss some opportunities you otherwise might have gotten in on. But, as I said earlier, I have no regrets about my years of focusing on striped bass.

As I go over my logbooks, I'm remembering many of those trips, the friends I went with, the fish we caught, and even the feel of the clean air and the look of the wild landscapes. I think I can honestly say I don't regret any fishing trip I ever took, whether for a few hours right outside my back door or off to Russia salmon fishing for two weeks. When I look at a year like 1989, I see an entry for almost every day from mid-May through the end of October. I remember June telling me on more than one occasion during those years that one or another of our friend's wives had told her they would never put up with their husband being away as much as Brad was. Our marriage survived just fine, though, and if I anything, I wish I had gone even more often.

In 1989, the huge bass that John Cole called slammers were definitely becoming in shorter supply in the Kennebec, and even though the fishing on fish as large as thirty-four or thirty-five inches was very good, I was used to catching stripers that were easily a foot larger than this, and I didn't really want to go backward. I also like the aesthetics of surf-casting. Some would say that one taken with your feet on the sand is worth any number caught while standing—even worse sitting—in a boat. So, as in other recent years I fished the Kennebec a ton during June and early July, and we had excellent catches, though of moderate sized fish. The river failed to produce much during the dead of summer, as was normally the case, but the big change was that there was also no real pick up in the fall. The fall had always been my favorite time, and the decline was tough to accept. I spent more and more of my fishing time on the beaches, mostly Reed and Popham, but also Scarboro and Higgins too. For whatever reasons I found the percentage of fish that were bigger than thirty-six inches was much better along these ocean beaches, and better still further south along Cape Cod and the islands. As a result I scheduled even more of my fall fishing time further south on Martha's Vineyard.

The 1990s

The 1990s saw the fruition of the striped bass recovery, and the Kennebec became one of the hottest destinations on the planet for striped bass. There were several aspects of Kennebec striper fishing that enabled this. First, the Kennebec's ecosystem was one of a lot of freshwater entering the river. This brackish makeup extended almost to the mouth if it rained, and it attracted large numbers of the striped bass's favorite baitfish, herring, which were there in abundance in all sizes. Second, the Kennebec was large enough to accommodate a ton of boats and anglers without the fishery becoming too unpleasant, yet it was still inside a river, and that meant you were protected from real ocean conditions. As crazy as it may seem, I didn't even bother to get a weather forecast most days I went fishing. Regardless of the conditions, I knew I could handle them inside the river, so I just kept some extra clothes and foul weather gear on the boat and was ready for anything.

Another very positive feature of the Kennebec River fishery were the prohibitions on killing striped bass, using lures with multiple hooks, or using bait before July 1. When we started stocking striped bass fingerlings in the Kennebec in the early 1980s, biologist Lew Flagg and I and then commissioner of marine resources Spencer Apollonio came up with a regulation we hoped would provide an extra layer of protection to the spawning population of stripers we were trying to build in the river. By prohibiting the retention of fish, we hoped to protect the breeding stock of the river, and by not allowing bait, we hoped to greatly reduce the number of deep hookings caused by swallowing natural bait. The prohibition of multiple hooks on one lure was designed to make the lure easier to remove from the fish so the fish would not have to be kept out of the water for long, enhancing its chances of survival. While we didn't foresee it, the new regulations themselves helped to create an atmosphere of respect for the resource and conservation that a great number of anglers found attractive. By 1990, if a fisherman illegally kept a bass in front of other anglers on the Kennebec, it wasn't tolerated.

I watched boats come up to other boats in which someone had just poached a striped bass and demand that they throw it back or they were going to call the wardens with their boat registration number.

In 1986, Maine, along with several other states, also made striped bass a game fish, meaning it became illegal to sell wild striped bass caught in Maine waters. The bill for Maine was put in by Spencer Apollonio, and he asked me to testify for it on behalf of the anglers. When I showed up at the committee hearing for the bill, there was no one to speak in opposition, and no one submitted any written testimony against the measure. Actually the only other public comments came from Bob Boilard, whom I mentioned in the first chapter. Boilard talked on and on until the committee were all either vacantly staring out the windows or had their heads in their hands, looking down at the desk. Finally the chairman told him to wrap up his comments. I tried very hard to understand whether Bob was for or against the bill, but in the end it dawned on me that all he wanted to do was to reestablish himself as the majordomo in Maine striped bass fishing knowledge. The reason no one showed up against the bill was because commercial striped bass fishing in Maine had never been more than a small percentage of recreational fishermen who sold their catch to pay for some of their fishing expenses. By eliminating it as an option, though, thousands of breeding-age female stripers were released to spawn that otherwise would have been killed.

The pleasant fishing atmosphere on the Kennebec, combined with the great fishing that started to build in the late 1980s, also put several tackle shops in business, sold a ton of new boats and outboards, and created a guiding industry that at one time had a couple dozen or more guides making their living by fishing the Kennebec for stripers.

The rules had their detractors. A culture of live-bait guides and local meat fishermen sprang up who couldn't swallow the idea that the government, supported by other anglers, was prohibiting them from their chosen style of fishing. Most years attempts were made to remove the regulations, and some of the arguments were bitter. Luckily the support to keep the regulations in place came from some of the more respected members of the fishing community and had a much larger group of supporters than the opposition, so the special conservation regulations on the Kennebec are still in place today.

Just as things were looking rosy, some changes were afoot with striped bass management at the Atlantic States Marine Fisheries Commission (ASMFC) that would have profound consequences for the future. When the moratorium on both recreational and commercial fishing for striped bass was put in place in Chesapeake Bay in 1985, it was determined it would not be lifted until the year after the Maryland young-of-the-year index averaged a count of 10 for the preceding three years. In 1986, the count was 3.7, and in 1987 and 1988 it was 3.9. These were three of the lowest young-of-the-year counts on record, and that meant that it would need to reach 22.5 in 1989 to average 10 for the period. This seemed unthinkable since it had only happened once during the previous forty years.

In 1989, one site, Hambrooks Bar on the Choptank River, had an astoundingly high count. Apparently the bar where the seining was done was now separated from the mainland and had become an island. Regardless of the reason, the number was an unparalleled anomaly. The one site drove the Choptank River count up to 97, whereas it had not been over 13 in the previous twenty years. The number of 97 was so great that it skewed the 1989 count to the point where the average jumped to 10.9. Three important conservationists of the day—Maryland waterman Jim Price, lure maker Bob Pond, and author Dick Russell—were quoted in a March 1990 *Sports Illustrated* article by Bob Boyle:

> But Price, Pond, Russell and others maintain Maryland's 1989 index was dangerously skewed by four extremely high hauls of fry from one site on the Choptank River, and does not signal a bay-wide improvement in rockfish stocks. In question is Hambrooks Bar, a nearly submerged sandbar below the Route 50 bridge on the Choptank, where Price said biologists caught 1,162 rockfish fry during two midsummer hauls and 536 fry during the final two hauls in late summer. The total, 1,698, amounts to more than half the total of 3,320 rockfish fry caught in all hauls all summer, Price said.

As if to offer further proof of the invalidity of the number, the count failed to reach 5 in either of the next two years.

The word was that Maryland governor William Donald Schaefer wanted the moratorium to end, and it did. The next year both commercial and recreational fishing resumed on a moderate basis, though the commercial quota was on a flexible footing depending on perceived year class strength, and it grew quickly.

This resumption of harvesting striped bass was probably not in itself capable of derailing the striped bass recovery. It was, though, a signal that the ASMFC was prepared to move forward on clearly suspect data and make the decision to increase harvests. This behavior would have a profound effect on the fishery, and it wouldn't take all that long to begin to see it.

Chapter Five

Martha's Vineyard and Block Island

Introduction to the Vineyard

Fishing on Martha's Vineyard started for me in 1978. I had heard stories about fishing the Vineyard before then from George Irving at the Portland Surfcasters meetings. George was definitely a different guy. In some ways I envied him. He seemed to be about the most patient and easygoing man I had ever met. In the years I attended and hosted Portland Surfcasters meetings—and there was just a small core group of maybe eight or ten of us at those meetings—George rarely missed one.

George owned a small sawmill near North Conway, New Hampshire, a pretty good poke from Portland, Maine. Late in the afternoon of the monthly meeting, George would get in his truck, along with his huge dog, and drive down to Portland. He always arrived in time to go to Cap'n Newick's

restaurant at 740 Broadway in South Portland. There, George would have a beer and order the captain's size fried seafood platter. Newick's prided itself on the heaping mound of fried seafood this meal amounted to. George ate what he could and took the rest out to his truck. His dog finished it. George dozed off and on during the meetings and essentially never spoke unless someone asked him a question. He was there to enjoy the comradery of other men who were fond of striped bass fishing, and for at least one night a month, he immersed himself in the striped bass fishing culture. It was enough for him just to hear the chatter: recollections of earlier trips and plans being made for the coming season. If his name was mentioned, he'd sometimes smile, even with closed eyes, and when the meeting was over, he'd very politely thank the host and hostess and head out to his truck and dog and begin the nearly two-hour drive back home. If he got tired, he just pulled into a parking area, pulled a coat over himself, slept until he woke up, and then continued on.

I'd known George for a couple of years, and then one Sunday in mid-February, he simply showed up at my door in Falmouth.

"I got tired of being in the mountains," he said, "and I brought the material to tie up some rigs for fishing on Martha's Vineyard. I thought maybe we could tie up a few this afternoon and talk about fishing."

The way of fishing George was talking about, which was popular with the crowd he fished the Vineyard with in those days, was surfcasting on the south-side, open-ocean beaches of Martha's Vineyard with a bait of freshly jigged squid. This was how most of the Martha's Vineyard Striped Bass and Bluefish Derby winners were caught over the course of many years. The rig was made with a huge single hook connected to a three-way swivel by a three-foot length of fifty-pound test nylon-covered wire. A large orange Portuguese float was strung on this wire, and it could be slid closer or farther from the bait, depending on how much you wanted your squid to move around in the undertow. I don't know how effective it really was in practice, but that was the idea behind it—and it did catch fish.

As we slid the wires through the corks and crimped on hooks, George talked in his very slow, friendly way about his buddy Coop Gilkes and his life as a Vineyard waterman and how he had made his living by trapping eels, raking quahogs, and dragging for scallops. George talked about fishing at night out on South Beach, fish that pulled so hard in Metcalf's Hole that they hardly allowed you to slide the rod out of the holder, what it was like to be at Wasque Rip on a black night, with the wind against the tide pushing the maelstrom of conflicting waves and current right onto the tip of the point, and more. To say I was intrigued would be a great understatement, and when George asked if I'd like to go some time, you can guess what my answer was.

I fished with George a few times on the Kennebec that next summer. When I'd head up to the Kennebec in June, I'd normally get up no later than 2:00 a.m. to be sure of being aboard the *Sea Beagle* by first light at around 4:00 a.m. When I'd wake up and turn my light on, I'd walk around the front of my bed and go by the bedroom windows in the front of the house. George would flash his lights on and off to let me know he was out there waiting. That was it. There was never a call in advance. If I already had someone to fish with that day, he understood and just moved on to Higgins Beach or wherever. I later learned I had inherited George from another Portland Surfcaster, Pete Matthews. George's unusual behavior had worn out his welcome with Pete's wife, and he needed another driveway to camp out in.

In September 1979, George invited me to go with him and Paul O'Donnell, Tony Fagnoli, Lou Zglobicki, and Clem Walton on their annual fall trip to Martha's Vineyard to fish in the derby. All these men were serious fishermen and had been making this trip for a number of years.

Everyone on this trip knew Coop, and George was particularly friendly with him. During derby time, Coop ran himself ragged running his shop, fishing, and giving everyone a little piece of his time. He loved it, and he pulled it all off very well. Once during our week on the island, Coop arrived with a bucket of big blue claw crabs he had netted from one of the island's salt ponds, and another day he showed up with a bucket of oysters.

The weather at the beginning of that trip was atrocious, with almost wintery cold and high winds. During those first few days, we fished South Beach with bait. To get fresh bait, every evening began with jigging squid from the various docks in Edgartown Harbor. This was before the deadly Japanese jigs made their appearance, and we were using jigs made by drilling a hole the long way through a small piece of wooden dowel, inserting a thick piece of copper wire, twisting it in a loop at both ends, and attaching a treble hook. The wooden dowel didn't stop the jig with its heavy copper wire core from sinking, but the wood slowed it down to a point just beyond neutral buoyancy so that, after you jerked it upward in the water column with the tip of your rod, it then sank slowly back down and wobbled from side to side as it went. Coop sold these at his shop, and they were painted white or red, usually with a couple of spots for eyes. Squid loved them. You jigged these lures up and down slowly with a small spinning rod. When a squid latched on, you would let it pulse a few times in the water to expel its ink, then lift it out of the water and put it in a bucket. This was an imperfect science, and any clothes you wore when you were squid jigging ended up with indelible black stains from the ink. When you had a couple dozen squid in the bucket, you would head for the beach. Some nights this took only seconds, and other nights you struggled to catch any, and you constantly weighed how many you had in the bucket against the available tide left to fish.

Clem Walton was a master beach fisherman. He was a short, thick man, a marine biologist by profession, and he loved fish and fishing. He did not love people, though, and because of his very competitive spirit and essentially ruthless fishing etiquette, he made some enemies on the island, including an equally ruthless and two-fisted local, Dick Hathaway.

In spite of the nearly unfishable conditions that kept most of us off the beach, Clem was out there virtually all night. He'd take off from the harbor with his bucket of squid, drive the three miles from Katama Road to the place where you turned off onto South Beach. A sign there demanded you reduce the amount of air in your tires for sand driving. The fishing hole made famous by the late Vineyard plumber Ray Metcalf that has produced a number of derby-winning stripers, including Ray's own fifty-one-pounder, is about a mile and a half distant from the turnoff. It is situated where Edgartown Harbor–Katama Bay breaks through the thin strand of sand dunes that separates it from the open ocean. This was where Clem did most of his fishing.

Clem set up two rods, both with squid rigs such as George and I had made that day in February. He carefully threaded a hand-selected squid of just the right size on the hook, along with a four-ounce pyramid sinker on a little wire fastener attached to a three-way swivel. He then walked to the edge of the surf and flung this thing as far into the ocean as possible, walked back up the beach safely away from any waves, and set the rod in a tube attached to a long piece of metal driven into the beach sand. He set a second rod similarly, but he made this cast much closer to the beach. Then Clem lay down on the beach and watched the rods until one got a strike, showed signs of collecting weeds on the line, or had been there long enough that Clem wanted to change his bait or reposition it.

Since Clem and I were both without fishing partners on this trip, I was assigned to fish with him. This was fine with Clem, because I was a total pilgrim to this kind of fishing, and he could work that to his advantage. Clem would do things like show you how to bait up. To do this he would reach into the bottom of the bucket and select from the oldest squid there. He looked for a specimen so large that it would be hard to cast, and then he would hook it in such a way that most of it was dangling off the hook, and if you did get a strike, the hook would most likely miss the fish. Then he would walk with you to the edge of the surf in a direction well away from where he thought the prime spot was, and he'd instruct you to fish there.

After a couple of long, freezing nights with absolutely nothing being caught, I opted the next night to hang around the house after dinner for the evening. Clem went out, though, and he returned around 2:00 a.m. and roared around the house that everyone needed to get up, get dressed, and come with him as he had found some fish. He had caught a really big one and vowed there were more there to catch. No time was to be wasted. Paul O'Donnell, though, had seen it before, and he didn't rise to the bait.

The rest of us piled into the various vehicles and drove over to Joseph Sylvia State Beach near what is called the Big Bridge over Sengekontacket Pond. There, all of us, except Clem—who was busy ordering everyone around—ran onto the beach and cast whatever old squid we had into the surf and waited.

It was a ruse.

Clem wanted Dick Hathaway and his friends to see him and the Mainers fishing in this unlikely spot so that when Clem weighed in his bass later that morning, Hathaway would think he had caught it at Joseph Sylvia State Beach, not at Metcalf's Hole, where he had actually caught it. I later learned that Hathaway was a terrific fisherman who knew every inch of the island and needed no help from Clem in finding fish. I've forgotten exactly what the weight of Clem's fish was, but I believe it was a very respectable fifty pounds or so.

Later in the week, Hathaway strutted to the weigh-in stage with a fifty-six-inch racer of a striped bass that weighed just over fifty-six pounds. That fish won the derby.

For the last few days of the week, I ended up fishing with Paul and Tony, and we went to a new area for our group,

Squibnocket Beach. I ran into a friendly guy about my age who was dragging a big bass that he said he had caught in the next cove over, around the corner. He shined a light on his white P-40 Atom plug of which all but the tip and the metal lip was inside the mouth of his bass.

"There are more of these in the rocks over there," he said. "But be careful. It's tough fishing."

A fellow surfcaster so free with his information isn't really all that rare. It is just the Clem Waltons of the sport that give surfcasters their tight-lipped reputation.

I walked a couple of hundred yards around the next point of land and into a cove where a group of men were sitting in lawn chairs and watching a half dozen rods in surf spikes dimly illuminated by a Coleman lantern. There were two parallel rows of boards there, a couple of feet apart, buried God only knows how deep on their ends in the sand, and leading right up to bank. This was the old herring run, and I would see it and the whole area many more times over the next decade. Shortly after going by the men in their lawn chairs, the water for quite a distance out in front of me started filling in with the tops of boulders. I imagined these were the rocks my informer was telling me about, and I began making casts. I used to remember exactly how many casts I had made before I had a strike, but it wasn't many, maybe four or five. My white Atom 40 plug was taken by a bass that felt absolutely indomitable. I had a rugged surf spinning rod and a big Heddon reel filled with about three hundred yards of fresh thirty-pound Stren line. The drag was set plenty tight. The bass headed off for deep water, and I swear you could practically see the spool decreasing in diameter.

When that run stopped, I probably still had plenty of line left, but one is never overconfident about these things when you have hooked a fish like the one that was now on the end of my line. I remember putting my finger on the spool for extra braking tension and feeling alarmed at how little line seemed to be left. Suddenly I felt something on the line that I have since felt a number of more times—and it always means big trouble. It was a rock, a very big rock, and the bass had the line around it and was trying to rub the plug out on its rough surface. Seconds later my line was all slack.

I looked over and could see the men still sitting in the lamplight watching their rods. They were blinded by their own light. I was invisible to them as my silhouette was hidden against a tall rocky banking in back of where I was standing. There were no witnesses to my just having hooked and lost a really enormous striped bass.

I remember reeling for what seemed like a long time, and finally the end of the line ran through my fingers. I slipped the line under the bail roller, wound it around my left hand, and started to pull off enough to thread it through the guides. I couldn't believe how much I had tightened the drag during the fight. It didn't seem possible for that bass to have run off way over a hundred yards against that strain.

Over the next twelve years or so I walked many times by that place in the cove where the big rocks began. The famous Bass Stand is just another hundred yards or so farther out at the end of that point. I've caught a few good fish in that stretch too, but I never did hook anything else in there that had the strength to make a run like that one did that night.

In later life, Atlantic salmon took over the greatest part of my ridiculous interest in fishing, but it didn't happen overnight. I went salmon fishing in Iceland almost twenty years before I became serious about the sport. To a degree it was like my striper fishing at what I will broadly call Cape Cod and the islands (loosely including Block Island). It wasn't that I hadn't known about the cape and islands for long before I started fishing there. I had read about the cape since my early issues of *Outdoor Life* in which George Heinold wrote about his trips to the island. I knew that, generally speaking, there were more large bass to be had there than in Maine, though during the 1980s not that many more, and Maine was where I lived. I could fish out of my proverbial back door, and in a half hour to forty-five minutes I could be at places such as Higgins Beach or the Kennebec River.

What the cape and islands did for me initially was to provide me with an extended season. There were always bass at Martha's Vineyard in May, and that wasn't always the case in Maine. And in Maine the season was really over by the end of the first week in October, and the equivalent fishing on the Vineyard continued into the first week of November, and on Block Island up until Thanksgiving. So starting and ending my striper seasons on Cape Cod and the islands was how I played things through the 1980s and into the late 1990s. After the great fishing of the Kennebec started to wane, though, I gradually devoted more and more of my fishing time to driving south.

Opportunities

In the last chapter about the Kennebec, I mentioned the great fishing Phil Perrino and I had on the Vineyard during the weekend of October 12–13, 1985. By then we were experienced hands at fall striper fishing on the Vineyard. The next weekend we were back "on-island" again. Phil and I worked out a routine where we would leave work at lunchtime on Fridays in October and early November, meet at my house, pack the car for the weekend, and drive to Woods Hole, where the ferry left for Vineyard Haven. I had already booked passage the winter before for the vehicle as well as two persons on and off the island every weekend for six weeks. We'd arrive at the ferry terminal, put the car in line, and start the important tasks of organizing our gear, tying new leaders, sharpening hooks, and making a plan for the night's fishing.

Making the plan for the night was one of my favorite undertakings. The plan was a blend of things such as the direction of the wind and its strength, the timing of the tide, what baitfish were known to be around the island, determining if any of the salt ponds were open to the ocean, what was the recent angling success, and a few other factors. One variable that made it especially interesting was the phenomena that it's always high tide somewhere on Martha's Vineyard.

The Vineyard is an island in a complicated area of relatively shallow, moving water and is under the conflicting influences of delayed tides from the Gulf of Maine pouring into Buzzards Bay through the Cape Cod Canal and a tide that arrives a solid three hours earlier, coming across the wide-open Atlantic from the east. It works out that, all on the same tide, you can fish the top of the flood at Lobsterville Beach, drop down to Pilots Landing and the pillbox at Gay Head for the beginning of the drop, keep up your counter-clockwise movement, and crawl up onto the boulders at Squibnocket—still with the pipes that held the Bass Stand—for roughly the same stage of the mid-drop, move a short distance to the mussel bar fishing into the bottom of the tide, get back into the truck and drive along the south side of the island and get on the beach at Katama for the run over the sand out to Wasque Point. If you hustle, you'll arrive for the beginning of the "rip."

Later, we would drive north on East Beach, around the lighthouse at Cape Poge, down the little ribbon of land that surrounded Cape Poge Bay and arrive at the Gut in time to fish live eels, all on the same dropping tide. When we got under the lighthouse dunes at Cape Poge, we always stopped the vehicle and listened for the sound of breaking bass. This area was a shoal extending quite a distance from the shore. Underwater it was made up of a mixture of sand and gravel bars separating some relatively deep, rock-fringed bowls. The habitat was usually too shallow for big fish during the day, but at night the baitfish would gather in these bowls protected by the comparative safety of the shallow bars, and sometimes the surf-loving stripers would come in after them.

In the early 1980s, Kib Bramhall, an early island fly rod ace with world-record fish to his credit, landed a forty-three-pound bass on a fly while wading off the point. Sitting in the truck with the windows rolled down, having a smoke, and listening the sounds of the night surf while the lighthouse's beacon passed occasionally overhead is about as agreeable a scenario as I can conjure up.

Most nights, though, Poge gave us nothing but the romance, and we continued on our way around the long, thin

sliver of land headed toward the Gut. This piece of ground is called the Elbow, and on a really high tide you can be left with almost no beach to drive on. Not far from the Elbow you reach the Gut. The natural architecture of this place is incredible. Looking at it on a map, it is very difficult to imagine how such a thin strand of beach could wind around for miles and end up nearly completing a circle. It isn't a really unusual phenomena for points on the end of sand islands to end up twisted around like this, but exactly how it happens, and how these circular points manage to hold together, is not easy to understand.

At the very end of the thin piece of beach is a narrow isthmus separating the beach from the Chappaquiddick Island peninsula and called the Gut. Through this tiny gap the sizable Cape Poge Bay and its appendages, Shear Pen and Pocha Ponds, drain and fill twice a day. On most autumn nights a small band of men make this long over-the-sand drive and park their trucks at a special location on the Elbow. From there they can wade out a fair distance over the shallow bottom to a position where a live eel can be cast into the mouth of the underwater funnel, which is the beginning of the Gut.

The baitfish from the ponds must leave the bay at some stage of the ebb tide, and they are gathered here by the current and the configuration of the bottom. By a magic calculation known only to the bass, they appear at the perfect moment when the baitfish decide the time has come to run the gauntlet, and the combination of water depth and current flow optimize the predator's chances of catching a meal.

Cape Poge Bay at night is a very quiet place. You have none of the loud sounds made by the ocean surf. As a result, I remember the whooshing sound made by the long surf rods lobbing an eighteen-inch eel far out into the pond. Often, during those years, we would begin to see the first light in the east as we stood flinging eels into the Cape Poge Gut. Assuming this was around 6:00 a.m., it would be nearly twelve hours of fishing on essentially the same stage of tide that we had begun fishing at dusk on Lobsterville Beach the evening before. As with all the fishing spots that we might find ourselves at on Martha's Vineyard, we knew to within a few minutes of how long it would take us to make it back to Vineyard Haven to be on the morning's first ferry off the island.

Beyond the handful that I just mentioned, there are many other great fishing spots on the island. There are the Chops (east and west), Mink Meadows, Tashmoo, and the Brickyard on the North Shore. The multicolored house, a lovely deep cut in the beach in back of the Jackie Onassis estate (irreverently named Jackie's Hole), Club House Point (overlooking the site of the old Squibnocket Club building), Stonewall Beach and Point, and among the great many more are my personal favorites, the pond openings of the south shore, namely, Edgartown Great Pond, Oyster Pond, Tisbury Great Pond, Chilmark Pond, and a number of other smaller ones. Actually the list of places on the Vineyard where you are unlikely to catch a striped bass from the shore is much shorter than a list of the locations with decent fishing.

To its great credit, there is no Shoreside Drive on the south side of the Vineyard. If you stand at Wasque Point (the southeastern tip of Martha's Vineyard) and look to the west, the south beach forms a very shallow curve that allows you to see the whole seventeen miles or so to Squibnocket. All but a mile or so of this very gently curved expanse of land is a great ocean beach, and when conditions are good, it can be driven in a four-wheel-drive truck with low tire pressure pretty much the entire distance. In back of this beach are, in addition to some ultra-expensive private estates, a network of brackish or saltwater ponds.

Salt ponds are not unique by any stretch, but these are distinctive because, unlike almost all others along America's Northeast coast, these ponds are almost completely undeveloped, and the times when they are open to the ocean's tides are largely regulated by nature. Most salt ponds have long since had their ocean openings permanently dug out and lined with rocks and crossed by bridges. Some on the Vineyard are like that too, but not these.

The storms of winter fill the ponds with fresh water, and the prevailing northerly winds of winter fatten up the sand margin between the ocean and pond. During spring and autumn storms, the high surf beats its way from the ocean back toward the pond. The water in the contained pond has several feet more elevation than the ocean, especially at low tide, and once the surf makes any kind of an opening, the fresh water pours out with such velocity that it cuts through the sand like a knife. Water pours from the pond into the ocean until the level hits an equilibrium with the sea level, and then the tides wash back and forth, restoring a brackish quality to the pond that will support marine growth such as clams, oysters, and blue claw crabs. With tamer weather, the water height in the ocean and the pond become roughly equal, and the sand seals off the opening. The pond once again becomes a brackish lake until the cycle repeats itself.

Whether they are open or not, the pond openings are potentially good fishing spots at any time. The theory is that some amount of pond water is always seeping out through the sand, and the bass are attracted to the smell. There is no question that striped bass are attracted to places where fresh water enters salt. In the springtime, the first schoolie stripers caught in the rivers I fished as a boy were always right up at the head of the tide. Places such as Augusta that stand near the head of the tide on the Kennebec would have bass in very early May, while it could be another month before bass would be commonly available forty miles closer to the ocean.

The times when the ponds really shine, though, is when they are open to the ocean. Herring enter these ponds in the spring through rain-swollen streams at places like the head of Katama Bay in Edgartown or Menemsha Pond in Chilmark. Creeks connect the various ponds, and herring find their way back to their natal body of water. After being spawned, the fry will grow up in the comparatively protected environment of the pond all summer and early fall. Then, when the autumn nor'easters breach the openings, the fry head out to the ocean and greener feeding pastures. Bass will station themselves near the outflows and catch the vulnerable young fish.

I remember an early November night at the opening to Edgartown Great Pond when small waves were depositing young herring in the process of exiting the pond directly onto the beach at our feet. We just bent over and picked up one of the flip-flopping silver shavings shining in the moonlight, slipped a hook through its lips, and tossed it into the wash a few feet away. There it would instantly disappear in the enormous boil made by a hungry bass. Sometimes the fishing at the pond openings is absolutely spectacular, and sometimes they are simply not there. But always the pond openings on South Beach are wild and beautiful places to be.

In the late fall the last of the migration moves down along the great South Beach. The bass are on their way south to warmer waters, but some of them take their time and stop and feed here and there, as nature provides opportunities. Fish coming along from outer Cape Cod can move south along Monomoy Island and toward Nantucket's Great Point. Once there, they can swim along the crescent of the island's east and south shore beaches, then follow the shoals by Tuckernuck and Muskeget Islands to Wasque Rip. Even during the bluebird days of midsummer, the south sides of these islands are relatively quiet, remote stretches. I'm checking my spelling of island locations with Google Maps, and the aerial photos show lots of boat traffic all around Cape Cod and the north shore of the Vineyard (easily visible when you zoom in): three boats on the south side of Nantucket, one lonely boat off the Vineyard's East Beach, and another just south of Gay Head, and not a single boat from Smith Point on Nantucket all the way across to Squibnocket, the extreme southwestern point of Martha's Vineyard—a distance of some thirty miles. And this is in the summer!

During one trip to the Vineyard in the 1980s, Phil and I stopped at Coop's and heard the news about the loss of a boat in the rips between the islands. It was a father, son, and family friend out for some nighttime bass fishing. I heard that the father and captain knew the ocean rips off Nantucket very well, but they are tricky and dangerous places. It was too rough, and presumably the boat took a big wave the wrong way and rolled over in the rip—a very sad end to a family fishing trip. I don't believe the boat was ever found, just some flotsam.

Perhaps my favorite piece of my own writing is the story of the Columbus Day Blitz that occurred along this remote Vineyard beach in 1982. It appeared in *On the Water* magazine in September 1999, and I just reread it for the first time in more than twenty years. I can't really improve on it, so I'm going to tell the same story again here. I remember I wrote this because I was already old enough then to know how quickly all memory of this extraordinary fishing event would be lost.

Phil Perrino, my surfcasting partner and I were on the *Naushon*, one of the Martha's Vineyard Steamship ferries. It was the weekend after the Columbus Day striped

bass blitz of 1982, and we were on our way out to the island for some surfcasting. Once aboard the ferry we caught up on the island's news by reading the fishing column of the *Vineyard Gazette*. The *Gazette* reported on fishing in the same editorial style that it covered things like the weather, gardening, or bird watching. It wasn't the kind of aggressive, how-where-and-with-what-to-catch-fish kind of reporting that you read in the city papers; instead it was a sort of conversational chronology of the comings and goings of fish around the island during the week that had passed since the last issue.

On the Vineyard fish are not regarded in the same way as they are in mainland, urban areas—almost alien things, smelly and covered with slime, that live over to the east, out in the ocean somewhere. On the Vineyard, fish are fellow citizens; they are a staple of island life, and that goes double for striped bass. For on Martha's Vineyard there are fish, and then there are stripers. No other fish that visits the island has historically been so abundant, so dependable, so delicious and so desirable. Perhaps this is because despite its great size, the stripers swim in the shallowest of waters, sometimes quite literally among the island's human inhabitants. It is therefore possible to stand on the beach and toss a short cast to a fish big enough to nearly tear your arms from their sockets. But in 1982 the striped bass reports were seldom very encouraging; striped bass were in trouble. Often the *Vineyard Gazette* made the simple statement that "stripers were scarce in island waters this past week." It was a representative statement from a culture in denial.

So it was with great surprise that Phil, perusing the paper while I sharpened the hooks on a lap-full of plugs that I'd brought with me from the car, read the headlines that proclaimed the Columbus Day Blitz. "Christ, Brad, will you look at this? It says here that all kinds of 40 and 50-pounders were caught on South Beach on Columbus Day. The bass drove the menhaden right up onto South Beach down by the ponds," said Phil, staring in shocked half-belief into the paper. "Thousands of pounds were taken, guys flying over in airplanes had spotted the fish. Goddammit, we missed it."

Phil, incredulous at what he'd read so far, feverishly perused a few more of the sordid details. Such a gathering of stripers, reasonably common once, was now, we had thought, almost an impossible dream. It was like Germany marshaling what was left of its once mighty army for the Battle of the Bulge, a last, desperate attempt that raised hell for a while, but couldn't be sustained, and afterwards left them more beaten than ever. Phil and I dreamed of great armies of stripers; in our imaginations they filled the moonlit waves in front of us with the splashes and wakes of their feeding. But these legions existed only in our minds. It was almost too much to bear, missing this great show, this glimpse of how it once was.

We used to play a game during our nights on the beach, with which we would breathe a little life into the productive-looking but fishless water that we flogged with our foot-long plugs and 11-foot surf rods. "How'd you like to have been here on the best night that ever was?" one of us would ask the other. Then we'd speculate on just what that would have been like.

"Perhaps there's some still down there on South Beach," said Phil, setting the paper down and staring out the window as we passed the rip at the end of Nobska Point. "Or maybe there'll be another school coming down along the beach." Perhaps, but we knew better; another Columbus Day blitz was even less likely than the first one. Besides, it would have been a mixed experience for us anyway.

For Phil and me, striped bass fishing was a religion, our link to a way of life where livings were made naturally, outdoors, from the sea. In striped bass fishing there were no quotas, no sales meetings, no industrial parks; there was just the beach, and the fish, the dark, wild nights, and the wind. We knew the striper was in trouble, and along with the fishery it was our dream that was dying. For the islands, though, it was a way of life, both social and financial that was disappearing. The *Vineyard Gazette*'s lack of editorial recognition of the striper's plight spoke for a lot of people on the island. "Fish come and go" was the paper's benign message—and when they are here you harvest them, and they did.

During the blitz, pickup trucks, island vehicles with bald tires for over-the-sand driving, and rusty springs from constant exposure to the ocean's salt, were filled to the overflowing with the giant stripers. Some of the trucks couldn't make it off the beach, and fish had to be left there for return trips, or placed in the cabs, down among the angler's feet. Courtesy of the blitz, the local auto dealerships did a brisk business in new four-wheel-drive pickup trucks: for about a week, a sort of "the good old days are back" euphoria pervaded the island's market fishing culture. Then it was back to sobering reality.

As I recall, winter came early that year, and what remained of the striper migration left the rips of Nantucket and the Vineyard a bit ahead of schedule. It must have seemed especially chilling to those who had been able to make the down payment, and now faced a slim fishing future, and a fat payment book.

I don't recall if it was the next fall, or the one after, that Phil and I ran into Eddie Medeiros over at a place called Windy Gates on the Vineyard's south shore. Windy Gates, also called Parker's and Stonewall Point, was reached by a winding dirt road that accessed mostly summer homes. Keep Out signs were on both sides of the gap in the stone wall that led in from the tar road, and many of the trees along its margin were similarly posted. The road ran through stunted oak woods and grown-over fields to a little parking area near the beach. None of us had permission to use it, but we did anyway. Like evolved blue-collar workers from [H.G.]

Wells' time machine, we surfcasters came out at night, driving with our lights out, and often during the cold, uncomfortable times of the year. The patricians kept to their beds while we had the run of the land.

It may have been Phil that asked, "Hey, Eddy, weren't you there for the Columbus Day Blitz?" "Yeah," said Eddy, his broad smile at the reminiscence clearly visible in the light of Phil's headlamp. "It was me, and Ed Jerome, and Coop that found 'em. We'd been up all night fishing down-island . . . just me and Coop, and Ed, riding down the beach, smokin', and drinkin' coffee . . . we came over the top of the hill and there they were . . ." Eddy turned and cast his plug into the surf, looked out into the nighttime sea, and slowly reeled the lure back toward the beach. He was obviously pleased with his recollection of the blitz: he fondly spun his story of what was perhaps his greatest day from a lifetime of fishing the Vineyard's shores. Phil and I leaned against our rods and listened intently.

Cooper Gilkes, Ed Jerome, and Eddy Medeiros had spent a long night slinging eels out on Cape Poge. Since they had been awake for all of a long, fishless October night, you might expect that they were ready for home and a few hours' sleep. The fall migration of stripers, though, does strange things to surf fishermen. There's a feeling that just around the next point, or maybe on the next cast, you'll luck into a ravenous school of big bass, fresh from the north. All that's required, you think, is perseverance, and despite bad weather, sleep deprivation, and unhappy spouses or lovers, the nights of autumn make it hard to stay away from the beach.

So it was that the three friends rounded Wasque Point, and instead of heading off the beach, inland to their homes, they decided that they had enough coffee left in their thermoses to last them on a reconnaissance of South Beach. "We'll just drive down to Oyster Pond," said one of them, "then we'll take Scrubby Neck Farm out to the tarred road." The sun was just rising clear of the dunes in back of them, bathing the way down the beach in the low, clear photogenic light of mid-autumn.

When they reached Edgartown Great Pond, about eight miles from Wasque, the narrow beach there forced them to detour in back of the dunes. They drove along the edge of the pond, and through the transition zone where the dunes, covered with sea grass and beach peas, met the upland fields that were still dotted yellow and red with splashes of golden rod and rosa rugosa. The three friends basked in the pastoral beauty of island morning.

Guessing that they had passed the narrow sand-cliffs carved from the beach by the surf in front of Edgartown Great Pond, Coop now changed directions back toward the beach. He drove through a little pass between the dunes, then came to the top of a small hill that marked the beginning of the broad ocean beach. As they crested the rise and moved onto the beach, they found themselves on a small protrusion along the wavy line of the dunes. From here they could see clearly up the beach to Oyster Pond, and in the distance all of the way to Squibnocket Point, a headland some 15 miles distant.

Here and there, clustered in groups along the beach, herring and black-back gulls either walked on the edge of the surf or maneuvered through the air, patrolling the water's surface. Occasionally, every gull in the immediate vicinity bolted toward a disturbance, either on the rolling surface of the waves breaking against the beach, or in the wash, where the last of the water petered out and the sand began.

Festooning the surface of the turbulent water under the gulls were the boils of feeding fish, some fully as large as the ample hood of Coop's full-size pickup. And frequently, from amid these disturbances, arose a silvery shower trimmed with white, reflecting brilliantly in the early morning light, a stark contrast to the ocean water's indigo surface, which was still unlit by the low-angled sun. These glimpses of the desperate menhaden leaping for their lives were often accompanied by the dark lines of the backs and tails, and the flashing sides of the attacking striped bass.

Sometimes the menhaden that had chosen the shallow wash for their escape from the deep-bellied bass ran out of luck. As they resisted returning over the lip of the beach and into the waiting maws of the predators, the frothy water running down the beach's face left them flopping on the wet sand. Here, they met a new and even less merciful predator in the gulls; since the baitfish were too large to swallow whole, the gulls held them down, and while still alive and wriggling, ripped them apart with the sharp hook at the end of their beaks. The sheer numbers of the menhaden were too great, though, and many escaped, gasping and writhing about on the beach beside their less fortunate schoolmates that were being eaten by the gulls. Then another wave carried them back toward the renewed danger waiting for them only a few yards from shore.

"Geezuz Christ, wouldya look at that!" exclaimed one of the men as he pointed unbelievingly toward the beach. The other two men leaned slowly forward in stunned, open-mouthed silence. This was the moment, perhaps the one moment, in the life of a hard-core soldier of the surf when things were perfect, beyond any expectation, and then some. For these were not tiny schoolies, chasing skinny sand eels in the wash of some quiet back-beach on a placid summer's evening. These were immense stripers, record-book kind of fish, those normally caught only in the dead of night at the rate of one or two a year by the best beach fishermen. For bass of this ilk are solitary beasts, not fish to be found charging the beach in waves, plainly exposing themselves to the clear sunlight of such a brilliant autumn morning.

Like all really unusual events this one was a combination of just the right factors. The stripers had probably been feeding for a few days in the tumult of Wasque Rip, over to the east, a place that possesses both the cover and the food to house a school of migrating bass of this caliber. The school may have wandered along South Beach with the vagaries of the southern migration that each fall pulls all of their kind toward the comparatively warm mid-Atlantic Ocean. There they would lethargically wait out the winter until the proper time arrived for them to ascend the rivers of their own beginnings. These were all cows, mature, breeding-age female fish that carried within them the beginnings of the roe sacks that in spring would be filled with millions of ripe eggs.

Moving along South Beach, the school of stripers undoubtedly caught up with the slower-moving menhaden. Also on the move southward, the menhaden may have paused to feed in the rich outflows of the recently opened Oyster and Edgartown Great Ponds. And of course there was the wind; it had been blowing hard from the south for days. This may have pushed the menhaden against the shore. Had it continued, the heavy ocean surf of South Beach would have been unfishable. Miraculously, as if it were all part of some Hollywood script, the wind had dropped off the night before, and it dawned cool but windless. It all seems so plausible, as if it must happen often, but it doesn't. Mother Nature had been waiting for some time before she served up such a perfect situation.

With coffee flying, Coop's truck fairly leapt across the beach, then slid to a cushy stop in the soft sand. All three fishermen had the difficult task of grabbing rods from the jumble in the back of the pickup without the benefit of eyesight, since their eyes were firmly focused on the chaos emanating from the surf not 100 feet distant. The action was now all around them; they were close enough to hear the splats of the bass's tails as they stunned the foot-long menhaden, and the frantic cries of the gulls, adding to the bedlam as they tried to capitalize on the bonanza.

Eddy remembers that he was the first to make it to the beach's edge. He could hear his companions cursing as they tried, with hands that had suddenly acquired five thumbs, to rig plugs onto rods that had been equipped only with a single hook for casting eels at Poge. Eddy's first cast, actually his first turn of the reel handle, produced a stunning belt from one of the leviathan stripers. Even a large bass will calmly suck in a delicate bait like a sand eel or small flounder, but they give a more robust bait like a menhaden a tremendous wallop, designed to knock it senseless, thus eliminating all chance that this nutritious meal might escape.

In its panic Eddy's hooked striper headed away from the beach toward the safety of deep water. The drag clicker on Eddy's reel screeched like a banshee, and it didn't stop until he was so close to being out of 30-pound test monofilament line that he put his hand firmly on the whiling spool. The stout rod bent straight out from the strain, and at the other end of the taut line, the curves in the heavy gauge wire that formed the large treble hooks that were stuck in the jaw of the great bass had pulled out straight as an arrow. Finally, even the barbs ripped out, allowing that fish to regain its freedom.

Eddy landed the next bass, a fish of about 40 pounds, but the one after that found a weak spot in his line and got away lure and all. Eddy was now vaguely aware that Coop and Ed had joined him, and it wasn't long before other vehicles started arriving. To his right, Eddy could see that other anglers had also found fish near the Oyster Pond opening. By later morning, a crowd was beginning to form, as word had undoubtedly filtered back into town from fishermen who finally had to go to work or risk losing their jobs. Some, though, decided to stay on the beach, job or no job.

The bass were beginning to pile up on the beach behind Coop, Eddy and Ed. This wasn't the time to be weighing fish, but Eddy knew that some of the morning's catch had to go 50 pounds. Soon a new problem arose. Few plugs are made to withstand every cast fishing for 50 pound-stripers; between lost plugs and hopelessly bent hooks, they were running out of fishable lures. Meanwhile the bass had the menhaden pinned closely to the shoreline, and every few minutes a fresh pod of them were stranded on the beach by a receding wave. "I took one of the hooks from my last plug," said Eddy, "tied it on, and picked up a pogie right off the beach. I just lobbed it 20 feet, then pow, a big striper grabbed it right there."

By early afternoon the action was starting to wind down. All three men were exhausted; their collective catch was stacked behind them like small logs, strewn from the truck down to the high tide mark. Rods had been broken trying to pull the heavy fish up the beach, reels had burned-out drags and stripped gearboxes, and there wasn't a plug left among them that had a full complement of treble hooks. The surviving bass had backed away from the beach. The school may have stayed off the ponds that evening. A few big fish were taken bottom fishing that night with bait, but it wasn't many.

By the next day the blitz was simply one for the record books, a new benchmark. The uneaten menhaden and uncaught bass had moved along. Perhaps for a day or two they dallied off Squibnocket, where they were less likely to be detected along the boulder-strewn shoreline, or maybe they moved on to Block Island or Montauk.

The fishermen loaded their catch and headed slowly off the beach in their creaking, overburdened trucks. The ever-present winds of the island's fall season soon obliterated their tracks from the beach, and the gulls, having eaten every scrap of menhaden, went back to dropping crabs and shellfish onto the paved South Beach parking lot. It had been a great day by any standards. The Columbus Day blitz, one day when everything was perfect, one day in living memory when the fishing may have been equal to—as Phil and I used to fantasize about during our long, often fishless nights surfcasting—the best day that ever was.

Wasque and Squibnocket

At the far eastern end of South Beach, on Chappaquiddick Island where the shoreline turns the corner to run due north and becomes East Beach is Wasque Rip, or more accurately where the rip comes closest to the shore. On each tide, the waters ebbing or rising along these two Vineyard shores rub together on this corner. The result is a spectacular, huge current seam that can be seen on a sunny, windy day from the point itself, running more or less southeast toward the horizon. Everywhere are treacherous sand shoals covered with breaking waves. It is all a spectacular habitat for game fish. The rip can fill with bluefish during the day, and dozens of anglers can sometimes be seen in front of a huge boomerang-shaped line of four-wheel-drive trucks, many with rods simultaneously bent by savage bluefish. In the fall, bonito, false albacore, and Spanish mackerel can be seen crashing frantically around, chasing small baitfish. And at night the place belongs to huge striped bass.

In the dark of night, as the rising or east-running tide slacks for a few minutes before it begins to run in the preferred westerly direction, vehicles start to gather at the point. Most of these anglers are members of a regular crowd that frequently fish this spot, and they have the equipment and knowledge to catch fish in this specialized environment. Generally speaking, the equipment is a long surf-spinning rod of eleven feet or more and a high-capacity spinning reel that will hold enough twenty- to thirty-pound test so that a really long cast can be made. Not that an extra-long cast is always needed. Depending on the direction of the wind and the size of the tide, the rip and the fish can be just a few yards off the tip of the beach.

The current can run at six knots here, and it is impossible—as you stand in the sand that is constantly disappearing from under your feet and look at the boiling tumult of white water that seems as if you can touch it with your rod tip—not to think about what would happen if you stepped just a little too far into that wash. It has happened, with fatal results, not only here but at Great Point, Nantucket, and the North Rip at Block Island, which is the most treacherous of all. At other times, though, actually more frequently than not, a really long cast will put extra fish on the beach.

The actual taking zone is usually quite narrow. It is sometimes possible to walk up the beach a distance in front of the rip and catch fish, but generally speaking this rip, like others, has a sweet spot just as a seam in a river does, and it isn't very wide. Because of this, the fishermen form a picket line at the rip, standing quite close together. These fishermen are often burly, hard-core types and a bit irritable from fishing in the middle of the night in close quarters. You fish the rip by making a cast, flipping over the bail, and letting the lure swim through the hot zone on a tight line. Then you reel in at a rapid pace and do it again. If one person is casting considerably shorter than the others or using a lure that sinks faster than the ones most other casters are using, then he ends up hooking the lines of the other casters. Some bad moments can take place. I never saw a fight, but I've heard it has happened.

Certain plugs were used at Wasque much more frequently than others, and the number-one choice was the Gibbs

Casting Swimmer. The plug is all wood, and the lower jaw of an odd-shaped head acts like the metal or plastic lip on most swimming plugs. It is also very heavy and streamlined and will cast into the wind far better than other swimming plugs. If you saw some rods sticking up in the rod rack of a vehicle over at Coop's Tackle Shop or parked the morning after in front of the Dock Street Café in Edgartown, you could tell if they had been fishing the rip, because the Gibbs Casting Swimmers on their lines would have all the paint worn off that lower lip from rubbing on the high spots in the sand bottom. Add to that some large bass scales in the truck bed or on the fish box in front of the grill, and you knew there were some fish in the rip!

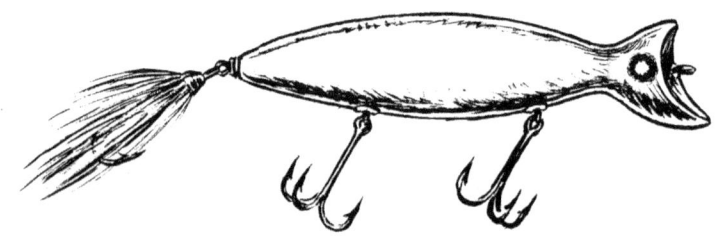

That isn't to say that only that plug was used at the rip, though it was the one most frequently found on someone's line. If the rip was being lightly fished that night, then you could use anything. And not infrequently, especially on the post-midnight tides, you were alone at the rip. One night a fisherman caught several nice bass while the rest of us struggled to get anything. Unless you want to be insulted, you never ask a surfcaster you don't know what he is catching fish on. Instead, you try and figure it out by watching for clues. But sometimes the fishermen are nice guys, and they just tell you. This guy walked over to me on his way back to his place in line and shined his light on the beach in back of us (you never shine your light on the water) and illuminated a bucktail jig he held in his hand. It was custom-made by him and had a head on it the size of a 12-gauge rifled slug. It would probably kill someone if they were hit by it.

The rip was running hard, and the bass were right on the bottom. I don't remember if I caught any with that bucktail jig that night, but I did at various other times. And I think I still have that jig along with others like it somewhere in my stuff.

At the beginning of the rip we would sometimes all be using live eels. Naturally you couldn't get a lot of distance casting an eel, but they are effective if you can reach the fish. Eel fishermen, or as island fisherman Kib Bramhall called them, "eel mechanics," developed a special swing for casting eels.

First, you had to hook the eel in the most favorable way or the hook would simply slice the end of the eel's head in half and it would be gone. The hook has to go in through the center of the bottom jaw and out through an eye socket. That gives you both of the eel's tough areas, the tip of the jaw and the eye socket, and they should stand up to the pressure of the cast. Naturally the eels don't like this much. We used to throw them on the beach, use the sand to grasp them by their slimy tails, and then swing them down onto the beach, pounding their head and upper body onto the sand. That would stun them long enough to slip in the hook and start casting them. The eel would live a long time when it was fished like that.

I have cast one for two hours, unhooked it, and watched it swim away. They don't have to be alive to catch fish, but the live ones seem to work better. You can reel in your eel to make a cast and hold the rod tip up against the moonlight. If your eel is still alive, you will see a little curl at the end of its tail, and that indicates it is fine to keep fishing.

The special swing I am talking about is one whereby the speed and load in the rod are built up with a very long motion that starts slowly and gathers momentum. You start by stepping backward with one foot and reaching with the rod far behind yourself, then constantly accelerate forward until you let the eel go after a forward step with your arms stretched far out in front of you. You have to make it all in a single smooth motion. We also used much larger eels at Wasque than in other places, such as Poge Pond. We were fishing for big fish, and we wanted the extra distance the weight would give us.

One inky October night, Phil and I arrived at Wasque Point a little early in the tide. Phil growled about being tired and curled up in the passenger seat for a quick nap. I sat in the cab for a while, but I got itchy and couldn't resist finding out if anybody was out there and willing to take a big eel. It just felt fishy. I selected a lively eel, about a foot and a half long, from a dozen we'd bought earlier at Coop's, slatted it against the beach to calm it down, slipped in the hook, and prepared to make my first cast. You have to make that first cast quickly with an eel, because if you don't, you are likely to have a real mess. Eels can actually tie themselves in knots, even with the leader still attached. When they are finished, you have a hog-tied bundle of slimy eel that can only be undone with a knife.

Coop sold his eels on an honor system, allowing customers to go out to a plastic barrel on the side of his shop, net out their eels, and leave their money in a small tin bucket hanging on the wall. This eel dispensary was advertised by the word *Eels* hand-lettered in black onto a small piece of weathered board and attached to a stake driven into the ground at the corner his driveway on the road from Edgartown to Gay Head. After closing the shop at night, Coop would take a rake and smooth out the dirt around the barrel. The next

day he could see if he had been visited by people who weren't paying.

I leaned way back, and made my cast in the long, smooth, accelerating stroke I described earlier. The eel landed somewhere out in the blackness, and I was pleased to note I could feel the current had already started sliding to the south. This was the perfect time in the tide for "eeling" the rip. The other great thing was that we were alone at the point that night. That gave me lots of room to maneuver, and I didn't have to worry about running afoul of a plug or a bucktail fisherman. I don't remember how many casts I made, but not too many before I felt a bass pick up the eel. It is possible to fish an eel by simple cast and retrieve. It seems hardly possible when you look at a large eel that a bass could take the whole creature and still reach the hook at the other end, but they can do it in one quick gulp. In fact I had been reeling in an eel at a fairly good pace when, *wham*, the line was hit hard by a bass that ended up hooked far in the back of its mouth.

All this notwithstanding, I generally like to make the cast, let the eel sink with a slack line, and then hold the line in my left hand, between my thumb and the middle of my index finger. When I feel a bass, I instantly stop squeezing the line and wait to feel the bass swimming away with the eel. I then put the reel in gear and set the hook. My spinning reel of choice for this sort of work is a Penn 706, a very large-capacity spinning reel that has a manual pickup rather than a bail that automatically gathers the line. For those who put in the time to become competent with the manual setup, it eliminates the possible malfunction of one more piece of mechanical equipment.

I could feel the bass rapidly swimming away from me with his prize, and I flipped the line around the roller and lifted the twelve-foot rod sharply. The hook went home, and the rod bent deeply as the line rapidly slipped out against the drag. You can tell if it's a really big bass, because its body is so long you can actually feel the rhythm of its swimming strokes. The bass headed straight out into the rip in the general direction of Nantucket. I hollered to Phil that I had a bass on. I knew he wouldn't want to miss it. But there was no response. After trying again with no luck, I turned and walked up the short, steep beach and a few feet across the flat sand to the truck. It was a distance of about forty feet. I opened the car door and Phil sluggishly came to.

"I've got a really big bass on, Phil," I said. "Here," and I reached in through the open door and put the rod in his hands.

"Jesus, Mary, and Joseph," mumbled Phil half sleepily and half excitedly.

After a few seconds I took the rod back, and Phil crawled out of the truck and onto the beach. The bass, meanwhile, had not changed course, and in spite of my huge reel, I felt down into the spool to see how much line I had. A lot of it had gone out, but I still had line left. When you hook a big fish at Wasque, you walk down and to the right, with the current, and in a fairly short distance you round the point. This gets you out of the way of other anglers trying to cast and retrieve and brings you to the slower-moving water of South Beach. This is where you work the fish into shore for landing. Phil was with me, shaking a little from the cold, since his body had been sleeping under a coat or two in the comparative warmth of the cab. He lit us each a cigarette and started to speculate about just what we had on the line.

For a long time after that big run ended, the fish just sat out there in the current. Occasionally I was able to gain a few yards of line, then the bass would summon its strength and pull it all back out again. Finally, though, things started going my way, and for the long distance back to the lip of the beach things went easily. When the big fish could feel the undertow from the waves breaking on the beach, it made another short run, but its strength and speed were mostly gone. Landing a big fish on the beach at night usually produces a few surprises as to exactly where it shows up. At places like Seawall Beach, up near Popham in Maine, there is a huge tidal range, and the beach goes out a long way and is relatively flat. Waves coming along this shallow beach have quite a velocity. You can easily lose track of where your fish is, and suddenly it is somewhere in back of you, and then where it will go as the wave recedes is an open question. The fish can easily get around an obstruction or a companion angler and break off.

At a place like Wasque, especially on a dark night with a large surf, the exact position of the fish can be hard to determine, and suddenly it is nearly head-high and then deposited on the steep beach. The backwash from the receding wave carries the fish back toward the ocean, and in some cases, especially if the fish is upright and swimming, it can seem to weigh a hundred pounds. Many anglers, this close to landing their prize, will try to stop the fish from going back into the sea and break it off or pull out the hooks. You must be in touch with the fish and feel if it is weak enough to be landed. When the wave starts to roll back down the beach, you apply as much pressure as you dare, but not enough to break things. Never straight line the fish. You can break twenty-pound test like thread if you point the rod right at a fish, something you are tempted to do to gain more pressure, but if you keep a bend in the rod, it is almost impossible to break the line. If you do things right, and it can easily take two or three attempts, the waves will recede and leave the fish laying on its side on the sand. You then have to quickly get to it, grab it, and drag it up the beach beyond the reach of the next wave.

When the wave left this fish laying on the beach, Phil and I both gasped. There was enough ambient light around to get a decent view, and it was a very large body lying there. I dropped my rod tip, ran over, and dragged the fish up the beach where we could get a good look at it. For the first time we flipped on our flashlights. The bass, like almost all of the really large stripers I have ever seen, was a perfect specimen. It had vivid black stripes and a huge eye looking down at the corner of its mouth, as if searching for the hook in the jaw hinge that had caused it all these problems. We didn't have a tape (we never did), and we wanted to waste no time in getting the fish back in the water. I lay my rod over the fish's back in the sand, put the butt by the tip of its lips, and agreed upon a spot up beyond the first guide as the location for the end of the tail. I spread my fingertips apart to measure the distance from that point to the guide, and then put my thumb in the creature's mouth and dragged it the short distance over the wet sand back to the wash. The whole process was probably around fifteen seconds. I held the fish to face the incoming wave, and with a shot of oxygen through its gills, it was gone. For a second we could see it swimming slowly off toward deeper water, then it was out of sight. What a thrill! The next day our best guess on the measurement was fifty-three inches. How much did it weigh? We don't know, but it was certainly upward of fifty pounds, and by its fat, perfect condition, it could easily have been into the sixties.

Squibnocket

At the far western end of South Beach lies Squibnocket Point (nicknamed Squibby). Between Wasque and Squibby, mile after mile of South Beach is basically the same: a great open-ocean sand beach with classic dunes and, in many places, an offshore bar structure. It ends as you come to Stonewall Point, a rounded gravelly nub strewn with boulders, some the size of a small car. The Squibnocket Beach parking lot, which was often the center of our operation, is about a mile farther, going west along Stonewall Beach itself. Unlike South Beach, Stonewall Beach is made up largely of semipolished stones ranging in size from baseballs to basketballs. It is hell itself to walk on. Luckily it can be decent fishing, especially in the area toward Stonewall Point.

We took our time and worked carefully along the beach, casting as we went. While we often fished both Stonewall Beach and Stonewall Point, we more often went west from the Squibby parking lot to the mussel bar, Herring Run Cove (where I lost the huge bass on my first trip to the Vineyard), and out to the Bass Stand. These are all excellent spots to hook a big bass. There are lots of likely places all along South Beach, and they often hold bass, but Wasque Rip, the mussel bar, and the Bass Stand virtually always hold some amount of fish. That doesn't mean it's always possible to fish for them. If the surf is up, exposed rocky places such as the mussel bar are impossible. The mussel bar is a sort of submerged and flattened version of Stonewall Beach. The bar is fan shaped, and some of the rocky shallows it encompasses reach out to the east, creating a little cove in front of the parking lot beach. That cove holds fish on some nights. It is generally relatively calm in that tiny refuge between the bar that absorbs the ocean waves and the sand beach. Peace-loving fish, such as spearing, butterfish, young herring, and menhaden, will take refuge in there on autumn nights. Sometimes it is so full of small fish that, if you shine a flashlight on the surface, the water just boils with them.

To fish the mussel bar you walk west a couple of hundred yards from the parking lot, and then wade out onto the rocks of the bar. This is a relatively shallow, flat area, and on calm nights, at the lower stages of the tide, you can walk out quite a distance both from shore and over to the east, where you can look back at the beach by the parking lot. You almost feel as if you're at sea while standing out there. In some ways the calmest nights are the most dangerous or, at least, the most uncomfortable. Waves coming ashore from farther out on the bar flatten out and pick up velocity as they are forced to race across the shallows. They are very hard to see coming in the darkness. One minute you can be completely absorbed in fishing, making long casts to reach deeper water, slowly reeling your plug back, waiting for an arm-jolting strike, and out of nowhere an express wave hits you in the groin hard enough to take your breath away, simultaneously giving you a stinging slap to your face with cold ocean water. Every time that happened to me, I vowed to be more careful and turn myself sideways, so any such incoming wave would break harmlessly on my shoulder. After casting for a while, though, I inevitably lapsed back into the more comfortable front-on stance, and then, *whammo*, I'd get whacked again.

In most nighttime beach fishing, it is not necessarily the longest cast that catches fish. The surf breaking on the beach, the undertow, and the deep-churning pockets between the inner and outer bars are natural feeding stations for striped bass, and often they are just not that far from where you are wading. But the mussel bar is different. Yes, occasionally a schoolie might grab your plug or fly in shallow on the bar (the mussel bar was one of the first places in the Vineyard surf where we did a lot of fly-fishing), and every now and then a big cow bass would slide into the shallows. Generally speaking, though, the mussel bar is where the longest cast you can make is none too long.

I remember a night there with Phil Perrino and Kenny Vanderlaske (we sometimes bunked in Kenny's house on Lobsterville Beach). The wind was blowing very hard from the northwest, and it carried our plugs directly offshore from the bar. By making a cast at a much higher angle than normal, the wind would grab the lure and practically empty a big spinning reel. Normally a northwest wind is death on striped bass fishing. One theory is that it cools off the surface layer of the water and turns the fish off. But in the late fall, everything can be different. On this night you could have waded well out on the bar and made one-hundred-foot casts with your fly rod and probably caught nothing. But even farther out on the bar, presumably at the point where it started to drop off into some deeper water, a school of jumbo stripers was feeding.

We made the longest casts possible, certainly well over a hundred yards, and started a moderate retrieve back to the shore. Almost every cast resulted in a powerful strike on the shallow-running needlefish plugs we were casting. Everything was taking place inches beneath the surface, and when the bass felt the hook, the water flew in all directions. In the wind and moonlight you could see these big splashes at what seemed like incredible distances from where we were standing. If you didn't get a hit, the time to reel the plug back in seemed to go on forever, and all the hits were coming in the first few turns of the handle.

After a while we smartened up, and if we didn't get a strike in ten or twelve revolutions of the handle, we lifted the rod tip high and reeled like hell so we could get the lure in and put it back out into the strike zone. The fish were taking in the northwest wind that October night, but they were on the edge of deeper water way offshore, and you needed a really long cast to reach them.

After you hook a fish on the mussel bar, you are presented with another relatively common problem for a surfcaster, what we called "rocked-up." A powerful bass, after being hooked, is instantly uncomfortable in the shallow water on the bar. It is similar to bonefish, whose fighting reputation comes from scorching across the flats to find their way to the refuge of deeper water. Those who have caught them on deep-water muds know that, in that situation, they are more content to burrow down and fight doggedly. While bass will frequently start out like a bullet on the mussel bar, they frequently stop and try to rid themselves of what has grabbed them by the face by rubbing the offending object on the rocks of the bar. You can't be sure of what they are doing, but you can feel what is going on at the end of your line, and once you've experienced it, you never forget the feeling. Many times, though, that throbbing, grating feeling indicates the bass is transferring the hooks from itself to a rock. Fresh twenty-pound-test mono will bend most treble hooks before it will break, and we pulled many hooks free from the mussel bar to find them still holding clumps of rock weed. How else could that have happened?

To combat this, we started by all but completely locking up the reels whenever a bass hit the line. The long graphite rods would bend perilously deep into the butt, and while we never broke one, I worried about it a lot. The immediate application of this full-court press strategy usually worked. Our theory was that while the bass could turn around and swim away against the drag, the pressure is too great for them to just hold their place in the water and rub their face on a rock. Anyway, once we started using the maximum pressure strategy, our landing percentages increased.

From October 30 through November 2, 1991, the mussel bar was the scene of what we called the Halloween Blitz. It is especially noteworthy to me because I missed the best night of the blitz. My wife had something I absolutely had to be home for, and it delayed my trip to the island by one day. Pat Abate and Fred Hart were out on the Vineyard, staying and fishing with Ken and Lori Lee Vanderlaske. On the night before Halloween they went over to the mussel bar to try their luck. Pat called me the next morning and gave me all the gory details.

"Brad," he said, "it was simply the best night for really big striped bass I can ever remember. I saw parts of the spool of my reel that haven't been uncovered since I wound on the line."

He landed ten fish over thirty pounds, with several estimated to be in the low fifties. The bass bent so many hooks that Pat was running out of fishable needlefish by the end of the night. He was definitely high rod, but the others had huge fish too. The pictures are incredible. The fish were as big as people.

I arrived later that day and we all went over to the mussel bar that evening. It was not a repeat of the night before, but it was still a great night, and I lucked into the best of it. It was slow at first, and the others were working the area right out front, where the best action had been the night before. I worked toward the east end of the bar, away from the others. It was a moonlit night, and after a while I could see a commotion on the surface of the water even farther off to my left. I cast over there and snagged a small bunker about six inches long. I reeled it in and unhooked it and started to see some big splashes on the surface of the water. A school of bass had found those bunker. According to my thirty-year-old notes, I ended up hooking ten of those fish and landing four. They were all big fish, but a couple of them were well over forty inches.

The other place of note that we fished a lot at Squibnocket was an area around the point itself that we called the Bass Stand. A number of stands comprised of wooden planks with metal supports strung between boulders had been assembled there in the second half of the nineteenth century by the Squibnocket Club. Like the rest of the historic old clubs of the mid- to late 1800s, the original Squibnocket Club closed when the striper population tanked toward the end of that century. During the 1920s, the property surrounding the point was purchased by new owners and became what was known as the Hornblower Estate. According to an article by Vineyard artist and fisherman Kib Bramhall, Ralph Hornblower briefly reerected some stands in the 1950s, but after his death in 1960 the stands were never deployed again. The pipes that held the planks of the stands, though, were still there, and on some boulders they were still strong enough to allow someone to haul himself up on the rocks to fish.

The Bass Stand was the scene of my most embarrassing experience as a surfcaster. Phil Perrino and I were still relatively young men and full of hell. We also shared an irreverent and what my mother would call a coarse sense of humor. We had modified the famous rape scene from the movie *Deliverance* and put it to surfcasting language:

> *Get them waders down, them fleece panties too*
> *Don't say nothing, just do it*
> *Come on now, get 'em down, squeal like a pig . . .*

Every now and then, in the middle of the night, on some desolate stretch of beach, one of us would roar that or some other bit of nonsense at the other, and we'd both practically fall over laughing.

Phil and I didn't always stick close together while we were fishing. We both loved to roam around, Phil probably more so than me, and we stayed in touch with hand-held VHF marine radios that we carried in waterproof plastic sleeves. I knew Phil was fishing somewhere to my west, and after working the mussel bar and the cove by the old herring run, I walked down to the point and saw Phil perched on one of the boulders that we often fished.

Phil was about six-foot-three and ruggedly built; his profile was obvious enough to me as it was silhouetted against the dark sky. He was intently casting away as I waded up undetected as close as I dared without risk of getting snagged in the head by his backcast.

"Get them waders off, do it now!" I bellowed in between waves.

Phil turned around carefully (it was easy to fall off those rocks) and looked back at me.

"Excuse me?" he thundered back over the sounds of the waves on the rocks.

It wasn't Phil.

"Oh, excuse me," I sheepishly blurted. "I thought you were someone else."

I quickly waded ashore.

There was one particular rock at the stand that was my favorite, and the man posing as Phil had been standing on it. This rock was just a little to the left of center on the tip of Squibnocket Point. It still had two roughly two-foot-high pipes sticking out of the rock. They were so worn with thirty-odd years of soaking in salt water and being pounded by ocean waves that they were somewhat flexible when you pulled on them. Even in waders, you could haul yourself up onto that rock with relative ease and the help of the pipes. Once you were up there, the top of the boulder was flat, and from there you could cover some of the best striped bass water the Lord ever made.

In the prevailing southwest wind, the surf coming in from the southwest direction of Nomans Island rolled and broke, leaving a large area of foamy water filled with submerged rocks of all sizes. If you put an hour in on that rock during an incoming tide on an October night, you could pretty much be assured of hooking one or two big stripers for your efforts. That was where we met Dick Vincent. He was about our age and just as nutty about stripers as Phil and I. We were seasonal pals for a few years, and Phil and I expected to run into Dick on the mussel bar or the Bass Stand whenever we showed up there. Dick went on to run a charter boat out of nearby Menemsha.

Autumn or Springtime

While Phil and I made the occasional Memorial Day trip to the Vineyard in the late 1970s and early 1980s, we didn't do a lot of early season fishing on the island. First, we had very good fishing at home in Maine, and we didn't want to miss out on it. Second, during those years, the spring and summer fishing on the Vineyard was often very poor. What was left of the big bass population liked to hang around the islands on their way south in the fall, but it seemed in the spring and early summer they stayed more along the mainland shore. We could guess that was because the inshore waters warmed sooner and the anadromous fish runs and inshore migrations of pelagic herring provided the bass with more nourishing food, but no one really knows for certain. I do know the beaches, bridges, and jetties around the Vineyard were almost devoid of anglers in June, and from late September to late October, the Vineyard was hopping with fishermen. I came to think of the Vineyard as a fall place.

Then, one October day, probably in 1986, Phil and I encountered a fisherman in the Squibnocket Beach parking lot. We were talking about how poor the fishing was, and he said the only fishing he had all year that was worth talking about was at Dogfish Bar, a very large fan of shallow, sandy bottom a mile or so east of Gay Head on the Vineyard's north shore. He said he had been snagging squid and live lining them out with the current, off the edge of the bar, and had caught several large bass one day in June. This information stuck with me because I had never heard many stories about June fishing.

That same year I was fishing the Vineyard in the late fall, just trying to get in one more weekend on the island before the long wait until the next season. It was early November and quite cold. I stopped by Coop's shop during the day for a chat. I told him about the guy we'd met in the Squibby parking lot about the June fishing he had at Dogfish Bar and how surprised I was to hear it.

"What about the June fishing?" I asked Coop. "Were there ever very many fish here early in the season or just a few passing along up the coast?"

"Oh, no, Brad," he said. "We used to think just the opposite. There were tons of bass here and all through the rips around the island in June. We thought it was the fall that brought us the stragglers of the migration.

"Really," I said, "and where were some of the places where you did well on them?"

"We caught them all over the island," Coop said. "All the good places you fish now in the fall, but the best of all was Lobsterville Beach. That place was always loaded."

I had fished Lobsterville Beach during the day on my first trip to the Vineyard, and I remembered it always seemed to have a lot of small bluefish hanging around, but I didn't pay much attention to it. Lobsterville is a back beach, meaning it is on the back or north side of Martha's Vineyard and isn't normally subjected to the ocean waves that hit South Beach. This means that other than a very small lip right at the water's edge, the beach is relatively shallow and gentle. It wasn't at all the kind of place I associated with big bass territory, but I was wrong. The ecosystem made up of Menemsha Bight offshore a short distance from the beach, the large Menemsha Pond and the attached Stonewall, Nashaquitsa, and Squibnocket Ponds, which flowed back and forth with the tides through Menemsha Creek, is one of the fishiest places on earth. In addition to holding bass, the beach and jetties at the outlet of Menemsha Creek are one of the best places on the East Coast to catch false albacore and bonito. And they are one of the few places you can consistently do it with your feet planted on the ground as opposed to the deck of a boat.

"Did you catch big stripers at Lobsterville too?" I asked.

"Oh, yes," said Coop. "Some of the biggest bass I've ever seen came off Lobsterville Beach in June."

Lobsterville Beach is a westerly extension of the beach outside of the outlet of Menemsha Creek. I thought of what an incredible thing it would be to catch big bass with my fly rod along a gentle beach like Lobsterville on a warm summer evening, as opposed to the cold winds of October and the slippery rocks of the mussel bar.

I didn't really do much with the information at the time, but I remembered it. When the striped bass population started to rebound on the Vineyard in the late 1980s, Lobsterville again became one of the most productive spots. The beaches around Menemsha Bight were visited by most if not all of the top names in East Coast saltwater fly-fishing. By 1990 every yuppie saltwater fly-rodder had come to think of Lobsterville in June as the holy grail of beach striped bass fishing. If there was a mother beach for the birth of the striped bass fly-fishing movement of the 1990s, it was Lobsterville Beach. During the late 1980s and 1990s most of the best-known names of the time, such as Lou Tabory, Ed Mitchell, Bob Popovics, Phil Farnsworth, Kib Bramhall, Coop Gilkes, and many more regularly fished Lobsterville Beach for striped bass. Just at the very beginning of that movement in 1988, I had one of my best nights of striped bass fishing, and one of the most unforgettable experiences of my time on the Vineyard.

Just before dusk on June 25, 1988, Phil and I arrived at Lobsterville Beach, got into our waders, snapped on our fly line shooting baskets, tossed a shoulder bag with a couple of wallets of flies over our shoulders, dangled a couple of flashlights around our necks, and walked down the path and through the dunes from Lobsterville Road to the beach. Just a couple of years later it would be nearly impossible to find a place to park near the beach at this time of the season, but in 1988 the word wasn't yet out about this place. There were a few fishermen scattered here and there along the beach, and all was quiet. I could see, though, a few hundred yards out from the beach, a large quantity of gulls, some flying reconnaissance and others just sitting on the water. Another fisherman walked by, saw where I was looking, and said that not that long ago there had been quite a bit of surface activity on the water out there. I waded in a few yards, stripped out some line, and started casting. As darkness approached, the southwesterly sea breeze that had been to our backs disappeared completely and a light northwestern breeze off the mainland started up. Bass soon became visible rolling here and there, well within casting distance of the beach.

The fish weren't easy to catch that evening, though they remained thick throughout the whole tide, which started high and dropped all evening. But you were never all that long without a grab, and this went on for nearly six hours. I didn't write down how many fish we landed, and I suspect that is because we were too busy to count, but it was a pile of fish. It does say they were between eight- and the low twenty-pound range. That kind of fishing went on for probably the next ten years before it started to slow down.

Around 3:00 a.m. or so, Phil and I had finally had enough, and we staggered off the beach and up to the road to stow our fishing rods in the car, lean the seats back, and get a little sleep before daylight.

We were still high from the night's nonstop action and chatting up a storm as we stuffed our fly rods into the back of my Trooper when we heard Kenny Vanderlaske's voice. Kenny and Paul Sharp were acquaintances from the Squibnocket mussel bar. During the same two weeks every fall, Kenny and Paul rented a house overlooking Nashaquitsa Pond and surfcasted the Vineyard, mostly the up-island section near

Squibnocket and Gay Head. Both men were from Long Island, near New York City, and both were longtime veterans of the Montauk surf. On a dark and foggy night, Phil and I might be taking a break in the Squibby parking lot. We'd be sitting there, having a smoke and drinking a little lukewarm coffee, and Kenny would simply appear from the blackness. Phil was better than I at seeing things in the dark. We'd be fishing and see other fishermen wading in the distance.

"That's so-and-so" or "He's using conventional gear," Phil would say.

I'd peer into the darkness and see nothing.

But not even Phil was always able to recognize Kenny's profile on those dark autumn nights out on the mussel bar.

"Any luck?" we'd ask the dark shape to the west.

"Brad, is that you? Phil with you?" Kenny would reply, and the friendship would be renewed for another year.

Kenny had just sold his business to his brother, and with his new wife Lori Lee and best fishing friend, they were going to make saltwater fly-fishing a way of life. Happy to be in each other's company, we stood out on Lobsterville Road, talked of striper fishing past and present, smoked, and drank the last of our cold coffee. These were the days when a lot of new tying materials and designs to accommodate them were coming into saltwater fly-fishing. Kenny was quite an innovator and was really into it. He went into the back of his vehicle to get some of his latest work to show us, and after rummaging around for a minute or two, he returned from his car with some flies he'd recently tied. It was nearly 4:00 a.m. now, and the blackness around us started to become gray. The dunes across the road took shape and then color, and birds started their morning singing.

Kenny opened his fly wallet and was talking away about some of the patterns he was now fishing and tying. After a while Kenny turned toward me a bit more with his creations so I could have a better look. The new light also partially illuminated Kenny's face, and suddenly the man I had talked with and fished with a couple of weeks a year for the past seven or eight seasons became a total stranger. I had never before seen Kenny in the daylight, but his friendly voice, complete with its Long Island accent, combined with his confident, self-reliant manner, had created for my mind's eye a face to match my impressions. I'm not known for running out of words, but I had to stop midsentence to gather myself. Kenny, seeing my hesitation, looked at me over the open fly wallet. In that second I recovered slightly and covered myself with a little laugh.

"Kenny," I said, "I just realized this is the first time I've ever seen you in the daylight. It's the first time I've ever really seen your face."

For a second no one spoke as we each reflected on our unusual relationship spawned by our devotion to meeting the striper on its own terms, in the dead of night, and in this perfect place to fish for them. Quickly, though, the conversation renewed itself, nourished by one more shared experience courtesy of striped bass fishing.

Surfcasting is many things to its lovers: A relationship with beautiful places at uncrowded times of the year. An opportunity for grown men, for a few days, to resume the carefree life of children. And, as we've discovered, an opportunity to make friends we did not even need to be able to see.

Block Island

At my grandparent's house in Friendship during the 1950s, there was a cream-colored, Bakelite AM radio on the kitchen

counter. It was generally on, rattling away with static and marginal reception but keeping my grandmother company. I think the station was out of the nearby city of Rockland, and it frequently broadcast the coastal weather. *Eastport* to *Block Island* and *out to twenty-five nautical miles* were the words that began many of the forecasts. They still do sometimes, but now they are said by a robot. I only knew that Block Island was to the south, and then my life went in directions for more than twenty years where I heard nothing about the place.

In 1983, Pat Abate was fishing with me in Maine, and he told me in some confidence that the hottest striped bass surf fishery along the coast was at Block Island and that it was a reasonably well-kept secret. The previous fall had been his introduction to the island, and if I were interested, he would try to find a few days for me to go out to the house that he and some friends had rented.

That finally happened in 1984, and I joined Pat, Tim Coleman (the New England editor of *The Fisherman Magazine*),

Art Lavallee (co-owner with his brother of the Acme Tackle Company in Rhode Island), and a couple of Pat's and Art's friends to stay in an old white farmhouse overlooking the eastern shoreline of Block Island. On November 8, I took the ferry leaving from Galilee and met Pat in the parking area.

That timing was the first big change to get my attention about this fishery compared to Martha's Vineyard or Cape Cod. Even though it is only about thirty-three miles from Squibnocket Point southwest to the north tip of Block Island, the timing of the fall fishing at these two islands is substantially different. While it is not at all unheard of to catch stripers at Squibby into November, I fished it quite a few times during those years, and it was very hit or miss after the end of October. At Block, though, things were just getting going, and, in fact, some years the fishing continued into early December, though you had to be very lucky to have comfortable fishing conditions that late in the season. There were a few years after this introduction that I was involved with renting a house on the island, and I left a car there for the month. It was a tiny Geo Metro hatchback, and I remember being in a fantastic mood when I drove it there full of groceries and fishing equipment, so elated to think I had yet another month of surfcasting to look forward to before hanging it up for the year. But those trips didn't always work out so smoothly.

The ferry ride to and from Block was a lot more exposed than the one across Vineyard Sound, and the weather in November was usually significantly nastier. On several occasions we had to leave early to avoid a nor'easter coming up the coast. We took the last ferry off the island one afternoon, just before they canceled all trips for the next couple of days. We rocked and rolled onto our beam ends, and I was greatly relieved to get inside the Point Judith Harbor of Refuge. When we got there, I looked behind the ferry and saw two guys in a twenty-foot Aquasport who had made the crossing by staying on our stern all the way across. It must have been one helluva ride. Later in the month there were several sessions when we fished in snow.

Block Island became a mecca for striped bass surfcasters seeking the holy grail of the Northeast surf, and many of the striped bass weighed in the high forties and even over fifty pounds. Every day during the season, surfcasters staying on the island would deliver bass to the ferry to be shipped to buyers at the Fulton Fish Market in New York. The fish were stacked on wooden pallets and marked with the dealer's tags. We would drive down to watch the ferry for the mainland load so we could see what was being caught and by whom. Lord, there were some massive fish in some of those shipments! Many of the anglers in the community knew each other, and there was a bit of a cat-and-mouse game among them to figure out if someone was onto a hot spot and keeping it quiet.

In one respect, Block was very much like the Vineyard, namely, virtually every inch of the island could produce catches of striped bass, though some areas were much better than others. Block itself is small, not much bigger than the up-island section of the Vineyard, that is, the part west of Menemsha and Stonewall Ponds. This meant it was a bit harder to hide on Block. Grove Point, Ballard's, Old Harbor Point, Southeast Point, the five or six points and coves on the island's south side, Southwest Point, Dory's Cove, Grace's, the Dump, and Sandy Point were some of the more important ones, but there are lots of little spots in between.

Some guys tried to do well by keeping in touch with as many of these locations as possible, and at night the island swarmed with fishing vehicles covered with rods and cooler racks. Tim Coleman was one of the guys who covered a lot of ground and kept up a fearful pace during a night of fishing. I fished with him one evening at one of his favorites, a spot named the Shit Chute, where a one-time sewer pipe exiting the island's east side had been protected from the surf by being covered with large rocks. The night we were there, you could barely stand against the heavy surf coming ashore. It was more than I was willing to endure for a shot at a striper, but it wasn't too much for Tim. He was still there, heaving away, long after I retreated to the house for a coffee and to dry out a bit.

On another night, Tim, who frequently fished alone because of his unmatchable energy, ran into some good fishing at Southeast Point. He desperately wanted a fifty-pounder from the beach. While Tim was one of the early anglers into releasing his bass, he had forgotten his scale that evening, and with no way to know for sure, he kept the fish that he felt were close to the magic number. At the end of his fishing, he couldn't carry them all, so he stashed them along the beach and fished his way from Southeast Point all the way back to the Shit Chute, where he walked up the road to the house. The whole walk was probably about a mile and a half, but much of it was through the surf and over some of the slipperiest ledges imaginable, and all the while Tim constantly kept casting. At the house he got some help to drive back and retrieve a good half dozen huge stripers, all at least weighing in the mid-forties. It took almost all night, but in the end, none of them weighed fifty pounds.

The most famous, and perhaps the hardest fished area, was Southwest Point. Like Wasque Rip on the Vineyard, the fishing spot on Southwest Point was not a physically large area, and the anglers clustered around the point to reach the prime water. Some of the New York crowd it attracted were pretty rough. One night at the point, a young angler fishing with his father got in the way of a disagreeable angler, who hit the kid and knocked him into the surf, and then told the dad that Southwest was the commercial fishing area on the island and they should get out. The father came back with the police, and the man was arrested.

What an incredible spot Southwest could be. One night, Fred Thurber from Providence and I witnessed a great blitz of bass at the point. It began right at sundown. Before dusk there were a lot of gulls flying over the surf, just off the point, and with the darkness the bass moved within casting distance of the shore. For a couple of hours the action was incredible, and there wasn't much room between anglers at the point. Fred and I took turns guarding each other's fish, because when released, if they didn't get going quickly enough, someone would step in front of you and try to gaff it.

After a couple of hours, the action slowed up a bit, and I needed a break. Other anglers had been piling their fish up on the beach behind them. When I turned around and walked back onto the flat rocky beach, I could hardly believe my eyes. The whole area was littered with the carcasses of dead bass, many of them the fish of a lifetime by almost any standard. I'm certain that several of the fish I saw were over sixty pounds.

Fifty-pounders were being caught every night. And another of Pat's friends had two over fifty in one night from a place called Black Rock on the south shore.

Of all the areas on the island, the one I had the most faith in was near the northern tip at a place called Grove Point. We always theorized the bass coming south along the coast from Cape Cod and Martha's Vineyard would be tolled in by the big tide rip off the north tip called Sandy Point, and then move south along the coast for the short distance to Grove

Point. I'll get back to the blitz at Grove Point in a second, but first I want to warn you against Sandy Point.

The big tide rip that forms off this thin finger of sand is famous with boat fishermen, and rightfully so since it has produced some terrific catches. There are lots of spots similar to this within the stripers' range, and they are all treacherous.

Exploring new ground, Fred Thurber and I waded out there one dark, rough night. We both knew what we were getting into, and we thought we were being cautious. I waded along the north side of the point, having made a pledge to stay in water that was knee deep. Fred was on the south side doing the same. One thing about Sandy Point is that you don't have to go very far from the high beach before you run out of shallow water. We didn't know this beforehand, and not much more than fifty feet from the beach, as I recall, Fred and I were both retreating up the sides of the bar to stay within our agreed-upon depth. We might have gone a little deeper, though, because our plugs were getting a nice swing, and we seemed to have good footing. Suddenly I heard Fred let out with a startled "Jeezus!" and he was coming my way. In the next second, the wave rolled over the bar, and I went from knee deep to near the top of my waders, and the velocity of the wave threatened to sweep me off my feet. Had that happened, I might not be writing this today. Fred stuck his rod over in my direction, and I grabbed onto it. In another second the wave crest passed, and I scrambled up onto the top of the bar, and we called it a night. I was tempted to try it again another evening under more gentle conditions, but I convinced myself there were better alternatives and never did.

One of my last trips to Block Island was on November 11, 1989. Fred Thurber, Phil Perrino, and I arrived at Grove Point a good half hour before dark. Again, as they had at the Southwest Point blitz, the gulls saw this situation in the making, and they were flying around and sometimes landing in the water over the rocky bar off the point. As darkness approached we could see small fish moving on the surface, and soon those fish were right in front of us in the wash. These were large herring and schooled up thick enough that we regularly snagged them on the treble hooks of our plugs. The bass were just outside of the herring, pushing them in, but for whatever reason, it was quite a while before we actually hooked a bass. In fact, I wasn't really sure any bass were present until we saw the first ones bust some herring on the surface, and then we began to hook up. I don't know if the bass were there all along and waiting for the edge of darkness to start feeding or if the herring were there on their own, and the bass just came along the beach and found them. The fishing for the next two hours or so was simply incredible, and many of the bass were well up in the forty-pound range. This night, though, our needlefish seemed useless. But if you used a big bottle-type swimmer, such as a P-40 Atom or a Danny surface swimmer, and retrieved it slowly, snaking it along the surface, it didn't take long for the bass to find it.

Within the next year or so, really with similar timing to the end of the big bass fishery of the Kennebec, Block started to dry up, and it was just too much aggravation to get out there without the reward of good catches of really jumbo bass. But those were incredible years, and I'm lucky to be one of a relatively small group of people who got in on it.

Chapter Six

Cape Cod and the Elizabeth Islands

Phil Perrino and I would come back from the Vineyard on Sundays so tired that we had to drive in shifts for the three hours it took to get home. We'd take the first ferry off the island from Vineyard Haven, land in Woods Hole, cross the Bourne Bridge, and take 495 up to Middleborough. There we would each get an Egg McMuffin and the largest available coffee. Whichever one of us was more awake (usually Phil) would drive from there north, and around Danvers we'd switch again. When we finally got back to Falmouth, we were both exhausted and close to useless for the rest of the day. This wasn't something my wife accepted readily, and often a full day was planned with the family for me to struggle through.

In the fall of 1986, an opportunity presented itself. June's parents were retired and spent their winters in Florida. They

decided to sell their house in Massachusetts and live full time at their winter home. June was not at all happy with this development, and really her parents weren't either, but in many ways it seemed the most realistic move for them to make. I suggested that if June and I bought a house in Falmouth, Cape Cod—the town that Woods Hole is in—then her parents could live there in the summer, meaning at least through the fall fishing season. Then, during the summer and early fall, June and our daughter Emily could drive down on the weekends with Phil and me, and we could drop them off at her parents. The following Sunday morning, Phil and I only had to make it the short distance from Woods Hole to the house, pick up June and Emily, and they would drive us home while Phil and I slept. Like almost all devious and self-centered plans, it was doomed to failure. I think we had just one or two weekends like that before June got tired of it. But at least I now had a house on Cape Cod.

The cape introduced me to a whole new relationship with ocean shorelines. My previous time around the waterfront, spent mostly in mid-coastal Maine, was in an environment of really large tides, expansive mudflats, and rocky, ledged shorelines. Our first house on Cape Cod was in a little community with frontage on Falmouth Great Pond. The south shore of Cape Cod in Falmouth is one salt pond after another, each of them flowing in and out of Vineyard Sound through a narrow outlet. I knew a little about salt ponds from my time on the Vineyard, but I had never explored their shallows on a summer day, or spent winter afternoons in them scratching up hard-shell clams, to have with my evening's scotch whisky. I was in heaven with this experience. I kept a fourteen-foot aluminum boat with a fifteen-horsepower motor on a trailer at the house. With this rig I sampled the clamming in several nearby ponds, went trout fishing in March and April at some of the cape's "kettle ponds," and fished Woods Hole when the bass, bonito, and false albacore were in. While the main channel through Woods Hole can get rough on a windy day, there are numerous little backdoor channels to help you get around without confronting too much open water, and most important, the very shallow draft of the tin boat allowed me access to the skinniest water without fear of hitting a deep-V hull or lower unit on a ledge, which was something I did all too many times with bigger boats during my years of bass fishing.

I remember my brother Jason asking me, "Don't you know which side of the buoys the channel is on?"

Jason wasn't a fisherman, and what he didn't realize was that to catch a lot of striped bass on a fly rod, you were going to spend almost all of your fishing time outside of marked channels.

My most important striped bass fishing venues were still the Kennebec and my fall fishing on the Vineyard, but things were evolving. I was interested in some exploring, and after the June push of striped bass moved out of the Kennebec, we started spending more time down on the cape. I learned all the little outlets along Falmouth's Menauhant Road: Little Pond, Great Pond, Green Pond, Bournes Pond, Eel Pond, and Waquoit Bay. All the ponds offered excellent May and, in some years, late April fishing. It was great in June too, but by then I was back on the Kennebec.

Our whole family started spending the Fourth of July week on the cape, and I got in lots of fishing early in the morning before everyone else was up. During the day the pond entrances were crazy with people, but they were deserted from about midnight to a couple of hours after daybreak, and there were very few fishermen and no tourists during that late shift. I'd drive up to each opening, jump out, grab my rod, and make a few casts. In the beginning, this was mostly done with spinning rods with small swimming plugs like Rebels or Hellcats, but this was also about the time that fly casting was becoming my equipment of choice, and unless it was bad weather, I started using a nine weight and carrying a stripping basket.

The stripping basket was made by The Surfcaster in Darien, Connecticut, and I still have it. The basket began as a Rubbermaid dishpan, and it came to me in the same box it had arrived at The Surfcaster prior to its conversion. The Surfcaster staff drilled or melted holes in the bottom and inserted a pattern of three-inch pieces of heavy monofilament line and glued them in place. Beyond just keeping your stripped-in fly line from tangling around your feet in the wash, the basket was designed to keep the fly line from clumping up in one spot as you stripped it into the basket. The thought was that it would keep the line from tangling as you shot it back out, which was the bane of saltwater fly-fishing. It helped some, I guess, but it certainly never solved the problem. A strap to go around your waist was pop-riveted to the dishpan, and some large holes were drilled in the corners to drain. I've since owned a number of stripping baskets, but none any better than this first one.

All the salt ponds provided some level of fishing. Probably the best one, not counting Waquoit Bay, was Great Pond. Waquoit Bay required a round trip walk of more than two miles over soft sand to fish it, and on top of the energy required, it takes a lot of time at night for surfcasting. Waquoit Bay, and to a lesser degree Great Pond, have some really large stone jetties at their entrance to Vineyard Sound. Those big jetties are no fun when you want to land a fish. You have to climb down over slippery rocks while wearing a dishpan strapped around your waist, which blocks your view of the ground. I used to spin it around behind me so I could at least watch where I was going. You have to bear down and pay attention to those rocks every second or you could get hurt. I never took a real fall, but I came close.

This was about the time the famous Clouser Minnow was becoming known. The extra depth provided by the lead-eyed Clouser, combined with the up-and-down hop it had while being retrieved, made it a killer. The other hot fly was a standard-issue Lefty's Deceiver. I don't think it really mattered which one you used if you found some hot fish. I generally liked the Deceiver better, because it didn't sink into the rocks and get caught if you daydreamed briefly. The best luck I had at night was on thin flies, and I found it hard to tie them too slim for the midsummer fishing.

The single thing that was most important on these finicky midsummer fish—beyond having a slim fly—was presentation. The fish were hanging out in some very specific spots, and that was where the fly had to go in order be taken consistently. Casts made out into the middle of the channel, between the rock jetties, would usually catch nothing, as would casts made far out into the sound off the end of the jetties. If a fish took it, it usually happened just as the fly got back to the edge of the rocks near the jetty. Casts made along the sides of the jetties and stripped back against the current were good producers. Clearly the fish saw this as mimicking weak-swimming baitfish that were using the slower current alongside the rocks to make their trip into the pond easier and also make them an easy mark for a hungry striper.

Another hot spot was the shadow line from the bridge. My being right-handed, to keep my rod and line away from the bridge, I had to stand on the west jetty, just a few feet downstream of the bridge, and cast a long line out into the channel. I didn't retrieve, but just let the fly swing with the current as you would a wet fly for Atlantic salmon. The streetlight on the north side of Menauhant Road cast a shadow of the walkway across the bridge onto the surface of the water. When the fly came out of that shadow, it was frequently taken by a bass that was trying to take advantage of a baitfish whose vision was somewhat compromised by the change of light. Similarly, you could cast from the jetties on the upside of the bridge and let your fly swing underneath. We stood on the bridge and spotted the bass that were laying in that shadow line, and that was as much fun as fishing. The problem with this technique was that if you hooked a good fish laying in the shadows on the up-current side of the bridge, it usually went under the bridge, with the current, and landing it might be impossible.

I caught many hundreds of fish in these pond openings, but other than one or two in the mid-thirty-inch range that I caught during the fall, they were all under thirty inches, and 95 percent were under twenty-six inches. This was true all through the 1990s and even into the early 2000s, when places like Woods Hole, the Elizabeth Islands, and the rips of Vineyard Sound produced bass as big as they come. Those places aren't far away, but they are a very different environment. They are bigger water, meaning they had some combination of stronger current, more robust structure to attract big fish, and better access to deep water. Catching schoolies was fun to a point, but I really liked a chance at bigger fish.

One of the great attractions to the Falmouth south-side pond openings for me was how well they performed at the ends of the seasons. During the summer, when there are stripers in residence all over the better New England habitat, there are stripers hanging in and around all of these pond openings. They get very used to boat traffic and angling pressure, though, and the fishing is often slow during the warm temperatures of summer. In both the spring and the fall, however, the bass are migrating, and the pond openings are like fast-food rest stops. With the resident bass either not having yet arrived or having already left for the south, just finding a productive place to fish for stripers can be the biggest challenge in late April and early November. With Falmouth's more than half dozen closely spaced ponds emptying into Vineyard Sound, it's likely that any bass moving along the shoreline will be attracted by the baitfish being swept out of the fast-flowing outlets. I often ended my season by hitting places such as Little Pond, Great Pond, and Eel Pond into the second week in November. On several occasions I caught stripers during snow squalls.

It was also true that when the bass population was at its peak in the mid-1990s, there were occasional large striped bass (i.e., over thirty inches long) in many places we would very seldom find one when the population had declined. I compared it to a glass of water. Think of all the large striped bass habitats as the glass and the large striped bass as the water. The best habitat for big fish is at the bottom of the glass, and the least likely places to hold them are at the top. That means that even with a small amount of water in the glass, a place like Sow and Pigs Reef off Cuttyhunk or Montauk Point will always have some big fish. As you fill up the glass gradually, there will be enough to inhabit other less-ideal areas.

In the early 1990s, I met Carl Breivogel, who was doing some work at the herring run where the Trunk River, a little stream, drained Oyster Pond on the south shore of Falmouth and near Nobska Point. In addition to being the town's alewife expert, Carl had a business on the side that cultivated beach grass. His main interest in fishing was about knowing more about the creatures and the environment they were part of than in simply catching them. His fishing specialty was using live juvenile herring to catch the large anadromous white perch that lived on the edge of salt water in some of Falmouth's ponds. These fish were once very common in more of the cape's salt ponds, where the brackish ecosystem brought them more, large, and nutritious feed than was available in the average freshwater pond. The educated speculation I repeatedly heard from people who have been close to this issue is that the headwaters of the various streams feeding most of these individual salt ponds have been turned into commercial cranberry bogs. These bogs are intensely cultivated, and that means applying chemicals in this way or that to fertilize the cranberries or eliminate competing plants within the bog. The chemicals it is believed have had a catastrophic effect on anadromous fish such as sea-run brook trout and white perch that live and spawn in the freshwater sources of the salt ponds. A couple of the ponds, though, such as Oyster Pond, don't have the cranberry bogs and still have populations of white perch.

Carl also made a science of live-lining herring for bass in his chosen environment. He told me the bass would wait in the shallow water at the mouth of the run for herring that were entering the pond to spawn. The herring were so compelled by their urge to spawn that, despite the presence of the bass guarding the entrance to the pond, a group of them would make a dash for it through the narrow channel, and the bass would often be able to pick off at least one. Carl said he had witnessed it many times. The bass, waiting in this shallow water, were particularly nervous. Big fish like the cover of deeper water, and it took only the slightest noise, shadow, or vibration to scare them away from the shallow stream mouth. Whenever Carl fished, he would walk carefully down to the area where the stream entered Vineyard Sound, stop well back from the beach, and lower his herring into the stream, where it would drop down with the current to a waiting bass. If he was fishing in the daylight, he would crouch down onto his hands and knees so the bass wouldn't see his shadow. He said there weren't a lot of big fish there, but he had regularly hooked and released thirty- to forty-inch bass.

When I saw Carl there again in the early 2000s, he told me that as soon as the commercial fishery quota for striped bass had been rebuilt, the good fishing had stopped, and that he hadn't caught a large fish there in several years. We saw the same thing in the Presumpscot River in Maine. Within a couple of years of meaningfully increasing the coastal commercial striped bass quota, we were back to fishing for schoolies. Fishermen from the Chesapeake Bay area during my time with the Coastal Conservation Association had similar stories.

In 1987, a couple of years after the moratorium on keeping striped bass went into effect, the fishery in Chesapeake Bay started to improve, and within a few years they were regularly catching thirty-plus-inch bass inside the bay during the summertime. That had almost never happened prior to that time. In fact, it was thought that virtually all the large bass had left the bay to feed in the ocean. That wasn't entirely true, though. When the population was large enough, and when the larger bass did stick around without being killed, the bay held decent numbers of large fish year-round. Those larger bass became almost nonexistent once the bay's quota was increased in the early to mid-2000s.

A notable exception to the "shallow waters of the salt ponds not holding large fish" rule occurred in the springtime, during the worm hatch. Even after Atlantic salmon had become my main fishing target, I continued to spend a week in May fishing at this event.

A whole book could be written about the complexities of so-called worm-hatch fishing. To begin with, worms don't hatch; they spawn. I've read there are something like twenty or more species of marine worms in the salt ponds of the cape. As with the behavior of all the striper's prey species, as well as the stripers themselves, I've always been curious to learn as much as I could about them.

What I found with the worms is that not a lot is really known. For instance, it is assumed that most or all marine worms emerge from the mud, and at a particular time of the year, under particular conditions, they swim en masse and spawn somewhere in the water column. But the particulars of exactly how that plays out and when, with all of the approximately two dozen marine worm species living in these ponds, are largely unknown.

The particular species of worm that creates the May worm hatches of the south-side Cape Cod ponds looks like the sandworms that we dig in Maine and ship to bait shops all over the Northeast. The ones in the Cape Cod ponds, however, are a lot smaller. Whereas a big Maine sandworm can be well over a foot long and as big around as a small finger, these worms are between one and four inches long. The larger ones, which I assume to be the females, swim erratically and spew a cloudy substance from their bodies, which I think are their eggs. The much more numerous and smaller worms swim through the milky areas, fertilizing the eggs.

Normally the worms arise from the mud late in the afternoon, sometimes very late, and swim just under the surface, frequently breaking the surface film and creating a disturbance that can be seen for some distance on the glass-smooth pond surface. But it isn't always that way. I've seen it when the spawning started at noon on rainy, overcast days, and I've seen it when, after two or three consecutive days of spawning, the worms seemingly take a night off and very little if any activity can be seen. Then again, the next night it may resume. Spawning goes on over the course of the month of May here and there on the ponds on the south shore of the cape, but it only seems to last for two weeks at any given pond. Different parts of the pond seem to host spawning activity on different evenings. While it is possible to see the worms appear amid mild wave action, generally speaking they like it calm and warm. If there is a heavy breeze from any direction, most of the spawning will occur close to the lee shore.

One of the things I like about fishing the hatch is that it can be done with minimal equipment. Grab a fly rod, a wallet of flies, a spool of tippet material and jump in a skiff and go.

There are places where you can wade right into a hatch, but a small boat of some kind is a wonderful advantage because it gives you the ability to follow the action. Worm-hatch fishing is also done very nicely with a six- or seven-weight fly rod and a floating line. Hooking a forty-inch bass on gear like this is about as much fun as you can get out of fishing.

One day in May in the late 1990s, I went out for an evening's fishing in my thirteen-foot Old Town Discovery boat. It was a particularly low tide and an absolutely flat, calm, warm, sunny day. I rowed into a shallow cove on Bournes Pond that I often fished and immediately noted that there was already a light density of worms swimming about. Typically, the first worms to arrive on the scene are the males, and they appear as different shades of red, pink, or orange in the water. But if you pick one up and hold it in your hand, it soon relaxes and becomes longer than its submerged length. The worm also changes color from pink to the dark drab green you would expect of a mud-living worm. This must have to do with the spawning, but I don't know the details. Often, in the early stages of the hatch, the bass will aggressively take these individual worms, and that goes for flies too.

This day I saw the boil of a bass that had just taken a worm, and I cast my fly into the area. The fly was immediately taken by a bass, which turned out to be about forty inches long. With no deep water to sound in and no rocks to rub things on, this bass headed straight for the nearest deep water, which was about a thousand feet away toward the other side of the pond. Anyone who has caught a striper in this situation knows just how fast these fish really are. As this panicked bass streaked for cover, it nearly collided with other stripers that were lazily gulping worms.

The water was barely deep enough to float my Discovery boat, and, in fact, it was hard to row very fast, because the oars contacted the weeds growing from the bottom. Swimming in these conditions, the bass left a big mud contrail, and every bass that my hooked bass nearly collided with in its flight also spooked and made a big mud. In short order, the bass and its startled companions turned a big path down through the cove into what looked like a battlefield. It was fabulous stuff.

On most days the hatch fairly quickly progresses in volume, and after about an hour there are worms everywhere. But as the volume of worms increases, the bass become much harder to catch. I don't think they are becoming more selective, but some of the bass are so stuffed with worms that if you lay one on the bottom of the boat to photograph it or unhook it, there are worms coming out of its mouth and a dark green ooze coming out of its vent. In the middle, the bass looks inflated, because it is so full. That never seems to stop them from feeding, though. It can be truly amazing how devoted the fish are to their gluttony.

The worms are extremely weak swimmers, and they are sometimes so thick on the surface of the water that the bass can simply wallow along on top with their mouths open, scoffing down worms in quantity. The bass can become so engrossed in their feeding that they seem oblivious to your presence, and you can touch them with a rod tip as they swim by lethargically. I've had them bump into my oars and even the sides of my rowboat. Some stripers can still be caught, even at this stage of the hatch, but it is very difficult. In some cases only a floating fly will take them. We make flies out of cigarette-filter-size pieces of foam, cast them out, and slowly move them along the surface. Sometimes this is like magic, and you can regularly catch fish with the crudest-looking floating fly imaginable, while a subsurface fly that appears to be the world's most beautiful worm is totally ignored. And then minutes later the bass seem to favor the subsurface fly. Our solution is to connect a small, sparse, subsurface fly with an eighteen-inch leader tied to the hook bend of the floating fly. This covers both bases simultaneously, and you even get a few doubleheaders.

What I have seen many times is that schools of similar-sized bass seem to stick together in the ponds. During a night of good activity, you can move around the pond and see the swirls of much larger bass and sometimes smaller fish. You are unlikely to be in a pod of fourteen-inch stripers and suddenly catch a forty-incher. But I've had evenings when there were sizable aggregations of fish in the high thirties and low forties present in the pond and feeding on worms.

During the prime nights of the worm hatch, the pond seems to be full of striped bass. I've always wondered how the bass know the hatch is going on. Sometimes schools that clearly contain hundreds of large stripers are found well inside these salt ponds in areas where, outside of the worm hatch, you would almost never find anything more than a few twelve-inch micros.

What causes them to search in these unlikely backwater shallows for something as obscure as a worm species that hatches in late evenings for a two-week period each year? Does the outgoing current of the pond carry the scent into Vineyard Sound, where it finds and tolls in a school of slammers? Do these big fish slide quietly into the pond as evening rolls around and shuttle back out as the worms return to the mud? Or do these thousands of striped bass simply drop into the eel grass on the bottom of the pond and wait until the next evening?

Some fish definitely stay inside the pond during the day. I've often rowed across the pond and seen spooked bass make boils on the surface as they swim away from the boat's shadow or noise. In an hour's worth of rowing, though, you may only see this once or twice, and then it often seems to be in the same confined areas all the time. It doesn't seem possible that the armies of bass that fill the pond during a good evening hatch are laying undetected under the boat during the day—but maybe.

Discovering the Elizabeth Islands

The Elizabeth Islands, which run to the southwest as an extension of the south shore of Cape Cod, are collectively one of coastal New England's greatest assets. Fishing or even just boating along the shoreline of the Elizabeth Islands is worth doing, no matter how good or bad the fishing is—though, thankfully, it is often very good.

The islands, with Cuttyhunk and a couple of smaller islands excepted, are all part of a large real estate holding that has a very few homes and cottages scattered across them. The more substantial cottages are clustered in a tiny village on the northern end of Naushon, while a couple more exist on Uncatena and Nonamesset, just across Woods Hole from the Cape Cod mainland. The remainder of the islands have an almost nineteenth-century feel with the very occasional old house or building surrounded by stone walls, rough fields, and shrubbery and trees, all of which are stunted by the constant salt wind blowing in off the ocean. The wildlife, too, is terrific. You might cruise along the island and see the antlers of a deer visible as it lays in some thick brush or hear and maybe see a pheasant cackling by in flight.

The islands are lightly farmed, doubtless to achieve some tax benefit, and one of the businesses is cattle, which often can be seen wading along the shoreline. There are thirteen islands, counting some very small ones scattered around the chain, and almost all of the shoreline offers what is at times terrific striped bass fishing and a fair amount of solitude.

In the spring of 1994 I was invited to fish the Elizabeth Islands with Pat Abate and Art Lavallee. Art came naturally by his passion for fishing as he succeeded his father, Art Lavallee Sr., as president of the Acme Tackle Company, makers of the Kastmaster lure, of Providence, Rhode Island. Art Sr. was well known in the striped bass fishing community, and he got around to many of the better spots for catching big fish. The Elizabeth Island chain, ending with Cuttyhunk, was one of those places, and he introduced his son to it too.

The Elizabeth chain runs seventeen miles in a southwesterly direction from Woods Hole to Cuttyhunk. At the tip of Cuttyhunk is a large shoal studded with boulders that is swept in both directions by the conflicting tides of Vineyard Sound and Buzzards Bay. Sow and Pigs Reef (also known as the Pigs for short) is perhaps the single best structure for jumbo striped bass on earth.

The Elizabeths in general are awesome big striper habitat. In fact, Charlie Church, a resident of Cuttyhunk in 1913, caught a world-record striped bass of seventy-three pounds here. The catch was unmatched until June 1967. Church's fish came from what he called a "pool" among the boulders of neighboring Nashawena Island. Church rowed over from Cutthunk to catch it. Millions of striped bass later, the fish that tied Church's record also weighed seventy-three pounds and was caught on the Pigs by another Charlie (Charlie Cinto), about five miles from Church's fishing pool. Cinto was on one of his regular trips aboard the *Junebug* with one of the last of Cuttyhunk's famous guides, Frank Sabatowski. Probably no place has more big striped bass karma than the waters around Cuttyhunk.

From what was once its iconic clubhouse, still standing today, atop and only slightly back from the eroded cliffs of the islands southeast facing shoreline, nineteen-century gentlemen lived the high life in summer, eating, drinking, and fishing for striped bass. They did this free from the supervision of their wives, who, by club rules, weren't permitted near the place. This exclusion spawned some members to leave and form the Pasque Island Club, situated overlooking Robinson's Hole, about seven miles back up the island chain toward Woods Hole.

Below the Clubhouse Cliffs on Cuttyhunk, just a few hundred yards from the beginning of the Pigs, is a boulder-covered shoreline very much like the one described at Squibnocket Point on Martha's Vineyard, but with one significant difference. Throughout the Elizabeth Islands, the tides run along the shoreline with a speed not unlike a tidal river. This is due to the complex interaction of the Gulf of Maine tides, which are squeezed between the tip of Nova Scotia and Cape Cod, constricted by a series of large underwater banks, and further confused by the backdoor flow of the man-made Cape Cod Canal. Thus the islands' tides lag almost three hours behind the tidal rise and fall measured just to the south of Cape Cod at Newport, Rhode Island. These conflicted waters meet on top of the Pigs, and with each change of the tide, a new rip line forms across the top of the reef.

Historically, the guides liked to fish the Pigs on the east running tide, that is, into Vineyard Sound from Buzzards Bay. The Buzzards Bay side of the Pigs is deeper water shoaling up quickly to the top of the reef. This allows the guide boats to fish in close to the rip line without as much danger of hitting a rock as they faced when approaching the reef from the east side. I preferred, however, drifting in from the east when I was fly-fishing there.

Fishing on the Pigs spawned its own boat design: the Cuttyhunk Bass Boat. Early versions of these boats were completely open from bow to stern, and the boats were steered from either of two rudder posts, one near the front of the boat and the other near the back. This allowed the guide to maintain some distance from the casting anglers by going to the front of the boat as well as being able to steer the boat from the back while gaffing fish hooked when trolling or running a distance in rough water. The boats never developed many creature comforts, but they were high-sided to keep out the rough waters, and some were double-planked on the bottom to withstand hitting a rock hard if the guide misjudged the sea bottom. That was all too easy to do on the Pigs, where a great deal of fishing was done in the dead of night.

The ride out to the Pigs, though, wasn't a very long one. The fleet was kept at a guide's dock in Cuttyhunk Pond, and from there, running around the normally smoother and less treacherous west side of the island, it is only a little over three miles to the heart of Sow and Pigs Reef.

Art, Pat, and I were going to fish with John Christian, who left Woods Hole with his twenty-two-foot Aquasport center-console, the *Susan Jean*. While John's time fishing Cuttyhunk does not run back to the heyday of the Sow and Pigs bass fishery, he didn't come along too far behind it. He fished alongside of, and learned from, some of the fishermen who made the place famous. In that one short trip with Captain Christian lies the basis for many of the things I adopted in my own approach to fishing the islands over the next decade. Some were just little things, such as going outside the nest of buoys surrounding the entrance to Woods Hole before turning the wheel southwest to run down to the lighthouse above Tarpaulin Cove, where John planned to start fishing. He did fish farther up the islands, but mostly in the late season.

I remember John's telling me that most of the fifty-pound or better stripers he had caught had come in early November, from the upper end of Naushon Island, not far from Woods Hole. He thought the water stayed a little warmer there in the late season. While John certainly knew all about trolling and pulling bucktails on wire line, his approach, at least with good casters like Pat and Art aboard, was to move surprisingly rapidly parallel to the shore of the islands while the anglers cast as far in toward the rocky shoreline as they could reach. I remember we did not catch any monsters that day, though, we had several thirty-six-inch class fish. But the number of sizable stripers that rose up and whacked the assortment of plugs and rubber lures—as well as some big flies I was throwing—seemed to me incredible.

We covered a lot of ground, and John, with his low-key delivery, kept up a constant dialogue about the fish that had been caught beside this rock or that and how large bass liked this stretch of shoreline and why you have to give this point of land a wide berth because of all the surprise rocks that reach almost to the surface. Art often added tidbits of knowledge and memory from his many previous trips to the Elizabeths, not only with John, but with other guides back to his father's time. That isn't to say, because of my photographic memory (cue lots of laughs), I filed every detail of this information and instantly knew the Elizabeth Islands. What I did come away with, though, was an understanding that this was a very special fishing place with a long and great history of producing huge striped bass, one that someone could just dive into and learn continuously about for many years to come.

I also saw John's basic, on-the-move technique for covering ground by tossing a few casts into likely spots here and there until he found some solid action. Even when we did hit a spot that seemed to have a concentration of fish, John didn't give it much more time than the others. He was coming back there the next day too, and he had developed an almost tour-guide style of giving you a good sample of the broad spectrum of potential fishing places rather than pound one productive spot until it got old. The invitation to fish with John and Art, who both had personal and family histories in fishing the Elizabeths, was a lucky break for me, and I was motivated to dig a lot deeper.

The Lund Alaskan

Fishing the Elizabeth Islands, though, requires more of a boat than the low-sided fourteen-footer sitting in my garage. One thing about the islands is that you can circumnavigate them and never be more than two hundred feet or so from shore. You can also choose your side of the islands to navigate. This can be handy at any time of the year, but it is especially so in the fall, when you frequently encounter stiff northwesterly winds from the seasonal cold fronts. In spite of occasional shelter from the land, trips up and down the islands can be hair-raising in certain situations.

In a pure southerly wind, you can run down the Buzzards Bay side and find a reasonable lee for most of the trip. In a southwest wind, though, it is hard to find real protection on either side of the island. The same is true of a northeast wind, though that wind often means stormy conditions and requires that you be a bit more careful about going out at all.

Over the years, I had many trips when a northeast wind was forecast but not yet present at dawn. I'd run far down into the islands, enjoy the great fishing that can come along with the conditions that often develop just before a storm, but then have a miserable and sometimes scary ride back to the shelter of Woods Hole and the Cape Cod mainland.

All things considered, the Vineyard Sound side is the worst in a northeast wind because of the potential for the wind to blow against the current. In some cases the current off the ends of the points can run several knots, and standing waves develop and stack up very quickly when the wind opposes the flow.

The currents in Buzzards Bay flow with much less velocity, and while a northeast wind rakes both sides of the islands, you have a little more lee by running up the west side.

Pat Keliher and a couple of the other young guides in the Kennebec had fished eighteen-foot Lund Alaskans at the beginning of their careers before they were bitten with the bigger boat disease. I thought about it quite a bit and got one that was tiller steered with just a twenty-five-horsepower Honda for an outboard. The boat certainly wasn't overpowered, but with two people and our gear, the boat would move along at close to twenty knots with a wide-open throttle, and that was plenty fast enough. While the boat was sufficiently seaworthy, and George Watson and I safely crossed back and forth to Martha's Vineyard on a number of occasions when we shouldn't have, the ride was mean.

For its size, the boat was light, and the back few feet are completely flat. The redeeming features were that, like my earlier small tin boat, you could tilt up the outboard when in Woods or Robinson's Holes and simply drift across the rock piles that were colored with the bottom paint from many collisions with deep-V hulls and outboard lower units. My Lund Alaskan was miserly on gas, and a ten-gallon tank would easily take you around all day long. It was laid out well for fly-fishing. I could simply stand up in front of my helmsmen's pedestal seat, flip a few feet for a back cast, water haul the head off the water, make a real back cast, and shoot out a ninety-foot cast. It only took a few seconds, and it was great for quick shots at bonito. My companion had a good seat two-thirds of the way forward plus a nice open space of his own from which to fish.

What was missing was one of the important features that John Christian provided, which was that *I* still had to run the boat. John, as he guided, was constantly nudging his boat in and out of gear to control the length of time he stayed in any one spot, and while he respectfully kept his distance from the inshore shallows, he worked the boat in and out to give his anglers the best shot he could at making a presentation close to the beach, which is often where the fish were. I couldn't do that in my boat and cast and retrieve a fly at the same time, so I came up with an alternative.

Around the time I got the Lund, both MotorGuide and Minn Kota were coming out with remote-controlled saltwater versions of their electric trolling motors. The freshwater bass guys ran these using foot controls as they cast. First, you can't have anything down around your feet when you are fly casting, because the fly line will inevitably lasso it. Second, I thought that trying to steer with my feet would be awkward. Somehow I came up with the idea of taking the large flat-foot control made by MotorGuide for the Great White series of motors, putting a strap on it, and wearing it like a chest pack. I put the small front deck available from Lund on the boat, bolted the motor to this, and now we were in business.

The first weekend we used the remote electric setup, George and I fished the area around Robinson's Hole. The islands have four of these holes—Woods Hole, Robinson's Hole, Quicks Hole, and Canapitsit Channel—and they are simply channels that lead between the individual islands. We never had great results around Canapitsit, though I know of others who have, but Robinson's and Quicks produced a lot of fish for me and a lot of other people over the years.

I'm told the old Cuttyhunk guides fished four places. The Pigs was their bread and butter, but they often fished the rip at Felix Ledge in Quicks Hole, trolled along the shoreline in front of the clubhouse on Cuttyhunk, then crossed Vineyard Sound to Devil's Bridge, a shoal that runs a long way out from Gay Head on Martha's Vineyard. They knew the most productive time in the tide for each spot, and depending on weather, tides, and recent fishing activity, they worked each of these locations.

To fish with the electric, we would pull into our intended position along the island shoreline, shut off the outboard motor near the position for our first cast, and tilt the lower unit out of the water. George, in the bow, would release the electric motor into the water, and from my control pad I would turn the motor on, steer the boat, and then adjust the speed. Because the motor was pulling from the bow, I found it stayed on track better than a stern-mounted setup. I could usually make a cast and retrieve it before I needed to correct our direction. Any adjustment took a second or so, and then I was back in business. After a while, quick adjustments to the angle of the electric motor became second nature. It was also a lot quieter than a gas engine. I don't really know how much difference that makes to fish, but it can't hurt.

Whereas a good spinning or conventional caster can throw even an unwieldly swimming plug close to two hundred feet, a long fly cast is ninety to one hundred feet. This means that to make effective presentations you have to bring the boat a bit closer. We found this setup did that very nicely, even though it required a lot of work on my part.

Perhaps the best acknowledgment of the value of this motor came on our third morning, when, after running down Vineyard Sound to the shoreline of Pasque Island, near Robinson's, in the dark, we found the electric motor wouldn't work. The problem turned out to be one of the finicky controls or connections (I have forgotten exactly what it was) that remote-controlled motors of the day were plagued with. The next time I tried it, the thing sprang to life and we started fishing.

George turned and said, "Did you feel the same touch of panic I did that we might have to fish without that rig today?"

I also learned the hard way with electrics that you can't be lulled into complacency by how quiet the motors are. One day at Robinson's Hole, we had drifted out of the zone, and I was standing up in the bow, running the electric pretty hard to get back into position. I wasn't careful enough with the length of line dangling from my rod tip, and before I knew it, the line was zipping off my reel. For a second I had no idea what was happening. It felt like a big fish had taken the fly right beside the boat. My reflex was to put my hand on the revolving spool to apply more pressure. That was just enough to suck the rod tip into the revolving blade of the propeller. With only the very mildest sensation, the electric broke the Sage 1090 RPLX rod right off at every guide before I could move to turn it off. I was left holding the reel, the handle, and about three feet of rod. The total time was probably less than two seconds. I thought about sending the rod back to Sage in a shoebox, but then I thought they might deny my claim because I was being a wise guy. I think their fee at the time for any repair was forty dollars, so that, plus shipping, was my cost for a new replacement.

The Kennebec Sinking Line Techniques Reapplied

We also effectively used the heavy sinking-line techniques we had learned in the Kennebec, but we took them to a new level. Whereas most Kennebec fishing was done with 300- and 350-grain lines, we found that many of the structures we were fishing in the ocean were much deeper. I found that while traditional wire-line trollers worked in as close as they dared to the kelp-armored boulders out on the Pigs, we caught a lot of fish drifting in toward the reef by starting well outside, in fifty feet of water. That was often where we found the fish holding.

We'd pulled up in position and made our first cast lazily into the wind. The surface of the water flows much faster than the water running along the bottom, and as the boat drifted, we could feed slack line into the cast while the fly and sinking-head fly line dropped quickly down into the water column. When I had all the fly line out, and it had come tight, I would point the rod directly at the fly so I wasn't wasting any energy by bending the rod, and I'd start to pump it back and forth to give the fly some action without stripping it in.

While this was going on, I'd eyeball the recorder, looking for fish on the bottom structure. After a few pumps of the rod, I'd make my retrieve. Very frequently it was only when I began to retrieve line that a fish would take the fly, and I assumed the bass saw it as a baitfish trying to escape toward the surface.

We did things just the opposite if we were being blown or were drifting from shallower water into deeper water. My first casts would be right up, almost onto the beach or into the rocks, and since I was using a sinking head I'd begin stripping immediately to keep from catching the fly on the bottom. The drifts can be made with the current or with the wind or with both. I could quickly calculate, depending on the tide and the wind, how to cover any particular area of bottom structure or shoreline.

I'd sometimes bring the boat in close to the shoreline and begin my drift so that, on the way offshore, I would pass over a particular bottom that I wanted to cover. I always had twelve-weight outfits to throw the big grocery or bunker flies on a floating line, if that was what was required. Sometimes I'd start off by making a few casts with a big surface fly, and then I'd reel that up and switch to a sinking line for the deeper parts of the drift. Oftentimes I'd then run back inshore or offshore, depending on the circumstances, and start from a position a short distance away from where I began the last drift, so I would cover a slightly different piece of the bottom. You learn that sometimes there are particular sections of the bottom that have a concentration of fish holding and that you don't have to miss them by much to miss out entirely.

We also used this technique on the sand rips of Vineyard Sound and at Devil's Bridge off Gay Head on Martha's Vineyard. The biggest kind of stripers often hold at Devil's

Bridge, far out from the tip of the island, in eighty feet of water. I fished with rigs as large as 750 and 850 grains, using a twelve-weight rod to cast them. I also tied special Clouser-style flies that had up to three sets of heavy dumbbell eyes to aid in getting rapidly down into the strike zone. This setup was more lobbed than cast, and it was only for the young and strong of arm. In spite of all this weight, eighty feet is a long drop through a water column. We would run the boat well up-current of where we knew or hoped the fish were holding, make our cast, let the fly sink for a while, then when the time felt right, we'd make our retrieve. It is nowhere near as positive as using a sinker, live eel, and conventional tackle, but it was still fly-fishing, and at that stage of the game, fly-fishing was the only way I wanted to fish. I really knew we had the technique dialed in when I caught up solidly on the bottom in ninety feet of water on the outside of Devil's Bridge!

The following story illustrates just how effective this big fly, sinking-line technique can be. There is a point of land just south of Robinson's Hole on the Vineyard Sound side that is a terrific fishing location. I have invested many hundreds of hours there. An old map showing the Pasque Island Club's bass stand locations was given to me by Rip Cunningham, whose great-grandfather was the club secretary. There were several stands around this point. The shallow water of the point becomes a bar that gradually deepens and broadens out underwater as it runs offshore. This point probably extends close to a thousand feet underwater, and it was a favorite place for the wire-line trolling boats to fish.

One fall morning, I arrived at the point just as a charter boat was making a pass in about twenty-five feet of water, probably five hundred feet or so off the point. The west wind that day was pushing me offshore from the point, so I went down to the southern end of the structure and prepared to make my first drift. I was going to drift out to the edge of the shelf, motor back to the shoreline, but not start my drift as far south on the next pass, and so on, eventually covering the whole structure.

As the charter boat trolled away from my position, I could hear the captain selling his sports. "What you're doing is the way to catch these bass." "Hell will freeze over before that rig he has will catch anything."

The fishing was very good there that morning, though the fish weren't monsters. On my first drift from the shallow to the deeper water, I released three decent fish. The charter captain made another pass over the bottom after I finished, and he zigzagged back and forth to cover the area more thoroughly on the second pass. On neither pass, though, did they manage to hook a bass. Finally I heard the captain say something about the fish not being big enough to bother with, the sports all reeled in, and the charter boat roared off toward Martha's Vineyard.

It's funny how every approach to the sports has its own perceived hierarchy. I remember John Christian telling me that he knew he could catch more fish out in the deep-water sections of the rips in Vineyard Sound, but that he no longer cared to fish in that way. To him, casting plugs into the rocks around the islands or trolling live eels near the surface without weights through those same areas was much more aesthetically pleasing, and that is how he and his clientele preferred to fish.

Likewise, Dean Clark, an old friend and a great fly fisher, found it hard to understand how I found any pleasure in my sinking-line techniques. He preferred to fish along the sandy stretches he could find here and there along the island's shoreline and sight-cast for his bass. He eventually ended up spending all his fishing time on the north side of the cape, fishing the pure-sand beaches of Cape Cod Bay and completely specializing in sight-fishing.

I have done a small amount of sight-fishing compared to many striped bass fly fishers of my level. I've enjoyed my experiences on the flats, whether they were for tarpon, bonefish, or striped bass, but sight-fishing never grabbed me the way it does some people. It is the same with Atlantic salmon and brook trout.

I have met anglers who are only interested in fishing dry flies for trout and salmon. Many of these anglers greatly prefer the crystal-clear waters of the Gaspé River to tannic streams such as the Miramichi or especially the Cains River in New Brunswick. I enjoy the rise of a salmon to a dry fly, but I do not necessarily prefer it to the solid take of big salmon on a wet fly in mid-swing.

For me there has always been a great attraction in searching out big fish in their element, often well below the surface, and feeling their strength telegraphed on the strike up the fly line to my hands. I get very excited to see the fins, boils, and flashes of surface-feeding stripers, and frankly I prefer that to seeing them ghosting along the sandy bottom, though I know that many excellent anglers feel differently.

Fishing brings satisfaction through its levels of accomplishment. If you are a pilgrim to the sport, just catching a striper is more than ample reward. From there it is the ability to understand your prey well enough to catch them regularly. Then it may be to catch them early or late in the season, when it isn't as easy. For me, it is to catch larger ones, especially on a fly rod. That's what drove me to get up in the middle of the night and run a small, open boat through the darkness to a place like Sow and Pigs Reef.

Actually, I loved everything to do with my time fishing the Elizabeth Islands, but had it not been for the huge cow bass I hoped were waiting for me down at the Pigs or the shoreline of the Elizabeths, I would probably have spent a lot less time fishing there. As my friend Brock Apfel liked to say, "One soon tires of catching tiddlers."

The House at Bournes Pond

One day in the winter of 1994 I took a call from the real estate agent who had brokered our purchase of the Cape Cod house. There was a downturn in the market at that time, and she had a deal on a terrific acre waterfront lot at Moonpenny Lane on Bournes Pond and wondered if we would like to look at it. I knew a little about the pond, both from fishing the jetties at the entrance and from doing a little clamming there. Looking at this property turned out to be quite an experience.

The vacant waterfront lot and the one adjoining it were owned by someone who had been implicated in a big fraud case, and the government had placed tax liens on it. This information didn't surface until we had it under contract and had already spent quite a lot of money on a sewer system design. Our agent was trying to untangle this mess so we could close, and out of nowhere a fishing friend called me and said he had seen a notice in the newspaper that the lot was to be sold at auction.

We showed up to make a bid for it among a crowd of real estate agents and other people with deposit checks in their pockets, which were needed on the spot if you made a successful bid. They were all looking for a steal, and once the bidding approached about two-thirds the market value, they all dropped out. For a minute it looked as if I might be able to buy this property for much less than what I had it under contract for. Then, a large man with a deep husky voice—he was the lawyer for the property owner and his name was McDermott—stepped forward and bid within five thousand dollars of what I had the property under contract for. I topped his bid by a hundred dollars and won.

Later, I learned I had probably thrown away nine-nine dollars. The property owner held a mortgage on the land, and the mortgage was in default. McDermott had foreclosed the mortgage, taken possession of the property, and thus could legally sell it. But I ended up with the lot and built a house right on the pond.

The views across the pond, over Menauhant Road, and off to Cape Poge on Martha's Vineyard were to die for. I put a mooring right in front of the house and kept my boat on it when I was down there, and I kept an Old Town Discovery pulled up on the bank for fishing in the pond. I was in heaven. Twenty years later the trips to the cape and driving around Boston got to June and me, and Atlantic salmon on the Miramichi were pulling me in another direction, so we sold it. It wasn't a bad investment.

If I walked through the backyard, along a little path through about seventy feet of pitch pine and scrub oak, and down the face of a low coastal banking, I came to the beach on Bournes Pond. About 150 feet along the beach, to the left, is a point of land that continues off into the pond as a shallow sand bar. On top of the bar, you can wade a good 75 feet into the pond. When you wade out on that bar, you are essentially surrounded by fishable water. On many late May and early June nights in the mid-1990s that pond was simply full of striped bass, including some really good ones.

On top of that bar is one of the few places I have seen striped bass turn on their side – assumedly to place the side of their mouth flat against the bottom for feeding. They would sometimes do that in the evenings, when the sun was directly behind me. Some call this winking. It was amazing what a bright flash their silvery scales made in the sunlight.

The pond forked right after the point, and a large cove branched off to the left. Up in that cove was the area where we usually saw the first worm hatches. I suspect it was a little warmer than the central channel of the pond, and the worms there were ready to spawn a little earlier than other areas. The other fork ran straight inland for a couple of miles as the pond gradually became smaller. During the worm hatch, I'd often patrol the pond, but I usually did better at the lower end, where I was within a thousand feet or so of the small bridge that led out of the pond and into Vineyard Sound.

The water moving through the small channel beneath the bridge, perhaps twenty-five feet wide, where the pond receives the tides from the sound, runs very quickly. It is very hard to row into the pond against that current and impossible for me during a moon tide. Where this flow enters the shallow pond, it has dug quite a hole. I often fished it quite successfully for fluke using live mummichogs for bait. That little hole was more than ten feet deep at high tide.

That deep channel runs back about 150 feet from the bridge, and then, as the current loses its speed, it can no longer push the sand it carries. That area is the scene of a considerable bar. Every time I came through this area in my Lund and later my seventeen-foot Parker, I would shut off the engine and tilt it up so I could drift over the bar. From early May to early November that bar always held a population of striped bass. You could see them spread across the bar, just waiting for baitfish to be swept into the pond with the current from a rising tide.

In addition to bass, fluke would bury themselves in the sand of that bar and wait for prey. The water was often only a foot of two deep, and sometimes, on a big moon tide, the top of the bar would actually bare for a while around low tide. If the water got low enough, the ospreys could see the fluke and would dive into the pond to get them. It was really an incredible sight, as the osprey would rise up from the pond with a fluke impaled in its talons. As ospreys do, they would sometimes circle the area a time or two before heading off to their nest with the prize. They reminded me of AWAC planes, only with that big disc positioned directly beneath them instead of on top.

For a few years some really great times were had at that house. I frequently brought George Watson and a lot of my friends to Bournes Pond, and we combined a little partying and cherrystone (clam) eating on the deck with fishing the cape and the islands. June's mother, Alice, was a great cook, and she was happy to have the occasional company. It was a really great period of time in my life.

Chapter Seven

The Glory Years of the 1990s

When 1990 rolled around, I had a lot of fishing options, too many perhaps. I knew I still wanted to be on the Kennebec in June. We had our first house on Cape Cod, and that was providing some good opportunities early in the season, and frequently during the season we would take a weekend trip down there from Maine. We now had three grandchildren for June's parents to enjoy, so June was often willing to head south for the weekend. I was in love with the fishing on Martha's Vineyard, so that's where I usually spent my weekends, beginning in late September. Also, there was always the Presumpscot River in my Falmouth backyard.

The Presumpscot, compared to the Kennebec, is little more than a guzzle, yet despite its comparatively modest physical stature, the Presumpscot is a fishy little river with historical significance in the world of fisheries. This river drains Sebago

Lake into Portland harbor, and prior to its being dammed, it was the route by which a great run of Atlantic salmon entered Sebago Lake and reached their spawning grounds on the Crooked River, which ran into the lake from the northwest. It is believed the Presumpscot hosted the three forms of adult Atlantic salmon: riverine (meaning they spend their entire life within the Presumpscot River), landlocked (meaning that deep, wide Sebago Lake was their ocean), and classic anadromous salmon (meaning they migrated down the Presumpscot and entered the sea). The riverine and anadromous runs were destroyed in the nineteenth century when a series of industrial dams completely blocked the salmon's access to their spawning grounds. Most of the dams are still there today, but the landlocked population that spawns in the Crooked River still survives.

My home in Falmouth is on the Presumpscot, and during the early 1990s, when I moved there, I fished the river most days from May until October. I kept an aluminum boat at a little dock I built, and all of my children caught their share of schoolie stripers. When I look back on more than sixty years of striper fishing, the 1990s stand out as the closest thing to perfect we ever had. The Presumpscot provided an interesting view of the striper population. It was small enough, and I knew it well enough so I was normally able to find a few fish. I could also get a good sense of the abundance and size of the fish. On any calm evening from late May to mid-July, if we had at least a half tide, and preferably it was going out, catching stripers was a given.

Both above and below the Interstate 295 bridge, you could usually see several schools of stripers on top at the same time. We would pick out the one that seemed to have the best activity and biggest splashes, motor over, and start catching fish. It was that easy. When the population of large stripers started to decline, I could see it almost immediately in the Kennebec. And when the great year classes of the 1990s also started to sporadically falter, I could see that reflected immediately in the decreased abundance of schoolie bass in the Presumpscot.

On top of my striper fishing habit, the 1990s were a time when I was able to sample a number of other kinds of fishing. I made annual trips to Minipi, Anne-Marie, and Crook's Lake in Labrador for monster brook trout and to Florida for tarpon, where John Cole had started the Key West Angler's Club. I also made occasional trips to Iceland, Quebec, and Labrador for Arctic char and Atlantic salmon. Reviewing my logbook for those years, I wonder how I ever worked, but I did, and, in fact, those were some of the most productive years in my life on every front. Hooray, I guess, for the energy of the comparative youth of our forties.

A good example of that energy took place on November 4, 1993. I was working in my Portland office when I received a call from Kenny Vanderlaske.

"Big fish last night at West Chop Beach, lots of them," Kenny whispered into the phone. "I got one over forty inches, and there were a lot of them there. They came in out of the rip."

The east end of the Middle Ground tide rip is a couple hundred yards off the beach at this location.

"I'm just letting you know," he said softly. "You're welcome if you want to come down."

There was a tone of subdued excitement in his voice that let me know this was an exceptionally choice invitation. Without hesitating, I told Kenny I'd be on my way as soon as I possibly could in order to be there for the evening's fishing.

I called June and told her about Kenny's call and that I was heading home to change and then head for the Vineyard. I asked her to fix me a sandwich for the road. I'd been pulling stuff like this on her for twenty years, so she wasn't surprised. I canceled the rest of the day's appointments and told the people in the office what I was up to and how to get me if there was an emergency. Fifteen minutes later I was gone. Probably forty-five minutes later I was on the road in fishing clothes and with my surf gear in the back of the car. Whenever June packed a lunch, I could never wait very long to eat it, so I probably ate the sandwich before I was out of Maine.

In July, even twenty-five years ago, taking your chances with the Vineyard ferry without a ticket is likely to leave you in the standby lanes for a long time. During the first week in November, though, at least in those years, you could often drive right onto the boat.

I only remember a few details of that trip. The fishing wasn't quite the hoped-for bonanza, but I did get one about thirty-eight inches on a dead-drifted Farnsworth slider. Spearing will often hide by floating in the surface film at night. If the bass can find one doing that, it is an easy target, and some of the spearing in the fall are as long as a ballpoint pen.

Phil Farnsworth had invented a fly that was a foam body wrapped in a reflective material with a wispy tail of anything from marabou to bucktail. Pulled, twitched, or even just dead-drifted on the surface, with the motion of the waves providing the action, the fly could be deadly in the right circumstances.

What I remember more about that trip than the fishing was spending time with Kenny and Lori Lee. Kenny and I got up at first light and slogged down the beach to the Mink Meadows jetties that drain a tiny pond and creek that butts up against the golf course. It was bitter cold, but at first light a handful of tiny bass were feeding there, and we managed to catch a couple before our freezing fingers drove us back to the house. We spent the day tying a few flies, looking at fly-fishing magazines (of which the Vanderlaskes had a huge collection everywhere around the house), and carving off an occasional sliver of the Entenmann's cheese Danish that Kenny always had on the kitchen table. The talk was about nothing but fishing: present, past, and future. We were totally relaxed and absorbed in the moment.

The short hours of November quickly brought us to the time to return to the beach. It was fabulous to feel the cool breeze on your face, smell the ocean, and know that you were still out there, catching fish, even after almost all the other anglers had hung it up for the season.

That's really how it was with striped bass fishing in the 1990s. There was good fishing almost everywhere along the coast, and because of the large population, the season started early and ended late. You even heard a lot about holdover fish. These are stripers that decide to spend the winter in places such as Scorton Creek on Cape Cod or the Providence River rather than migrate south in the fall. Some were occasionally killed by a cold snap, but others survived, and on a warm, sunny day the fish could be active enough to provide some decent activity. These holdover fish seem to only happen in times of a large striped bass population. Also, in the early 1990s, there were very few of the high-forty-inch and larger stripers that we had up through the 1980s. But it appeared that new ones were on the way, and it seemed certain we would again have oodles of really large bass in just a few years.

This great fishing started an entire new movement in saltwater angling. Certainly the old standby conventional tackle and techniques were still in use, and that part of the fishery really didn't change a lot. There were just more people doing it. That's one of the great things about stripers: their versatile feeding habits lend them to a wide variety of fishing approaches. There was definitely some modernization of tackle, as graphite replaced fiberglass in rods, and super-thin and abrasion-resistant Gel Spun lines became common. I think it was in the early 1990s that I first saw this material.

Brock Apfel from L.L. Bean was just back from San Mateo, California, and what was then the largest U.S. fly-fishing show. I told him how much I liked using a small reel by Orvis, called the Battenkill Multiplier, for bonito fishing. Bonito have a habit of rapidly changing direction and causing your line to go slack, often resulting in a lost fish. The speed of retrieve on the multiplier is a big help in this situation. The problem is that bonito and even more so false albacore (the two are often caught together off the Northeast in the fall) frequently make long blistering runs. If you can't follow the fish for some reason, you need some serious backing. The Battenkill held less than two hundred yards of twenty-pound-test Dacron backing plus an eight-weight fly line.

"Try this," said Brock, handing me a three-hundred-yard sample spool of thirty-pound test Tiger Braid he had been given at the show.

I reeled on the whole three hundred yard spool plus my fly line and had more room left than I did with just two hundred yards of twenty-pound Dacron!

Some of the surfcasters at Montauk used braid in up to eighty-pound test to cast weighted treble hooks across the lines of fly fishers who get too close to what they perceive is their turf. Then they pull the fly lines to shore and cut them off. I saw this on my trips to Montauk with Steve Bellefleur, and I lost a fly to it. We dreamed up some tackle to combat the braid, but we never bothered to follow through with it.

Lures improved too, with things like Japanese Yo-Zuri crank baits with unbelievable paint finishes. Even conventionally designed wooden plugs went through an evolution. You could drive down the beach at a place like Island Beach Park in New Jersey and see custom plug makers parked by the inlet to Barnegat Bay displaying their inventory for sale. These were most often wooden, metal-lipped swimming plugs modeled similarly to the historic plug designs from makers such as Atom, Goo Goo Eyes, Creek Chub, and Stan Gibbs. These, however, were hand-made, with the best materials and finishes that looked somewhere between fine art and a custom hot-rod paint job with multiple layers of clear coat. The prices started at several times the price of mass-produced lures, even though most agreed they wouldn't catch any more fish. Instead, some people began collecting custom plugs as a hand-made art form.

But of all the advances in lures in the last hundred years, nothing compares to the story of plastic baits led by Slug-Go. One ad claimed: "Weightless Slug-Go or Slug-Go with a couple of nail weights is pure magic. The only lure with a totally random action. All other baits have a repeating mechanical action (crank bait, metal-lipped swimmer, SP minnow, etc.) or no action at all (bucktail, needlefish, etc.)." The ads are wrong about no action with bucktails and needlefish, and we'll get to that below.

My first experience with the Slug-Go lure was with Pat Abate. He showed up for a morning of fishing at the Elizabeth Islands carrying a small plastic double-opening suitcase that contained about a thousand Slug-Go lures of different descriptions. Pat had some hooked to jig heads for deep fishing, others with some weight added to cast and retrieve below the surface, like swimming plugs, and others that by their own density were heavy enough for him to cast into the rocks near the beaches and retrieve on the surface as we maneuvered slowly around the island shoreline.

I was standing in the back of the boat, running the motors (gas and electric), and fly casting. I thought I was hooking up at a respectable clip, and out on Sow and Pigs, fishing deep, I did as well as Pat. But farther up in the sound, along the rocky shoreline of Naushon and Pasque Islands, Pat's rig was several times more effective. He would cast a footlong white Slug-Go way in by the beach and rapidly reel it back in, right along the surface of the water. Fish after fish would come up and take a swipe at that thing, and there were some really big ones too.

Just what it is about the Slug-Go action or, for that matter, any lure action that causes fish to strike is not only a fascinating subject but one I have found poses as many questions as it does answers. Some believe a "totally random action" makes the most desirable lure, and perhaps it is, all things considered. On the other hand, some lures and flies with apparently subdued actions also can be really big producers. The Slug-Go ad claimed the bucktails and needlefish had no action, but if they are used in the right situation, both of these lures are absolutely deadly. The lead head on the bucktail jig allows it to be kept in close contact with the bottom, produces a hopping-up-and-down action when jigged, and because the bucktail fibers breathe, they move just enough in the water to be incredibly deadly. Needlefish plugs wander slightly back and forth in the water, and treble hooks swing back and forth much like the fins on fish. Night after night on Popham Beach, Martha's Vineyard, and Block Island, I watched needlefish plugs markedly outfish swimming plugs with much more exaggerated swimming actions. This unexplained preference can also be true in flies.

In the early 2000s, I was fishing in late May with Dave Rimmer on Sow and Pigs Reef. There were small herring around, and the bass were randomly coming up here and there and making a boil on the surface. The fish were very spread out. I couldn't see any concentration on my fish finder either, but if we did enough casting, we'd get enough strikes to make it worthwhile. I was using an old standby "Grocery Fly" and so, I thought, was Dave. After a while it was clear that Dave was getting at least three times the number of strikes I was, and he offered me one of his flies.

The fly was almost entirely synthetic. A body and tail of various flash materials and crinkle hair was stiffened as it went along the hook shank by running an epoxy-covered dubbing needle through the material. The head was made by slipping a short length of Mylar braid over the material and binding it down around the eye with tying thread. Then the braid was coated with more epoxy. In the water, the fly had little of the seductive swimming action you look for in normal deceiver-style flies. It actually pulled through the water like a stick. It was just another reminder that it is not what we think of a fly's action but what the bass think of it that matters.

Saltwater Fly Casting

Of all the developments caused by the huge increase in striped bass availability, the most dramatic came in fly-fishing activity. Striped bass fishing with flies is nothing really new. Nineteenth-century Atlantic salmon anglers from Eastern Seaboard cities practiced their love of catching big fish on fly rods by casting for striped bass in waters near their homes. Some of these anglers even favorably compared the fight of the striper to that of salmon. I've caught many of both species on flies, and I'd say that if you take the jumping out of it, they are fairly comparable—but I really like the jumps. Interestingly enough, stripers can definitely jump. I've only witnessed it a handful of times out of thousands of bass on the line. The few jumps and tail walks I've seen took place immediately upon being hooked. I had a small schoolie, just at dusk in the Presumpscot, hit my streamer fly in about a foot of water right on the edge of the shore. The fish put a good two feet of air between itself and the surface of the water. Another time, on the Kennebec, I hooked a bass of approximately forty pounds trolling a Danny plug in between the twin ledges at the lower end of Goat Island in Phippsburg. Instantly on hookup, the bass came to the surface, and at a sixty-degree angle from the water's surface, with not much more than its tail still in the water, swam about twenty-five feet across the surface before going back underwater. It was an incredible sight, but I would say that it is one-in-a-thousand fish that does it.

In the 1940s, Harold Gibbs tied the famous Gibbs Striper Fly for his home waters on the Warren River in Rhode Island. In the 1950s, Lefty Kreh tied the Lefty's Deceiver fly for striped bass fishing in Chesapeake Bay. The fame of both flies carries down to this day.

In spite of this localized fly-fishing activity, if you went striped bass fishing almost anywhere on the East Coast between 1950 and 1990, you would still have to look hard to find anyone with a fly rod. There were some, enough so that the Atlantic Saltwater Flyrodders Club started up in 1960 at Seaside Park, New Jersey, and spawned similar organizations in a number of states. The Rhode Island chapter was formed in 1963 and continues to this day. But it was a very small movement compared to what took place in the 1990s.

One could easily write a long and heavily researched book about the 1990s striped bass fly-fishing movement. There would be a lot to look into.

For instance, Brad Gage, now retired as the manufacturer's rep for Far Bank, which owns Sage fly rods, told me in the mid-1990s that Sage had gone from practically no sales of saltwater fly rods in the Northeast to their being something like 50 percent of his sales. He added that virtually every new point of distribution during that era (new fly shop) was a saltwater fly shop.

And it was all due to striped bass. The very successful fly-fishing shows of Marlboro, Massachusetts, and Somerset, New Jersey, were spawned by saltwater fly-fishing for striped bass. The reason was all really quite simple.

In 1977, the year the first Atlantic Saltwater Flyrodders Club folded, if you went down to the Great Pond jetties in East Falmouth, Massachusetts, on Memorial Day, and cast a fly into the outgoing current—even if that tide had coincided with good conditions and early morning light—you would probably have seen and caught nothing. With the same scenario in 1995, you probably would have caught several striped bass between ten inches and maybe thirty inches, would have seen other fish busting bait on the surface, and watched other anglers hooking up. On your way off the shore, someone would probably ask you how you had made out, and you would have spent some time making a new friend. You would have pulled out your fly wallets or boxes and compared your favorite killer pattern, probably tied and maybe designed by you during the winter months.

All of this activity was taking place in about as attractive an environment as one could hope for, and once you have a modest amount of equipment, it costs no more than a couple of gallons of gas to go fishing. That scenario scratches a lot of itches. On top of all that, millions of people could enjoy this fishing within less than an hour from their homes, most in just a few minutes. It sure put following the hatchery truck to shame, and tons of freshwater fly fishermen came over to the salt to give stripers a try.

L.L. Bean

Through my conservation advocacy work with the Coastal Conservation Association of Houston, Texas, I was introduced to Brock Apfel, who was running the fishing department at L.L. Bean. And we started fishing together.

Brock was trying to build Bean into a nationally known fishing brand beyond just being a large tackle retailer. Since its inception, Bean had always had some fishing equipment with their Double L brand on it, and Brock wanted to significantly expand that concept. He hired Lefty Kreh to be the face of Bean's fly-fishing. Brock had a series of rods made for Bean at various price points by G. Loomis and St. Croix, including some high-end models. In addition to Bean's historic association with Hardy, who made freshwater models for them, Brock made a deal with the new Islander Reels of Vancouver to make L.L. Bean Tidemaster reels, which were high-end, bar-stock-machined reels with a terrific drag system. He also copied the concept of the Jim Teeny steelhead lines with short, heavy, level sinking heads measured in grains (250, 350, 450, 550) that Bean called the Superhead. Orvis came out with essentially the same thing at around the same time and called it the Depth Charge. Much of this equipment Brock and I tested hard on stripers in the Kennebec.

Brock had earlier been a geologist, and he worked for the oil industry and had fished in a lot of exotic locations. He told me that all the tarpon he had caught on flies would fill the room we were sitting in. Brock was a terrific fly-caster and an innovative fly tier who coined the term "Groceries" to describe the specially tied Lefty's Deceiver–styled flies we were tying and fishing. Man, did he love to fish!

Brock fell in love with the Kennebec and bought a seventeen-foot Lund that he fished from when he wasn't aboard my boat. There was considerable friendship, mutual respect, and a degree of competition between us that made us both better fishermen. All of that made for a lot of good times. He retired from Bean and moved to Florida around 1997, just in time to avoid the beginning of the decline in the Kennebec fishery.

One thing I loved about Brock was his irreverent attitude toward conventional wisdom. He wasn't obnoxious about it, but he'd quietly think things through and come up with his own approach to fishing questions. It started with things like leaders. Brock would just peel off five feet or so of thirty-pound test, and that was his striper leader. He was quick to pick up and utilize innovations in fly-fishing, for instance, the Gel Spun backing he gave me before anyone else was using it, constructing his grocery flies using thinned Shoe Goo to attach spread-out bucktail fibers to the sides of his flies so they were tall and flat sided, the profile of an actual herring, and using new materials such as Big Fly Fiber when none of the rest of us had even heard of it. He used to carry a little Barbie comb for grooming flies.

We would meet for lunch at the Muddy Rudder restaurant in Yarmouth during the winter and pull out the latest flies we were working on for each other's comments. In order to get them to look their best, we would run doll combs through them. Actually, I used a plastic brush from my daughter's My Little Pony toys. The mane and tail on the pony were made of a material similar to Big Fly Fiber, and the brush was perfect for smoothing out snarls. We would sit there, with flies all over the top of the table, both of us combing them and gabbing like a couple of old ladies. Our activities generated more than a few raised eyebrows, but no one bothered us.

One time, not long before he moved away, Brock and I were fishing at Robinson's Hole in the Elizabeths. It was first light, and we had just arrived after the twelve-mile run in the darkness from my mooring in Bournes Pond. We were nearing the head of the little tide rip inside the hole, where we planned to fish. The boat was down, off a plane, but still moving along at probably seven or eight knots. Brock was moving toward his casting position in the bow, and his grocery fly was skipping along the surface about six inches from the side of the boat. A bass that had to be in excess of thirty pounds grabbed it right there and made one helluva commotion before finally getting some traction and disappearing underwater. Brock and I both practically came out of our skins. Unfortunately, it was not a great hook set, and the bass got off.

The new saltwater fly-fishing movement had its leaders. Bob Popovics (perhaps the industry's most innovative saltwater fly tier who invented the use of epoxy to make fly bodies), Lou Tabory (writer, tier, and fisherman), Ed Mitchell (writer, fisherman, and photography professor), and quite a few others (including me) put on fishing clinics, gave slideshows and talks to fly-fishing clubs and appeared at various events from Maine to North Carolina, all made possible by striped bass.

Among all the sport's personalities, none had any recognition that remotely compared to Lefty Kreh, who had been doing this sort of thing for a long time and was known from coast to coast. Lefty wore a flats hat around in the way most people wear a baseball cap. When not fishing in the sun, he kept the back brim folded up. Lefty's profile – always wearing that hat—became so famous that almost any serious fly fisherman in the country instantly recognized the silhouette as Lefty Kreh. No one else, including Lee Wulff, ever achieved that level of recognition.

The 1990s striped bass bonanza gave everyone a shot in the arm. Lefty's relationship with L.L. Bean was a perfect example. Had it not been for striped bass, Brock would not have seen the opening for Bean to try and advance itself as it did, and Leon Gorman, who loved fishing himself, would not have allowed it to go forward.

Lefty went to Freeport a couple of times a year to consult with Bean about the fly-fishing industry and to go over their marketing plans for the upcoming year. It was no coincidence that one of these meetings was in June. I had a twenty-five-foot Hydra-Sport center-console moored in the Kennebec, and I was free to make my own schedule. Brock asked me to set aside a couple of days to take him and Lefty fishing on the river. So I got to know Lefty a little.

When I first fished with him, he was in his midsixties and, as most people who have gotten there can tell you, throwing rifle shots with a ten-weight, a 450-grain head, and a foot-long fly is something for younger joints and muscles. Lefty was still pretty damned good, though, and he seemed to love it as much as a twentysomething year old.

I remember a day when we were drifting into a place where a fairly strong current was carrying water up from about forty feet in depth to fifteen feet as it swept over the rock pile of a long-abandoned dock. An upriver wind was stirring up a standing wave that marked the position of the structure, and all around that rip line, bass from big schoolies up to forty-inch fish were tearing up the water as they used the structure and broken water to pick off herring that were dropping downstream with the current.

"Oh, would you look at that!" Lefty squealed as he hopped around the bow, stepping on his own fly line, trying to get into position for a good shot. No young man could have been more excited.

The Kennebec provided plenty to be excited about. My 1994 notes say that Brock was called back to Bean for business on the afternoon of June 21, and Lefty and I fished the rest of the afternoon together. We landed thirty-six striped bass between high-twenty-inchers and forty-inchers.

Lefty talked about the business of being a fly-fishing personality. He took me by surprise with that, particularly when he spoke about some of his competitors. He was very candid. This guy knew his stuff and was a great guy or that guy was a total bullshit artist who would backstab you for ten cents—or words to that effect. I was a veteran of the rough-and-tumble sales world of the office machine industry, but I hadn't expected it of the fishing industry. Later, after I'd spent a little time in the fishing industry myself, I learned just how naive I had been.

Lefty was friendly and helpful to me over the next twenty-five years before he passed. He sent me a lead-core shooting head made with his own hands, and whenever I'd call and ask for a few flies for a conservation event, he'd just reach into his fly boxes and send something along.

Brock introduced me to Jim Rowinski, who took over for him at Bean. Jim enthusiastically continued Brock's support of the Coastal Conservation Association in Maine, New Hampshire, and Massachusetts, and we had some large, successful dinners that were attended by over three hundred people some years, including almost all of Maine's top politicians at the time.

In 1995, I sold Kemco, the business I had started in 1982, to a large outfit named Danka Office Imaging, which was buying copy machine dealers all over America and Europe. I used to joke that we were a slightly smaller acquisition than their largest one: Kodak. Suddenly I was free of the nine-to-five world and turned to my favorite hobby to fill the time. Jim told me that L.L. Bean was going to have Nick Lyons produce a series of handbooks on some popular outdoor topics, and I pitched him on letting me write the one on striped bass and he agreed.

Ten years prior to this, I'd met John Rice while fishing at the Vanderlaskes, and I hired him to illustrate the book, which was titled *The L.L. Bean Fly Fishing for Striped Bass Handbook*. Given the times, and with L.L. Bean's name on it, my lack of notoriety as an author didn't seem to matter. We sold a ton of books, and it was reprinted several times. Clerks in Bean's fishing department told me that, during the fishing season, it was impossible to keep them on the counter. Occasionally the warehouse would bring over a couple of cases, they would put a huge stack on the counter, and in a few hours they were gone. More often, though, they were simply out of stock, and they would sometimes have to wait a while for Bean's corporate machine to get more in. Even today, with the book out of print for twenty years or more, the Amazon sales ranking is way ahead of my Atlantic salmon books that are only a year or three out of print. A lot of people are still interested in striped bass.

Writing the Bean book gave me a little notoriety. I put together a slideshow on fly-fishing for striped bass and appeared at some of the fly-fishing shows as well as doing a fair number of speaking engagements at fishing clubs around the Northeast. It was fun, but there isn't a lot of glory in driving home from Boston to Maine at ten o'clock on a snowy winter night, and there definitely wasn't a lot of money in it. I never pushed it very hard.

The best part of talking to these groups was in getting to spend a little time with some of the people I met at these events. One of them was Walter Fondren, the chairman of the Coastal Conservation Association in Texas.

Walter's great-grandfather was one of the founders of Humble Oil, and Walter was also a member of the Texas

Football Hall of Fame, as well as a scratch golfer with numerous championships to his credit. As the organization's lobbyist Bob Hayes often said, taking Walter to see one of the Texas politicians of the day was pure magic. Walter was also a very shrewd man. He was not a CPA, but Walter could look through a complex financial statement and, in short order, point out exactly what the financial strengths and weaknesses of that organization were.

After a couple of years of my going to board meetings in Texas, Walter told me that he'd like to see what Northeast striped bass fishing was all about, and I invited him to come to Maine and fish with me. Walter caught lots of stripers, including one really good one of twenty-six pounds, and we got along very well. Walter always stuffed a couple of bags of turkey jerky from his favorite Texas barbecue restaurant in his suitcase, and we chewed on that while we fished. I almost never took any food out with me when I was fishing, but that turkey jerky was a treat.

Walter invited me to fish with him for the traditional "specs and reds" at his place in Port O'Connor, Texas. I made several trips there, and Walter also made several trips to Maine. He was very interesting company and an excellent fishing partner. As a young man he had spent endless hours fishing the big saltwater lakes of the Texas coast. He loved being out on the water. In his early sixties he could still gracefully climb onto a poling platform and push a boat around all day. He was good at it, and he had an excellent eye for seeing fish.

In the summer of 1997, my friend Mason Morfitt was raising money for the Nature Conservancy and invited Lee H. Perkins Sr., chairman of Orvis, to come up to Maine for some striper fishing. He asked me to guide Lee, and I readily accepted, since I thought it would be fun to meet him and because Orvis was an important contributor to the Coastal

Conservation Association. I already knew Paul Fersen, Pip Winslow, Tom Rosenbauer, and some other folks at Orvis, and I knew this could strengthen the relationship.

We again had some pretty good striper fishing. If you've ever read Perkin's book *A Sportsman's Life: How I Built Orvis Mixing Business with Pleasure,* you have a pretty good window into his personality. The Perkins family inherited a fortune made in the robber-baron days of the late nineteenth century, and as a young man, Lee worked in one of the family's businesses, experiencing life several notches below his inherited social level. Some of the rough men he was working alongside tried pushing him a bit, and Lee proved he was just as comfortable trading punches as he was talking situations through.

Much later in life, even though he could afford the best of everything, Lee would take off for bird hunting in the Midwest with a dog or two, his guns, a blanket, and a few changes of clothes. He'd drive until he was tired, sleep beside the road, and take his hunting where he found it. I suppose some of that is a generational thing, but I find a lot to admire in it. At the same time, Lee built Orvis by shrewd marketing practices, like being one of the first to swap direct mail lists with other companies to extend the reach of his business.

Lee H. Perkins was also a terrific caster, and like Lefty Kreh, Lee was another guy who made his own shooting heads and was generally into his tackle. A few days after his trip up here, a package arrived from Orvis with a new nine-foot Whisper Tip prototype nine-weight. I lined it up and went out in the backyard. I immediately was casting farther than I had ever been able to with my favorite rod of the time, a Sage RPLX. A couple of years down the road, the tip of the Orvis rod broke in an accident. I sent it in for repair and received a free replacement rod, but it wasn't the same as the prototype that I'd been given. They never did come out with that exact rod. I don't know why, but the Whisper Tip sure was light-years ahead of its time.

1996: The Peak

I've been searching my records to see if I can pick what year was really the peak of the East Coast striped bass fishery. Naturally, not everyone is going to agree on it, and one reason is that the migration doesn't follow the same pattern every year. Tagging records have shown that a fish caught in June one year may be two hundred miles farther south at the same time the next year. Assumedly, that is true of some or all the fish in its school. Also, not everyone agrees on what constitutes the best fishing. If I had to pick a year, though, it would have to be 1996.

The Atlantic States Marine Fisheries Commission (ASMFC) keeps track of a statistic called the spawning stock biomass (SSB), which is the estimated combined mass of all spawning-age striped bass. It is probably the best overall indicator of how robust the striper population really is. The ASMFC shows that the SSB peaked around 2004, but between 1996 and 2004 the numbers were fairly similar. It was a rapidly improving fishery until 1996, then it plateaued, and, after 2004, it began to steadily decline.

Another important measure is called recruitment, which is the number of young bass that survive to become adults. That number also peaked around 1996 and has dropped steadily ever since. We're going to talk about that decline more in the next chapter. Let's just say that 1996 was a great year.

In the mid- to late-1990s we still had strong numbers of small bass coming into the fishery every year. I noted in my logbook that in the spring of 1996 we had great schoolie action on Cape Cod and also in back of my house on the Presumpscot River. In the Presumpscot, the fish showed up early, on May 7, and before Memorial Day we were regularly catching them as large as twenty-eight inches. The only problem with the early fishing is that was the year the elver fishery really blossomed. Both sides of the river, for two hundred yards below the site of the old dam, were one elver net fishing inside the next all the way down the shoreline. It was almost impossible to find a clear place to cast.

On Memorial Day weekend, George Watson and I slayed bass, lots of bass up to around forty inches along the Pasque Island shoreline, just outside of Robinson's Hole, and for the first half mile or so of Nashawena Island after leaving Quicks Hole. If you made a cast in toward the rocks, almost anywhere along that stretch of shoreline, when you retrieved the fly, you either hooked a bass or had several following it. The hot fly was the black groceries. I also tied some groceries up specifically for that fishing in which I tied the head like a huge muddler. The rest of the fly was a standard groceries. I used a twelve-weight floating line to cast this fly into the rocks, where the spun-deer-hair head combined with the floating line to keep the fly pushing along the surface. It kept the fly from hanging up in the rocks, and the bass really loved it. We fished it primarily at night and during the early light.

The Presumpscot had a good charge of four- to five-inch sea herring early that summer, and on June 15, I caught bass up to thirty-five inches wading just off the grass in my backyard.

The Kennebec was absolutely full of bass that June, but the biggest I caught only happened to be about thirty-six inches long. It got a little better later in the month, and my notes record that on June 22 I caught six or eight bass that were thirty-four to forty inches, but I complained a little in my log about the lack of surface action.

On June 28, I fulfilled the trip that Leon Gorman and his wife, Lisa, had bid on at last winter's CCA banquet in Portland. Leon, the grandson of Leon Leonwood Bean, inherited his grandfather's love of fishing. He caught a nice thirty-six-incher from the boat out in front of the Sprague River and a few more up inside the Kennebec. I also noted the feeding of the baby swallows in the nesting boxes in the field beside my house was creating quite a commotion. You couldn't walk down the driveway without being dive-bombed. The first white-tailed deer fawns of the season appeared in the field on June 29, which was a little late for me to get my first glimpse.

I can see, looking back through my log, that it was fishing on Cape Cod that was largely responsible for my no longer doing much nighttime surfcasting on the beaches around the mouth of the Kennebec. I'd been trying to juggle my time between Maine and Massachusetts. Most of my beach fishing in Maine had been from July through September, after the Kennebec water temperature became too high to hold many bass. For many reasons including the new house on Bourne's Pond I wanted to spend more time on Cape Cod, and often I was able to get my family to go with me. Once August rolled around, the cape really called, because bonito were added to the fishing repertoire. I got to like bonito fishing as much or better than I did striped bass, plus they are incredibly delicious. I suppose it is also possible that, at forty-seven years old, I no longer cared much for driving an hour to Popham, fishing for a couple of hours, and getting home at two, three, or four in the morning. It would take me two days to recover from that. It was also true that the ability to fish the Elizabeths from my boat in the fall had replaced my Vineyard and Block Island surfcasting. In the barn now my spinning and conventional surf rods are hanging by their tip tops from hooks on the ceiling, right where I left them in the late 1990s.

I remember the last evenings I fished the mussel bar. I loved being way out on the eastern end of that place. I was far enough offshore to see a good distance up South Beach. I could see the lights shining in people's homes, and I thought about them watching television or having a cocktail, and how much more I felt that I was getting out of life by standing out there in the ocean with the wind and the fish and the big night sky. But I got away from it, and I doubt now I'll ever have that view again.

On October 9, Phil and I were back for our annual fall trip with Steve Bellefleur. The three of us were all about the same age and shared the same rough sense of humor and the same love of fishing. It was always a great time. This trip was of special note, because on this day I caught a New England Grand Slam on a fly: a bass, a bonito, a false albacore, and a bluefish.

My last trips for the season were the next couple of weeks back on Cape Cod. It was tough, though. Some years you just get dealt a bad weather hand, and the northeast wind blows day after day. The northeast wind tends to keep fish down, and when that wind gets up to twenty knots or more, as it so often does in the fall, it makes Vineyard Sound virtually unfishable.

1997

Nineteen ninety-seven began with a cold, slow start. I noted the water in Buzzards Bay was 49 degrees Fahrenheit on May 25, when 55 degrees is closer to normal. I did get a nice bass of forty-four inches in Robinson's in early June. On June 14, I fished the Kennebec and wrote a short note in my log: "Fishing okay but not quite as good as previous seasons."

I see in my notes that a couple of friends, Dave Rimmer and Pip Winslow, were on the Kennebec at the end of June. Pip was then the Orvis rep for New England, and Dave was and still is a great fisherman and part-time guide. They both lived on the Merrimack River, but the Kennebec was the place to be. Tom Fote from Toms River, New Jersey, came up and fished with me for a few days. Tom, more than anyone, was responsible for New Jersey making striped bass a game fish when Maine did in the mid-1980s. We were comrades in conservation, he with the Jersey Coast Angler's Association, and me with the Coastal Conservation Association. I would drive down to ASMFC meetings and bunk at Tom's, and we'd ride on to Virginia and back together. Often I'd stay a couple of extra days and we'd fish Island Beach State Park. They were good days, and we were trying to extend the game fish designation to the rest of the coast.

I wrote this in my log: "Scraped a few off the Hump and Green Point at the beginning and ends of the tides. Ram Island, Goat, etc. etc. have produced zero. We had a good tide or two where Back River meets the Kennebec just below Bald Head, but a big bust of large bass is rare despite a very good bait situation."

This was a definite change from just a couple of years before, when the turn of every high tide saw schools of bass surface feeding all over the river.

Duncan Barnes, at the time the editor of *Field and Stream* magazine, who I had met through John Cole, had become a regular fishing companion a few years back. I see that we caught a couple of bass in the low forty-inch category at Lower Hell Gate on the Sasanoa on June 30 but not a lot else to brag about. Duncan was so taken with the Sasanoa that he built a home in which to retire on its shore overlooking the upper end of the Back River.

On July 1, the season that allowed baitfishing for striped bass opened on the Kennebec. The good fishing of the past few years had given the river a huge reputation, and on July 1 the whole character of the fishery changed. During the catch-and-release and artificial-lure-only season of May and June, there were lots of people on the river. With the exception of the occasional outlaw, they all knew they were there to enjoy the world-class fishing and to revel in seeing with their own eyes just what nature was capable of providing.

On July 1, the fly fisherman and plug casters were largely replaced with eel fishermen whose mode of operation was to fish in free spool and let the bass run-off line under no tension while they swallowed the bait. The bait fishermen would then throw the reel in gear, stand up, and rear back on the rod three times as hard as necessary to drive the hook home. All too often the hook was placed back in the esophagus, gills, or stomach of the bass, where it was nearly impossible to remove. They would cut the line and tell themselves the bass would simply shed the hook in a few days. This was of course often untrue. I caught a large but thin bass off a ledge at the lower end of Long Reach in Bath that had a foot of heavy mono covered with green slime trailing from its vent. There was nothing I could do but trim off the line. During leaner times in the winter, this fish would not have the reserves to survive.

The boats were drifting in a fleet so close together as to almost touch. Many of the boats had several anglers, and at times it seemed like everyone on board was hooked up. I'm sure that in a single hour more big fish were killed than from the hook-and-release mortality during the entire previous conservation season. For those of us who had watched this fishery come back from a veritable handful of big old fish to a river loaded with stripers of all sizes, this scene was simply too much to bear, and many of us started to turn away from the Kennebec fishery.

I spent the rest of the 1997 season fishing the cape. I had the additional reason of having outfitted a seventeen-foot Parker especially to my fly-fishing specifications the winter before. *Fly Fishing in Salt Waters* magazine, for which I had become a masthead contributor, published an article about it, "The Ultimate Skiff."

I sold my Alaskan to another comrade in conservation, Mike Nussman, who was then a vice president and lobbyist for the American Sportfishing Association. Mike drove north from Annapolis, Maryland, and I drove south, towing the Alaskan from Falmouth, Maine. We had agreed to meet in Nyack, New York, on Mike's side of the Hudson. There we swapped boats and money, and each headed back home. I haven't spoken with Mike in a couple of years, but last thing I knew, he still had the Alaskan.

The Parker was powered with a tiller-steered fifty-horsepower four-stroke Honda, and I ran it from a single-pedestal seat. We mounted a simple set of gauges and a fish finder to the inside of the starboard side coaming. About two-thirds of the way forward, I had a sturdy fiberglass box seat mounted to the deck, and that is where my guests sat. Right in front of both seats were large open areas to stand and fly cast. The most powerful Great White trolling motor I could buy was mounted on the front casting deck. In many ways this was the same set up as the old Cuttyhunk Bass Boats. They were set up with front and rear tillers for steering, and anglers sat in either chair or on top of the engine box. There was no windshield and no superstructure of any kind.

I wrote an article about "Wearing Your Windshield" in which I mentioned things such as sunglasses, fleece-neck gaiters, good foul weather clothing, boots, and warm, waterproof gloves as protection from everything from salt spray to rain and biting northeastern winds.

The Parker was no deep-V ride, and it was only seventeen feet long, but it was sturdy and wide, with reasonably high sides for its length. It proved on a couple of hair-raising trips up Vineyard Sound when we had no business being down there that it was a very capable little sea boat.

That fall I was working on the L.L. Bean striper book, and I neglected my fishing a little. A friend from Barnstable, Dick White, who took a lot of the photos in the L.L. Bean book, called on October 30 to tell me there were tons of school bass a half mile offshore in the sandbar tide rips that stretch from outside Waquoit Bay east to New Seabury. He said it was incredible how many there were. My log notes recorded my disappointment: "Damn, I should be there."

Later that fall I followed the migration south to do a little fishing with Tom Fote at Island Beach State Park. This included daily breakfasts in waders at Betty and Nick's. I gave a slideshow to Bob Popovics' Atlantic Saltwater Flyrodders in Seaside Park. After that, I was on to see George Reiger in Locustville, Virginia.

George was the conservation editor for *Field and Stream* magazine, and he had written several important books about hunting and fishing. He had visited me in Maine when he was researching *The Striped Bass Chronicles*, and we hit it off. George set up a terrific trip for me to fish with Claude Bain, who had the enviable public relations job of taking people to fish on Chesapeake Bay for the state of Virginia. We fished for a while on a flat, just inside the north end of the Chesapeake Bay Bridge-Tunnel. There were a couple of boats drifting live eels there, and they were very surprised when, while we drifted between them, I landed two approximately twenty-pound stripers on my grocery fly and 450-grain sinking head. We didn't see another fly rod all day, and Claude was also quite impressed with how effective it could be. I enjoyed that trip immensely and picked up a lot of great material for my book.

1998 Through 2001

To begin 1998, Duncan Barnes and I drove down to Kingston, New York, on the Hudson River with the hope of observing the striped bass spawning event. The Hudson River population, like that of the Chesapeake Bay, had explosively recovered since a low in the late 1970s. In some recent years, big schools of stripers had been observed spawning in the general area of Kingston in mid-May. Through a friend of a friend, we found someone who was happy to take us out on the river to look for bass. He was perfect in that he had a bass boat with a gigantic engine and really enjoyed covering the river. Duncan observed that our mild-mannered friend totally transformed when he sat behind the wheel of that overpowered boat. We spent a couple of days cranking up and down a good-sized section of the river and asking folks we ran into if they had seen any spawning bass, but we came up empty-handed.

After that we had an excellent worm hatch in Bournes Pond and some decent fishing for fish up to thirty-six inches or so that were chasing squid at Middle Ground. Back in the Kennebec, though, we weren't so lucky. On June 7, I fished all my good spots in the Kennebec and came up with a big fat zero. On June 14, just as we hoped the big bass would arrive, it began to rain and did so continuously for four days. The Kennebec became a river of mud, and it was near the end of the month when it cleared up enough to fish. I did get fish of forty-four and thirty-nine inches from Robinhood Cove on the Sasanoa, but that was the odd bright spot.

I received a call from Steve Bellefleur, who said the terrific fishing on the Watch Hill Reefs that he was used to in June had been slumping in recent years. This year they had tons of beautiful squid, but there were no big bass in the rips to feed on them.

The rest of the summer was lackluster. I caught plenty of stripers, but getting anything in Maine much larger than thirty-four inches was a difficult order.

Nineteen ninety-nine started with a good worm hatch on the cape and some fish there up to thirty-five inches or so. I had several great days in late May at Quicks and Robinson's Holes, catching a good number of fish between thirty and forty inches.

On June 9, the large stripers made an early arrival in the Kennebec, and I had a couple of hot tides up in front of the old wharf in front of the Flat Top Cottage, where Lefty Kreh had been so excited a few years before. The action was confined to a relatively small area, though, and those big surface blitzes that had been the norm for up until the last year or two were nonexistent now. When I got to the Flat Top, there was nothing showing, but I made the drift, connected with a fish, and saw on my fish finder that there was a school hanging there. I often compared notes with Pat Keliher, a local guide who some years later ended up as the head of Maine's Department of Marine Resources. He told me that he had recently made three trips for a total catch of two small stripers.

My reaction to the great decline in the Kennebec fishery was to spend more time on Cape Cod and the Elizabeth

Islands. I see in my notes that fall fishing from the boat had also replaced my Martha's Vineyard beach fishing. I now knew the Elizabeths quite well, and I could usually manage to find a few good bass, even though the numbers there weren't nearly as consistently good as they had been just a few years earlier. I was discovering some of what John Christian had told me, that later in the season I seemed to find more fish on the upper shoreline of Naushon. The areas around the French Watering Hole and inside of Woods Hole were quite good to me too.

Another change I made, almost subconsciously, was to do more freshwater fishing. George Watson and I purchased a camp for brook trout fishing on Nesowadnehunk Lake (pronounced Sowderhunk) on the western edge of Baxter State Park, and we were putting some time in there. For a few years, we finished the freshwater season in Maine around this time by fishing the extended catch-and-release season in the East Outlet of Moosehead Lake. These fish, both brook trout and landlocked salmon, are small fish relative to stripers, but the aesthetics of the fisheries are very nice, and I didn't have to watch people gaffing the declining runs of striped bass.

I really don't like to be a bleeding heart about fish. They are good to eat, and I eat them. You must kill them to do that, and I accept that as a part of life. I don't like, though, to watch people killing exceptional fish, such as big striped bass, with an apparent disregard for what these creatures are. I realize that is a very strong statement to make. For one thing, how do I know that the people killing these fish lack appreciation of what a 40-pound striper represents? The accusation is not made lightly or without considerable thought. I've fished side by side with all kinds of people for years. I watch how they treat other people at the boat ramp, or how they approach them on the water when they think the other boat is on fish, or how generous they are or aren't with a little bit of information, or how they handle the fish when they catch it. Too many anglers just don't realize what a prize a big bass is, or how important it is as a spawner in the population.

I annually made a trip in late April and early May, before the striped bass season really got going, with a group of guys to Pete Dube's Motel Restigouche in Matapédia, Quebec. The fish we were catching were in many cases as big as striped bass and plenty tough on the end of a line. Even though we were fishing for kelts (salmon that had spawned the previous fall and stayed in the river without feeding for the winter), they were still excellent fighters. We caught them with the same ten-weights and heavy Teeny-style lines we used to cast grocery flies for striped bass. Not only did I enjoy the fishing, but just as importantly I enjoyed the people and the culture. You weren't allowed to kill these fish, and no one there would have given any consideration to doing so if they could. It was all about being out on the water and occasionally connecting with one of these magnificent creatures.

In November 1999, I decided to go back to work and opened a business in Portland, Maine, called Portland Computer Copy Inc. (PCCI). It was a second go-round in that industry for me, and this time I had more capital in my pocket from the beginning. The effect of that was I didn't have to bear down quite as hard all the time, and if I wanted to go fishing, I could.

Chapter Eight

The Unraveling and the Future

In May 2000, we had some good fishing in the Elizabeth Islands as well as the rips out in Vineyard Sound, especially along Middle Ground, which is about two and a half miles long. Parts of it are quite deep, with water rising from one hundred feet or more in depth up to less than twenty feet at the top of the sandbar, where the rip line forms. The easterly section is much shallower. Some boats anchor just above the rip line and cast in. I never liked that kind of fishing, and instead I would run up to about 150 feet above the rip and get in two or three casts before I had drifted out of the zone.

The rip moves sideways over this bar, so as you drift and then run back up, you are gradually moving down-tide and covering a large area of the rip, increasing your chances of finding hot fishing or a school of large fish. One of my favorite

things to do, if there were few boats around, was to run the boat barely on a plane, along the glassy surface, just up-tide of the standing wave, and look for surface-feeding fish. It was productive from a fish-finding sense, but it was also simply a wonderful thing to do.

On a clear day in May, you were aware that the season was still fresh and new, and looking ahead, you could see miles of foamy white rip line unfolding continuously in sunshine. The contrast of the white wave top against the bold ocean blue of the still-cold waters of Vineyard Sound was a glimpse into heaven. Sometimes in May and early June, you could see squid schools being swept up in the rip and the bass chasing them. The squid would squirt well out of the water, and on many occasions I saw really big striped bass come clear of the water to chase them.

When the prime time in mid-June rolled around, though, the Kennebec was again a total disappointment. There were a few schools of small fish here and there, but large fish were in very short supply. In fact, I saw things in my notes such as "zero today" or "skunked except for a couple of rats." Finally a note simply said the Kennebec was probably no longer worth doing. Then I received a call from Steve Bellefleur, and he had the same complaints about his areas off the Watch Hill Reefs.

Things never got much better in 2000 in the Kennebec. I went to Crooks Lake in Labrador for a week, and when I came back on June 27, I ran into Dave Pecci on the Kennebec. He said it had been terribly slow. In the mid-1990s you could almost walk on them in late June. The decline in just five years was really profound.

On August 27, I was on the Kennebec, this time at the invitation of Dave Pecci, who wanted to show me the action they were experiencing in North Bath near Thorne Island Ledge. Dave grew up within sight of this spot, and he and a few friends had been quietly enjoying much better fishing in this area than was occurring downriver, which for me was totally unexpected. I did know that stripers went all the way up to the dam in Augusta, but I believed the much larger body of migratory fish hung down in the saline lower estuary.

The wide, straight stretch of the Kennebec crossed by the Bath bridge is called Long Reach, and throughout this 3.6-mile stretch, the river turns from brackish at the lower end to completely fresh at the upper. Thorne Island is slightly upriver from Long Reach and in a completely freshwater section of the river. The anglers here were drifting with marine worms for bait, and they discovered that, using smaller pieces, they were able to hook and land stripers as small as six inches in length. This was very important, because fish of that size are only half the size of the smallest migratory stripers that would make the swim from the Chesapeake or the Hudson to Maine, and we were always searching for evidence that the tiny bass born every year in the Kennebec were surviving to establish what we hoped would become a substantial fishable population of native Kennebec stripers. But by all the information we had in 2021, that still hadn't happened.

Action at Thorne Island had been quite good just before my trip with Dave Pecci, though almost exclusively on schoolie-sized stripers. We hit a day when the fish were off the bite, and we caught only a handful, and none were over twenty-four inches long.

In September of that year, I did a little of everything, including making a trip up to Ungava Bay for char and brook trout, as well as a fair amount of fishing for bonito and albies in and around Woods Hole.

George Watson and I had an incredible experience while we were fishing Woods Hole. George was in the bow of the boat and I was at the helm when we saw a pile of birds diving in an area called the Gates of Canso. I assume this narrow passage of very fast running water is named after the Strait of Canso in Nova Scotia, but I don't know for certain. I had caught a lot of small bass in this little thoroughfare, but mostly I used it as a back door on windy afternoons to escape the rough, rock-infested water ripping through Woods Hole. This afternoon, though, the area was hosting a sizable school of false albacore, and they were really tearing the place apart.

We came up on the edge of the school, and George fired out a cast and immediately hooked up. The albie took off like a rocket. The excess of line George had stripped out leaped off the deck and came violently tight to the reel, the impact spun the spool and instantly caused the kind of backlash you need to sit down and calmly take a few minutes to pick out. We didn't have a few minutes, though; we had a hard-charging ten-pound false albacore on the line. We had to make the best of it, and I hollered to George to brace himself against the thigh-high front deck while I attempted to follow the fish closely enough to keep from breaking the line. George had on some fresh fifteen-pound Maxima Chameleon tippet, which is mighty tough stuff.

I cranked the tiller-steered outboard motor this way and that, turning violently, accelerating then shutting down, all to stay on top of the fish. On his end, George would bow to the fish and stretch out as far as possible, trying to absorb the fish's frantic surges. At times I was sure the rod would break, since it was bent at what seemed like straight out from the butt. But in the end, it all held, and in probably less than five minutes we boated George's albie.

In early October, Phil Perrino and I were again with Steve Bellefleur at Montauk. There were a lot of bay anchovies that fall, and the bass pushed them into tight pods, so dense that their bodies changed the color of the water to look like big brown stains. The bass feeding on the anchovies were also more tightly packed than I had ever seen, even when feeding on a worm hatch. Getting anything bigger than thirty inches out of these surface blitzes was difficult, but I found that if I fished a big grocery fly and let it sink a few feet before starting the retrieve, I could pick up much larger fish than by casting the little epoxy-and-fly fur bay anchovy patterns into the surface action. One or two days a year of that fishing is more than enough for me.

There were several boats crowded around the point where the hottest action was. Some of the boats accelerated wildly to intercept the pods of anchovies. Boats deliberately cut off other boats to put themselves in the best position to catch fish, and big, deep-V hulls threw up tremendous wakes that were magnified by the speed of the water ripping around

Montauk Point. I saw boats pull up alongside each other, and their captains with beet-red faces scream threats at each other that could be heard even over the noise of the wind, screaming gulls, breaking waves, and racing engines. It created a lot of uncomfortable and dangerous situations, and I understand that boats running into each other and people getting hurt was not all that uncommon.

Looking back at my notes, I see that the last couple of trips to Cape Cod were the most enjoyable and productive of the many I made down there all that season. We had developed a pattern of getting up long before light and leaving the mooring at Bournes Pond in time to be at our first fishing spot before full daylight. Late in the season that spot was most often Woods Hole or down around the French Watering Hole. The October winds are very frequently from the northwest, and by staying fairly close in the lee of the cape mainland, and then Naushon Island, the ride was reasonably comfortable. Once you get down in the vicinity of Robinson's Hole, the sound starts to broaden out, and you can run into a swell from the ocean that makes things a bit less pleasant.

We continued to have decent fishing on the morning trips, and when the early morning bite petered out, we'd ride the southwest sea breeze back to the house for lunch and a break from fishing. In the evenings we fished the inflow and outflow of some of the nearby salt ponds and the Vineyard Sound beaches. There was one little stretch of shoreline at the west end of the Menauhant swimming beach that we could walk to from our house on Bournes Pond. There is a formation of large underwater rocks out there that must have been left over from some construction years ago. I can never recall catching a lot of fish there, but there always seemed to be a few, and every now and then a good one would be hooked in those rocks—a testimony to why the Chesapeake folks call stripers "rockfish."

Parts of this beach have experienced a lot of erosion within living memory. Not far to the east, off Eel Pond, a row of jetties that at one time was built right on the beach now sit about two hundred yards offshore. It is quite amazing to circumnavigate these rock piles in a boat and know that they were attached to dry land less than a hundred years ago.

After a few hours in the evening at the ponds and the beachfront, we'd hit the rack to get up before light to do it again the next day. I loved the variety of being in the boat by day and at the beach at night. The essentially undeveloped Elizabeth Islands are as pleasant a place as any on earth to spend some time, and their shorelines, especially the holes between the islands, provide excellent opportunities to hook a big striper. The nighttime beaches, including the shores of the salt ponds, are a magical environment.

I love the way that summer hangs on into the fall on the southside of the cape. You could be out on the beach, standing in the surf, and walk just a few feet up onto the high beach and hear the creaking of the crickets living in the cover of the beach roses and bayberry. Sometimes I'd sit on the beach and rest my back against a rock. If your fingertips dig down just a few inches into the sand, you can still feel the warmth of the day's sunlight well into the night.

We fished all the way into November that year, and our last trip was made running down to the French Watering Hole at dawn in flat-calm conditions with a temperature of 58 degrees Fahrenheit. In the fall those mornings come along just like those that are below freezing. We landed a number of husky bass, including one of thirty-eight inches, and when I saw John Christian off Pasque Island later that morning, he told me that on a charter a few days before they had trolled up fifteen fish between eighteen and thirty pounds at Sow and Pigs.

Two thousand one was a year that, in retrospect, held a lot of the evidence of the changes that were coming. I again started the year with some spring salmon fishing on the Matapédia, and then, in May, I was down on the cape fishing the Elizabeths and Middle Ground while spending my evenings on the worm hatch inside Bournes Pond. It was all reasonably productive, but my notes say the largest fish I landed was thirty-four inches, except for a couple of forty-inch salmon on the Matapédia. What really stands out, as I look through the summer log entries, is that there isn't a mention of the Kennebec, so I guess that is the year I just decided there were better places for me to spend my time. The other thing of note is that, between May and September, I made trips to Quebec, Labrador, our camp at Nesowadnehunk Lake, Rick Warren's salmon camp on the Upsalquitch, and a trip to the Little Cascapédia River for salmon and sea-run brook trout. Looking back, it seems to me that I was searching for the next Cape Cod or Kennebec in my life.

On the weekend of August 10–11 I invited Rip Cunningham to visit the house at Bournes Pond to fish for bonito. I see by my notes that we ran all over, looking for bonito, but the good fishing we enjoyed was off Robinson's Hole for striped bass. In a shallow area just to the east of the hole, we could see the surface of some glassy water was covered with the dimples of some small baitfish that turned out to be sardine-sized herring. We used the electric motor to slide into this shallow water and, using the seven- and eight-weight rods that we had set up for bonito, landed several thirty-six to forty-inch bass. This is relatively light tackle for bass of this size, and each one of them threatened to show us the bottom of the spool. I had to run the electric hard to try to keep from getting cleaned out while minimally disrupting the shallow area where the baitfish were schooled up.

"Next year," said Rip, "you've got to come up with me and try some salmon fishing at Black Brook."

The rest of the fall fishing season was a mixture of fresh and saltwater. George Watson and I made several trips to the camp at Nesowadnehunk Lake, and on one we ran into an afternoon blue-winged olive hatch in Nesowadnehunk Stream. It was a day I will never forget. We were wading down through the stream, fishing the beaver-dam ponds as we came to them. George liked a particular place where we caught a couple of nice fish, and he decided he would stick it out there for a while. I walked out of sight downstream to the next pool and found a good number of eight- to twelve-inch brookies, nicely colored up, and with the males sporting their hooked jaws. I caught a few fish before it slowed down, and I sat down beside the stream to give it a rest and see if George would show up. Finally I became curious as to why George hadn't arrived and decided to hike back and see what was going on. When I got there, George was sitting on the edge of the bank and tying on a new fly.

He looked up for a second and said, "It's been absolutely fabulous! There's a big hatch going on."

I looked out at the stream in front of me and realized it was solid with tiny emerging blue wing olive mayflies. Here and there among the insects were boils of feeding brookies. The hatch lasted almost another hour, and the fishing was nearly continuous lights-out activity. To our left, upstream, the river was narrow, shallow, and fast running. At times the little mayflies would emerge there, and any kind of a small dry fly was instantly taken. The fish were in less than a foot of water, and you could clearly see them flash on their sides as they darted up to take the mayflies. In less than a hundred feet the water slowed down and deepened as it flowed into a bend in the stream that was blocked by a massive beaver dam immediately after it turned the corner. The fish in this slower water were a little fussier, and it took a while longer to get a take—by that I mean less than a minute compared to instantaneously up in the run.

It was classic northern Maine fall weather—dark, cool, and drizzly—and set in an alder lined-stream running through a forest, with mountains visible here and there peaking through foliage. As we fished, we were intermittently joined by a cow moose and her calf, which would now be near us, and then they foraged their way out of sight. Even though the calf was the size of a small horse, the cow eyed us wearily, as we did her. The whole experience was just superb.

For the rest of the season, the striper fishing in the Elizabeths was okay but quite unremarkable. I hunted here and there between Robinson's and Quicks Holes, with an occasional trip to Sow and Pigs as the weather allowed. Some falls it just seems to blow all the time, and this was one of them. On Columbus Day weekend, my notes say it blew fifty miles per hour from the west on Saturday, but I was able get out on Sunday and got a few small to medium bass at Robinson's. When you try to fit trips in between forecasts like that, you are bound to get beat up by the tail end of something or fooled by the early arrival or just unexpected change in direction from another system.

2002

I received a call from Rip Cunningham in March, offering me a week's fishing at the Black Brook Salmon Club in New Brunswick. The relatively small amount of Atlantic salmon fishing I had done by that time had been at commercial lodges. This would be my first time at a private club and my first trip to the Miramichi River. The last couple of days in June through the Fourth of July was the time that was available, and I accepted. I planned to mix it with a few days of brook trout fishing at Nesowadnehunk on the way.

Black Brook itself is a large, cool brook that flows a few miles from a big bog east of the Southwest Miramichi. The brook enters the Miramichi about a hundred yards downstream from where the Cains River, the largest tributary of the Miramichi, also enters. The three streams then combine into a broad, deep, slow pool, the tail of which was the home fishing pool of Wade's Fishing Lodge—for many years an institution on the Miramichi River.

For those not familiar with it, landownership in New Brunswick largely stems from a system of Crown grants. The grants were used by the king of England to encourage homesteading on these rivers in order to develop and populate the area in the early to mid-1800s. Subjects received a decent-sized piece of land, usually fifty to a hundred acres, on which to farm and cut wood for fuel. Ownership of the exclusive fishing rights out to the center of the river in front of their property was also granted by the crown. Those deeded rights stayed with the land unless sold off separately, and so the clubs, commercial lodges, and private homes situated on the land in these old grants enjoy deeded ownership of the exclusive right to fish on the property. The fish themselves are not owned, since they are merely passing over the private property, and the government reserves the right to manage the fishery as it sees fit.

Life in the camps and clubs can be very comfortable, with good food, comradery, lovely views, and the peace and quiet of the wilderness in contrast with the hustle and bustle most people endure near their homes. The fish, Atlantic salmon, are one of the world's most desirable species to catch. Ted Williams, the Splendid Splinter, wrote a book titled *The Big Three* about the triple crown of fly rod sport fishing: tarpon, bonefish, and Atlantic salmon. Williams caught over a thousand of each, and his first Atlantic salmon came from Black Brook in the 1950s while he was still a relatively young man. Many anglers with lifetimes of experience settle on this fish in their later years as the exclusive focus of their fishing interest, because it is such a fascinating quarry.

We didn't catch many fish on my trip to Black Brook, because the water was too warm. Salmon fishing is like that: too warm, too low, too high, too dirty, high barometric pressure, low barometric pressure, dropping water, rising water, etc. A few years back I jokingly made a list of the excuses for why salmon aren't taking flies, and I numbered them. I told my guests to save time and just use a number.

Nonetheless, I was attracted to what I saw. On our last day, Lew Smith came by from Wade's Fishing Club next door and told us that the club was disbanding and that they had a couple of pools for sale downriver. He asked if any of us were interested? That invitation started me on a journey that finds me twenty years later owning several salmon pools and a couple of camps on the Miramichi and Cains Rivers, with striped bass claiming a much lower priority in my fishing schedule than the unchallenged number-one slot they had for the first fifty years of my life. But it didn't happen right away, and I didn't completely abandon striped bass fishing.

One of the things I instantly grasped about the Atlantic salmon fishery on the Miramichi was that virtually all the participants were more interested in good fishing than they were in making money by killing and selling fish or in eating them. Perhaps more important, the political system was behind salmon conservation. In response to a crashing salmon population in the 1980s, nets, which had historically made the river almost impassable to salmon, had been outlawed, as well as the selling of Atlantic salmon. They had become strictly a game fish, and the population was enjoying a considerable rebound. Also, while the Miramichi had been thought of by many as a grilse or small salmon river, specimens of over twenty and even thirty pounds were regularly being taken in 2002.

Striped bass along America's Atlantic coast were going the other way, and someone such as I, who had fished for stripers over a long span of years, could see it very clearly. Painfully clearly.

Two thousand two wasn't without some great moments of saltwater fishing, though. One of them was the terrific worm hatch experience I had in early May. I fished with Jim White in Greenwich Cove, Rhode Island. Jim had fished these waters with his father in the 1950s. His life's work had been as a mail carrier, and he had retired and was following his passion for striped bass fishing by starting White Ghost Guide Services. He had a pretty good run at it too, including guiding some of the sport's best-known personalities, such as Lefty Kreh.

It wasn't striped bass, though, that had me most anxious to fish with Jim. It was weakfish, also known as sea trout and squeteague (reportedly their Indian name). They had historically been numerous at times in Narragansett and Buzzards Bays. There was even a Squeteague Harbor on the eastern shore of Buzzards Bay. Vinny Kiernan, who built our house on Bournes Pond, recalled as a boy in the 1950s catching squeteague in Green Pond, the pond west of Bournes Pond. For just a little while in the late 1990s and early 2000s, it looked as if weakfish might be making a comeback, and modest to decent catches were reported from several of the fish's old haunts. I hoped to write a story about it and ran the idea by the editors at *Salt Water Sportsman* magazine.

On the evening of May 10, Jim and I were on Greenwich Cove, and a light worm hatch was taking place. There were definitely enough worms coming out to spawn, so that we could see a few swimming by the boat every now and then. But as time wore on, the hour when you would expect the hatch to hit its peak came and went, but the density never picked up. Jim was casting a light spinning rod with some sort of rubber bait, and I was using my fly rod. I began to notice fish occasionally surfacing that I couldn't identify. They porpoised partially out of the water, very much the way a salmon would. Stripers will roll on their side and will often show a dorsal fin and a tiny patch of their back, but these fish were humping up, and a substantial curve of their back was breaking the surface. On top of this, they appeared red in the evening light. There weren't a lot of these fish, and there was no concentration to try to get near, so we drifted with the tide and cast.

We were catching a few small stripers, and then Jim got a grab from what seemed like a pretty good fish. After a nice fight, the fish appeared beside the boat. It was a large weakfish, which folks sometimes refer to as a tide runner. As a guide, Jim was equipped with a boga grip and ruler decal glued to his hull. The fish was thirty-two inches long and weighed ten and a half pounds, a really terrific specimen. It was sure a thrill to see that fish!

The little uptick in the population, however, disappeared right after that, and I haven't heard even a rumor of weakfish in Rhode Island for the last twenty years. This is another saltwater game fish that was unbelievably numerous off the mid-Atlantic coast, and then it was netted into oblivion under the ineffective watch of the Atlantic States Marine Fisheries Council and has never regained its niche.

The rest of the year passed smoothly, and we pecked away at stripers on the cape, made my annual trip to Bellefleur's with Phil, and a trip with George Watson to Victoria Island in Nunavut, where, along with a slew of big lake trout, we landed a number of large Arctic char, including a forty-one-inch fish estimated at twenty-two pounds from the Nanook River. The char was an incredible thrill, and George and I later made a trip to the Tree River, also in Nunavut, which is the place where most of the world records have come from, but we weren't able to top that one from Victoria Island.

The char have an unusual spawning schedule. They arrive from the ocean dark green and silver colored and spend a full year in fresh water before spawning the next fall. Unlike Atlantic salmon, though, they do feed. After getting into fresh water, they turn color to an incredible electric orange, pink, or red—it is impossible to exactly describe the color. It starts with the belly but eventually colors the whole fish. When a big orange-colored char chases a fly or rises for an insect, they are visible a long way off and at quite a depth through the water. They seem to actually glow.

2003

This year started for me on a very sad note with the passing of my longtime friend John Cole in January. He loved all kinds of fishing, and in addition to our years together on the Kennebec, he had been with me at the house on Bournes Pond a number of times. One of my regrets is that I never spent time with him on the Miramichi. Few striped bass fishermen, and probably no young ones, know that it was John's book *Striper* that motivated his college friend, Senator John Chafee from Rhode Island, a Republican, to push through the Atlantic Striped Bass Conservation Act of 1984. Provisions and funding from this act were credited with turning around the crash of the late 1970s and early 1980s.

The next thing I did in 2003 was to make a deal to buy Campbell's and Keenan's Pools on the Miramichi, the property the man from Wade's Fishing Club had told us about in July at Black Brook. I made an offer in September to purchase it, but it was lower than the owner expected, and he didn't bother to acknowledge it. He took my call in early January, though, and we negotiated a deal.

In March 2003 I received an email from someone saying that an effort to get a larger commercial quota for striped bass in Rhode Island had led the commercial fishers to approach the Rhode Island Marine Fisheries Council with the idea of shortening the recreational fishing season. The estimated recreational catch for that period would be calculated, and that number of fish would be added to the commercial quota for the upcoming season. My informant was very upset with this development, and since he knew I had been active in the Coastal Conservation Association's attempts to build an organization in New England, he wondered if I had any thoughts on what could be done to combat this proposal.

I didn't know much about Rhode Island's fishery council, but I had met Steve Medeiros who had recently started the Rhode Island Saltwater Anglers Association (RISAA).

"It's terrible," said Steve in a phone call, "but there is nothing we can do about it. The whole committee is stacked with commercial interests, and if we try and fight this, they will just go after even more."

On top of that, the required public hearing was only a week away, so there was no time to organize a resistance.

The power of email was just beginning to be understood at that time. I had a fair number of friends in Rhode Island, and of course they all had friends etc. We made up a Take Action Letter announcing this atrocity and asking everyone to send emails or letters to the governor's office opposing the quota grab. We also told them where and when the meeting was to be held and asked them to attend and speak in opposition.

And it worked.

We later heard that the governor's office had to assign a staffer just to answer the emails. Rhode Island has a big charter boat industry, and one out-of-state charter boat customer sent copies of a number of canceled checks that he had paid for guided fishing and lodging. It all added up to several thousand dollars. This angler said that he would never fish in Rhode Island again if the state cut the recreational quota to give extra fish to the commercials.

The hearing was held the next week, and Dave Preble called me from the back of the room.

"Brad," he said, "it's incredible! The hall is packed, people are standing outside and waiting to get in, and they're all recreational anglers." He added, "I see a small group of commercial anglers sitting together, and they don't dare to speak."

The governor's representative had told Preble that no matter what was said that evening, there was no way this quota shift was going to take place. It turned out the governor was a recreational striped bass fishermen himself, and he instantly grasped what an appalling piece of public policy this would be.

In the aftermath of this political action, Dave Preble, Rip Cunningham, Fred Thurber, George Watson, Jim White, and a few others whose names I apologize for not remembering started Stripers Forever with the concept of using email and the internet to organize a movement to designate striped bass as game fish—meaning no sale of wild striped bass would be allowed—in every state from North Carolina to Maine. It has been a tremendously time-consuming endeavor that I'm sorry to say has been only partially successful, but the current situation in which we have again allowed this incredibly valuable fishery to wither to a remnant of its potential may eventually allow us to get the job done.

My friend Walter Fondren used to say that one of the great things about recreational fishing advocacy was that you could never truly lose. There is no finish line, and all political policies can potentially be changed eventually. Stripers Forever is still fighting that battle, and membership is free. (You can join online at stripersforever.org.)

My full intention with Campell's and Keenan's Pools was to do a little salmon fishing at the peak times and continue with my striped bass fishing largely on Cape Cod, because the cape in 2003 showed me what I'd be missing if I abandoned the fishing there.

George Watson and I went there on May 27, and our fishing at Robinson's Hole and on Middle Ground resulted in a forty-four-inch bass along with several others from thirty-four to thirty-eight inches. Earlier in the month we had excellent worm-hatch fishing, with many fish up to the mid-thirty-inch range, that is, once we discovered the secret of the floating worm fly.

Late one mid-May afternoon, I was standing on the sandy point in back of the house and looking for bass and worms. We had been watching some sports on television and drinking scotch. Every now and then, one of us would get up and walk to the beach for a look. When I got down to the beach this time, I saw little red worms zigzagging all over the surface and boils of feeding stripers just a few yards off the bank. I hurried back to the house, alerted George, and went back onto the deck to get into my waders and grab my rod and flies.

George was watching a tense moment in the NBA playoffs and was a few minutes behind me.

Once I got down to the pond, I started fishing one of the red velvet worm flies that were in vogue at the time, but even though I tried every retrieve I could think of, I could not get a strike. The boils of large stripers were everywhere right in front of me, and I was using a fly that had caught lots of fish during previous hatches, but I was having no luck.

George showed up a few minutes later, sat his drink in the sand, peeled off some line, made a couple of false casts, and plunked his worm fly about forty feet from shore. By luck he landed it right on top of the huge boil where a bass had just taken a worm. George's fly, identical to mine, was still completely dry, and it sat high up on the surface of the water, where it was instantly taken by a huge bass.

George was completely unprepared and, in fact, lifting his rod by reflex to make a longer cast. The lifting motion set the hook powerfully into the fish, and the fish instantly dove and headed for the deeper parts of the pond. George was so startled he just held onto the line firmly with his left hand. The rod was yanked down straight toward the direction of the runaway fish, and the twelve-pound tippet promptly parted. It was over in less time than it takes to read this sentence.

We had the secret, though, and now we tied on new dry flies and managed to catch some nice fish. The next day I sliced open the end of the velvet tubing on several of the flies, slipped in pieces of tubular foam that I had on hand for tying sliders, and stitched up the openings. The floating worm hatch fly was born.

In mid-June, George and I made our first trip to Campbell's Pool for bright salmon, and we landed six salmon between twelve and twenty pounds. We also lost several, including a real monster that George had on. I remember that fish vividly. George never got to turn the handle of the reel. It fought, as a few of those early run fish will do, for its entire thirty seconds or so on the line, without running downstream of the position at which it was hooked. The fish grabbed the fly and ran upstream, towing the fly line hissing through the water, and then it jumped about five feet into the air. I could see its expressionless eye as it suspended in the air, parallel to the surface of the water. I'm not sure it ever went back under the surface went it landed. Instead, it rushed back and forth, half in and half out of the water, with the drag on George's reel screaming madly. Suddenly it was gone. The fish was only about forty feet away from George as the crow flies, but the entire fly line was outside of the rod tip. The fish had been swimming so fast that the sheer drag of the line in the water was enough to pull the line out against George's drag.

After the fish came off, George looked at me, not far away in my canoe. "What happened?" he said.

Massachusetts Commercial Striped Bass Fishing

My notes from August say that the Massachusetts commercial striped bass quota for the entire year, 1.2 million pounds, was caught in five weeks—with no fishing allowed on weekends. For those who are not familiar with the Massachusetts commercial striped bass fishery, and not to single out Massachusetts, because most of the other states are similar, the name is a misnomer. I guess that it's true that since the fish are sold, it's a commercial fishery. But with very few exceptions, this fishery was not and is not undertaken by commercial fishermen. It is largely fished by recreational hobbyists who sell their catch for the old expression pin money, thus they are nicknamed pin hookers.

Is there anything wrong with that?

Perhaps there wouldn't be anything wrong with it if we were not talking about a fragile resource that a lot of people must share. I don't want to spend a great deal of time preaching on this point, but clearly by the repeated collapses of this resource, there aren't enough and never will be enough of these fish to support commercial fisheries on the scale they take place and, at the same time, allow millions of recreational anglers who fish for them to take home an occasional fish for their families to eat. Trying to manage any fishery for two user groups with different goals does not work satisfactorily for either the users or the resource.

I used to request spreadsheets from the Massachusetts Division of Marine Fisheries (DMF) that provided some analysis and data on the Bay State's striped bass commercial fishery. These provided a lot of interesting information about the fishery. The spreadsheets showed that only a handful of the license holders reporting any catch at all made more than a couple of thousand dollars for the season. Roughly half the license holders reported no catch. When you combined this with the common knowledge that striped bass were being sold to restaurants all over Cape Cod for cash, it was abundantly clear the legal licenses just served as a cover for the fishermen who didn't want to deal with income taxes or to report their catch so that it could be counted against the commercial quota. By owning a license, you could legally transport a commercial quantity of striped bass. In the unlikely event that you would be found with these fish, you could say you were on your way to sell them at the market. As long as you had a commercial license, you were protected.

Just how indifferent the Department of Marine Resources was to this activity became clear when, in 2012, the Atlantic States Marine Fishery Council (ASMFC) Law Enforcement Committee strongly supported a policy of tagging all striped bass at the point of capture and additionally designed a scheme to send tags out at the beginning of the season based on the volume that had been reported the year before. Additional tags could be acquired based on proof of having sold enough fish to cover the tags already sent out. The Massachusetts DMF lobbied hard and effectively for the tagging to be done at the point of sale, which continued to enable fishermen to possess and transport commercial quantities of untagged bass that might very well be headed for under-the-table sales. As the saying goes, you can't make this stuff up!

It's important to note that while the commercial striped bass quota was quickly caught in 2003 and for several years after that, the areas in which the fish were caught continually shrank on an annual basis. In the early years, after reopening the commercial fishery, landings came from pretty much all over the coast of Massachusetts. In later years, very high percentages of the quota came from just one or two locations each summer.

Clearly the population of the over-thirty-four-inch fish was in decline in the early 2000s. A big school might appear off Chatham or Provincetown, and with modern communication systems, everyone knew. Hundreds of boats were so compacted that a person could almost jump from one boat to the next. The cluster of boats would hover over the schools pinpointed by fish finders and GPS, very heavy tackle was deployed, and the fish were winched quickly to the surface and gaffed.

To rapidly get the bait down to the bottom, a dastardly setup, called a yo-yo rig, was often employed. This consisted of a dead menhaden stuffed with a heavy sinker and rigged with two big treble hooks connected by a steel spring that would keep the baitfish straight but allow it to be somewhat flexible. The yo-yo rig could be jigged more or less straight up and down in the water column, which was necessary to fish within the tight group of boats. It was deadly and relatively inexpensive. The inexpensive part was important, because the bass often swallowed these things, and there was no easy way to get them out of the fish. So the line was just cut off at the mouth of the bass and a new rig was tied on.

A big problem with the yo-yo rig was that the minimum-size striped bass allowed in the Massachusetts commercial fishery was thirty-four inches in length, and of the nearly seventy thousand legally caught, the average size was about thirty-five and a half inches. This meant an awful lot of fish smaller than thirty-four inches were caught on these devices. When the fish got close to the boat, the angler gaffed it, measured it, and if it was too short, they just cut the line and threw the fish back. Lots of striped bass were recaptured, having temporarily survived gaffing, with one of these yo-yo rigs still hooked to the inside of the fish's gullet or stomach. They might survive with the rig in their stomach for a while, but it would interfere with their feeding, and in times of stress, such as over the winter, the fish would die.

It isn't hard to see the damage that can be done to a school of striped bass with a large flotilla of boats constantly drifting on top of them, locked in position with state-of-the-art electronics, and fishing with this barbaric but extremely effective device.

2004

In the very early 2000s, a few sharpies began to realize that during the peak of migration, some striped bass that were migrating north could be found on the surface when they came up through Buzzards Bay and Vineyard Sound. I remember from old how-to books on striped bass that during the fall fishing off Montauk, you could intercept the migrating schools coming south and cast to them.

On the weekend of May 21, I was fishing with John Rice, and we had reasonably calm conditions. So we decided to give this old advice a try.

We were at the south end of Vineyard Sound, a mile or so off Cuttyhunk, when we ran into several good schools of stripers. The fish were well away from any land, in nearly a hundred feet of water, swimming slowly north and feeding on herring that were two to three inches long. The fish were easy to locate under the big flocks of gulls, terns, and gannets. The herring actually tried to hide all around our boat, and the fish that we released were spitting up the small baitfish. Fish like bonito or albies are normally found in the open like this, herding up bait and then ripping through it. Because of their great speed, they don't need any structure to hold on. Opposite of this would be fish such as cod that live very attached to rocky bottom structures and largely depend on that structure to limit the escape paths of their prey. Striped bass, by virtue of their mixture of dark- and light-colored muscle tissue, a deep body shape, large fins for maneuverability, and a big square tail for rapid acceleration in turbulent conditions are hybrids of these two designs. You won't find them spending a lot of time on the surface chasing fleet baitfish, such as mackerel. On the other hand, they can and do feed in this manner for short periods, and they can do it for prolonged periods if the baitfish are weak enough swimmers, as small herring are.

We found the bass and herring easily, and we had some great action that day. But the next day they were almost entirely gone from the area, and we spent a lot of time simply roaming around and looking for fish that weren't there.

The rest of the May and June shoreline fishing down through the Elizabeth Islands was largely so-so, and I spent most of my time that summer running back and forth to do more New Brunswick salmon fishing.

My last trip to Cape Cod for the season was September 5–7. Duncan Barnes and I landed bass of thirty-two, thirty-five, and thirty-five and a half inches, along with a few smaller ones, but it wasn't good enough to keep me from heading north on the weekends for the rest of the salmon season.

Two thousand five was the year of my only really solid fishing for school bluefin tuna on the fly—ever. On August 6 we went to Sow and Pigs Reef where a month earlier we had decent fishing for striped bass of up to forty inches long. I had heard about school bluefin being around inshore in good numbers off Rhode Island, and at the south end of the Pigs we were essentially in the same neighborhood.

Dean Clark called and told me that he had heard of some tuna the day before by Devil's Bridge on the Vineyard. We were in the twenty-five-foot Hydra-Sport, so heading across the eight miles of open water to Gay Head was no problem. As we approached the outer edge of Devil's Bridge, we could see birds working, and even from a great distance we could make out the white water being thrown up by the surfacing bluefins. We approached it just as we would if we were fishing for albies, except we had some twelve-weight outfits that hadn't seen much use, since I had stopped tarpon fishing a few years earlier.

While it doesn't always seem like it, Steve Bellefleur claims that fish such as bonito, albies, and bluefins feed into the tide. Successful presentations are most often made by running the boat alongside and slightly up-current of the school and casting back to and across the leading edge of the fish so that the fly appears to be running away from them.

The tide was running hard into Vineyard Sound, and the fish let us get very near. I tossed the boat into neutral so it wouldn't run off in one direction or another, stepped out from behind the console, and prepared to cast off the port side of the boat. From almost beside the boat to a couple of hundred feet distant, the surface of the water was broken every few yards by a whirlpool roughly the size of the engine hood from a full-size pickup truck. I could see the flashes of moving fish, and here and there a tuna launched completely clear of the surface and headed straight back in as if it had been fired from a cannon.

My cast went out about a hundred feet, and when it landed in the water, there were at least a half dozen visible surface eruptions between me and the fly. I didn't see how I could fail to hook up, and I wasn't disappointed. These tuna ran between twenty and forty-five pounds, and the fights were all pretty much the same. On the strike, whatever line you had stripped in seemed to elevate all at once from the deck, and in a split second it disappeared through the guides and came up tight against the reel. Once you felt that take, your one concern was to get that line clear to the reel, because nothing was going to stop that tuna or give you a moment to clear a tangle. If the line tangled, it was going to go out through the guides or something was going to break. That was all there was to it.

The tuna would take off away from us like an express train, and peel about 100 yards of backing from the tightest drag we dared to use. I was fishing with an old Sci Anglers System 3 12/13 reel, and we had the drag on the maximum setting. Shortly after the fish took off, smoke was coming from the reel. A few of the bigger ones might have gone 150 yards, but that was definitely the maximum run we experienced. Then you started pulling and cranking on the fish, all of which, somehow, ended up swimming in circles on the bottom.

We were rigged with straight thirty-pound test for tippets, fifty spectra backing, and Sci Anglers intermediate tarpon lines. This setup could take quite a lot of strain.

Invariably, after a few minutes, we ended up with the fish directly under the boat, doing everything it could to stay deep. I hardly used the rod, instead I pointed it almost at the fish and simply lifted it straight up, then bent back over, and cranked in a foot or two of line. In a surprisingly short length of time we could see the fish near the boat.

No matter which of us had hooked the fish, George would then take the rod and pull the fish to the surface, and because I was a little more flexible and lighter than George, I'd bend over and grab the fish by the tail, then slide my other hand under its belly and lift it out of the water. Our relative body weights were an issue because, on the larger ones, George would grab my belt to keep me from going over the side. I could never seem to get a clean shot at grabbing that tail quickly enough, and invariably each fish gave me a soaking as it beat the surface to a froth when I tried to grab it. Once I got the tuna over the rail, George would yank out the hook with a pair of pliers, and the fish went back in the water, headfirst, seconds later. They hit the water swimming a hundred miles an hour.

We had the fish for three days, and I remember looking across the mouth of Vineyard Sound, between Cuttyhunk and Gay Head, and being able to pick out five or six schools of surface-feeding bluefins. We'd make a decision based on how far away they were and how many looked to be in the school, and then we'd go crashing after them. The first day we had them all to ourselves, which was simply an incredible luxury, and by the third day we were sharing them with another dozen or so boats, but that was it. I hope to experience the likes of those days again, but I'm not counting on it.

I ended my season on the weekend of October 22–23, fishing the pond openings in Falmouth, Massachusetts. My notes say there were decent quantities of small bass around, but a northeast storm kept me out of the boat.

2006 to the Present

By 2006 I had settled into a pattern nearly completely focused on Atlantic salmon. I started my years in March, fishing for what are called springers in Scotland (very early run, bright salmon), then back to Miramichi in April for kelts (salmon spawned the previous fall and wintered without feeding in the river). Between the end of this fishing in early May and the arrival of the first bright salmon in mid-June, I would make a couple of trips to Cape Cod, mostly for the worm hatch, and occasionally during the summer, for a family weekend or to get some use out of our house there. In the late fall I'd get in a few nights of fishing the pond openings in Falmouth, trying for a late bass or two. In between trips, I'd hit the occasional tide in Maine on the Presumpscot.

I was also very active in Stripers Forever, and through that I was always in touch with several people who were actively fishing for stripers, so I knew what was going on. It wasn't good. One of my favorite sayings is that stripers are a school fish, and if you find yourself fishing on a school of bass, things may be just great, but how far away is the next school?

As the striped bass spawning biomass has been depleted, the overall quality of the fishing has gone down. Yes, there are bright spots, but places that have historically offered good fishing became far less dependable, large fish became much scarcer, and soon the young-of-the-year count, that indispensable measure of the future of the fishery, started to falter, with the good years becoming less impressive and the poor years becoming increasingly concerning.

Just how far the stock of large stripers has slipped is clearly illustrated by the Massachusetts commercial landing data. In the Massachusetts fishery, all striped bass must be landed by hook and line. As I pointed out in some detail earlier, it is a recreational fishery masquerading as a commercial fishery. Using just hook and line means it is difficult to keep catching the volume of fish once the population starts to decline. With nets you can put out more nets or larger ones, but with rod-and-line angling, you would need to increase the number of anglers, and that isn't likely to happen with fewer fish out there to fish for.

To illustrate the declining success of the fishery, I've created this table of the last ten seasons with listings of the pounds of fish caught in thousands:

YEAR	QUOTA	LANDINGS Pounds(in thousands)
2011	1,062	1,164
2012	1,057	1,218
2013	1,003	999
2014	1,155	1,138
2015	869	866
2016	870	938

YEAR	QUOTA	LANDINGS Pounds(in thousands)
2017	801	823
2018	847	753
2019	870	586
2020	735	386

The quota stayed quite stable up until 2015, when in response to strong evidence that the stock was declining, the quota on the coast was reduced by 25 percent. The quota within Chesapeake Bay was only reduced by 20.5 percent at that time, because the bay areas argued there were lots of small bass coming into the bay, and they shouldn't be reduced as much as the coastal fishery, where the large fish were more depleted. The Atlantic States Marine Fishery Council (ASMFC) is well known for this sort of political compromise based on how it crunches the data.

The Chesapeake Bay commercial fisheries for striped bass are predominately a gill-net fishery. While there are a lot of part-timers in that fishery too, it is much more of a traditional commercial livelihood fishery than the coastal rod-and-reel fishery, and there is a history of greater and better-organized resistance to conservation measures than seen in the coastal fisheries.

The entire Massachusetts annual quota was eventually caught through 2017, but it took much longer to catch it then the few weeks required in the early 2000s. It is well known that in the early 2000s many extra fish were sold under the table to both avoid income taxes and to keep from catching the quota and having the season ended. As the fish became less numerous, and anglers had to work much harder to catch their quota, some or all of this behavior disappeared. Defenders of the commercial fishery will dismiss this statement, but the reality off substantial illegal sales is validated by the number of arrests and convictions coming from virtually all the states up and down the seaboard.

In the 2020 season, only 33 percent as many pounds of stripers over thirty-four inches were landed in Massachusetts as were reported in 2011, even though the season was allowed to remain open until the fish had migrated out of the state. The large fish simply weren't there to catch.

During the debate on the 25 percent commercial quota cut proposal in 2015, which took place at the ASMFC meeting on October 29, 2014, Paul Diodati, the director of Marines Fisheries for Massachusetts, said:

> I put aside all the questions about bias and age and what the reference point might do and just look at the facts. Let's look at what catch statistics are telling us. In Massachusetts alone, since 2006 to 2014, our recreational catch has decreased 80 percent. That has already created the most significant economic impacts I can imagine on our recreational fishery; and it is not just the for-hire fishery. We're talking about the tackle shops, the boat manufacturers. Everything that I'm hearing about today, if we take any rapid cut it might result in an economic impact. Well, where do you think we've been since 2006? We've taken some pretty drastic hits and not to mention the hit that the stakeholders, the public has taken in terms of lost public benefits from this resource. This is a tremendous fishery. I've seen it at its height after the recovery. There is nothing like it along the entire Eastern Seaboard. I think it is clear that our management plan, Amendment 6, tells us exactly what to do when we're at the point we're at today. Actually, we

were at this point three years ago; and that's when we should have taken an action.

My path had crossed with Diodati's quite a few times over the previous forty years. Paul was at one time the recreational fishery coordinator for Massachusetts, and he eventually worked his way up to being the top fishery executive in the state. Paul understood, in Massachusetts, the home of Gloucester and New Bedford, a couple of the nation's largest commercial fishing ports, that the concept of commercial fishing had immense political support. The CCA's Walter Fondren used to say, in national politics, the commercial fishing industry had some politicians who would "lay down on the railroad tracks" if that were needed. Recreational fishing had supporters too, but no one who would take the cause of fish conservation to those levels. Politicians such as Congressman Barney Frank, whose district included New Bedford, was well known as someone who would champion the cause of commercial fishing regardless of how indefensible his position seemed. This was because Frank knew he would be supported by the voters in his district for doing it, and that was all that mattered. They were the people who elected him. The so-called commercial striped bass fishery in Massachusetts, though, had a much less dedicated political constituency. The recreational fishery was much more financially important, and Diodati knew it. He was just telling the truth.

The Meduncook River: Summer of 2021

The Meduncook is not a typical striper river. Rivers come in all shapes and sizes, and the currents and food chains found in their often-brackish-water environments are generally very attractive to striped bass. Most Maine rivers I have fished for stripers start with a substantial freshwater source, and then have miles of a relatively narrow channel before finally emptying into a broad saltwater estuary. The Sheepscot, Damariscotta, Kennebec, and many others are such rivers. Compared to these, the Meduncook is more a bay than a river. The freshwater head consists of a couple of small streams that can easily be jumped over or walked through, and they empty into what is called Salt Pond. I believe this pond of a few acres in size became a pond only because, at some point, a thin ribbon of land was filled in across its lower end to accommodate a road from East Friendship to Cushing.

There is a very small bridge in the middle of this ribbon of land, or causeway, and the tides run back and forth under that bridge into and out of Salt Pond. The height of the land directly under the bridge is a greater elevation than the bottom of the salt pond, so the water in the pond only partially drains out, and with the streams pouring water in 24/7, the salinity of the pond is brackish and not pure salt. It is just three miles from Salt Pond to the southern tip of Crotch Island, where the Meduncook River enters Muscongus Bay. This whole distance is very much a saltwater environment, complete with rockweed, clams, and lobsters. A very modest current runs through this distance of the river as it empties and fills with the tides. This bit of flowing water, combined with the little taste of fresh coming out of Salt Pond on the ebb tide, is enough, though, to hold a good array of forage for striped bass, including grass shrimp, several species of marine worms, smelts, various minnows, pelagic herring, and, during many summers, pogies.

In the spring of 2016, June and I had had enough of the drive from Maine to Falmouth, Massachusetts, to reach our house on Cape Cod. Our children were grown and had their own families, and they didn't have the time to fight Boston traffic. Striped bass fishing no longer presented the opportunities it had, and a big house that far away becomes a bit of a problem. We received a great offer on the house, and with sadness and some relief, we decided to sell. For a few years we were very happy to have to maintain only one house in Falmouth, Maine but the call of the less-developed and more informal mid-coastal Maine was always there.

A frequent Sunday drive at almost any time of year would find us heading up to Boothbay, South Bristol, Pemaquid, or Friendship. For whatever reasons, the time was right in the winter of 2020, and we found a home in East Friendship with a dock near the mouth of the Meduncook River. This was just around the corner from the commercial fishing harbor of Friendship, which is lined with docks and filled with hundreds of lobster boats. As the crow flies, our new house was only two miles from the house in which I grew up. It felt like home to me, and in exploring the water there I was reminded of the things my parents and especially my grandparents had told me about East Friendship, and the Meduncook River. It was known for clamming and for a channel on the backside of a nearby island that had sea scallops and for a deep hole near the mouth of the river that my grandfather said offered good flounder fishing.

Some stripers were also caught in the Meduncook. My grandmother drove me there a couple of times in the late 1950s, when people first reported catching stripers in the area, and I cast bucktail jigs into the outflow of Salt Pond but failed to catch anything. In the winter of 2020, when we were looking at the house, the sales agent said there was good striper fishing in the river.

"Where?" I asked.

He laughed and said, "Right in front of this house."

I thought it was just a sales pitch, but whether or not I had striper fishing there didn't matter a lot to me. This was just before the 2020/21 pandemic hit, and I expected to be in Canada, salmon fishing for most of the summer. I could always scratch what was left of my striper itch in the Presumpscot. Still, it would be a nice plus, I thought, but it dropped quickly out of my mind.

One day in early June 2020, I was in Friendship to do some work around the new house and on my boat. I stepped onto the back deck for a daybreak coffee. A veritable cloud of birds—herring and laughing gulls and terns—were milling over the surface of the water and making quite a racket. Suddenly all the birds in one area turned their attention to a section of ripply looking water, and the tension was broken by a big splash or two and a shower of baitfish. I had seen it thousands of times in my life, and it had to be striped bass.

The fishing was quite good there during June and into early July, though the fish were almost entirely schoolies of twenty-five inches or less. It was a chance to see them in an environment where I had not done a lot of striper fishing. This is the famous rockbound coast of Maine, known as a cold place at the far end of the normal migratory range of the striped bass. On top of that, it is big: the coast runs some 230 miles—about the size of the rest of New England—and much more, if you take into consideration the hundreds of inlets and long, thin points of land. I have always marveled that stripers, a fish that in large part is spawned in a few moderate-sized areas of Chesapeake Bay, can manage to fairly densely populate huge sections of the coast of Maine as well as the rest of New England. But in the good years they do.

On the Fourth of July weekend, my youngest daughter, Caroline, and her husband and their two daughters were visiting. The oldest, Lydia, is interested in fishing, much as her mother has always been. Caroline could throw like a boy, and, in fact, she won the softball distance-throw contest for her class one year in school, girls and boys. That strength and coordination carried over to casting. I took Caroline and Lydia out on the river in the *Sea Beagle*, and we trolled a small silver spoon right through areas of breaking school bass. A hook-up was a sure thing, and Lydia caught her first striped bass, then repeated it several times. It was a great day!

During the dog days of late July and August, the stripers were still around, but they were quiet during the day, unless it was foggy or drizzly. In low light, the bass could still erupt out in front of the house at just about any time, if the current was moving a bit. I noticed when I was out clam digging or going for morning rows that the bass were all over the extensive mudflats that surrounded the river channel. I'd be digging a flat at low tide and get back in my rowboat to head home when the water started to rise. Often I'd see schools of small bass moving in and waking all over the flats as soon as they were covered with just a few inches of water.

As stripers do everywhere, they reacted to the cooling waters after Labor Day by feeding more actively. The seabirds were now up and looking for breaking fish very frequently, and the fishing was pretty good. There were no bragging-sized specimens or record numbers of fish to be caught, but I was long beyond caring about that. I just loved seeing a few stripers feeding on the surface out in the channel, or popping a pod of bait they had corralled off the end of my dock. I didn't run for a rod at every opportunity. More often than not, I was content just to watch them and to know they were there.

Then one late September weekend, cold and with a stiff northwest breeze, I saw only one or two little breaks on the surface, and after that they were gone completely. I looked through early October. With our warming environment, we have come to expect the seasons to last much longer, but it it doesn't always happen. By my childhood experiences in Damariscotta and my years of living on the Presumpscot, late September was the time for them to leave, and they did.

I can hope for them to be back next spring, undoubtedly some will, but how many, and what number will grow to be large bass? Last summer I fished the Kennebec several times. I hadn't been there in twenty years. There were a few more homes along the shoreline than I remembered, but all in all, the appearance of things hadn't changed much since my last visit. I launched my fourteen-foot Lund aluminum boat with a fifteen-horsepower outboard from the state ramp on the old Burgess Marine property, in fact, on the exact spot where John Cole and I had walked down the dock to go out on my twenty-four-foot Aquasport the first day we ever fished together. Burgess had failed, the building was torn down, and the site became a state access point to the river.

Being in the middle of the Kennebec River with the big eddies and fast-moving currents throwing your small boat this way and that is a bit intimidating, but I had been on the river before in such a boat, and I hung on tightly and kept the throttle well under control. I had picked the very start of the dropping tide to fish my way down and then back up the river. I planned to hit most of my old favorite spots in this section of the upper river: Fisher's Eddy, the Flat Top, the Hump, Green Point, and Ram Island's Lower Unit City . My plan was to spend just a few minutes with the deadly bucktail jig in what I knew to be the prime part of each structure, and that is just what I did. When you've done enough of it, you can almost sense if the fish are there. Often you have a little help from telltale signs such as a sprinkle of nervous baitfish, the persistent circling of a couple of gulls, or the scattered breaks of surface-feeding bass. I saw none of that, but I quickly fished each spot, feeling the bucktail bounce off the bottom and getting a decent retrieve through areas I knew would have held many stripers in the 1980s and 1990s. There were almost none now. I even put on the Danny deep diver and pulled it through a number of historically productive places. No luck. I did catch a few schoolies, and I saw a pod or two on the surface down by my old Marr Island fishing ground, but John Cole's army of slammers was just a memory.

My next trip a week or so later went much the same way. There were no crowds, but there were a number of other boats on the river, and I chatted up a couple of fishermen back at the ramp.

I was rusty, no question, and some of them did much better than I, but still, the largest one I heard anyone talk about was just below the twenty-eight-inch keeper size. Everyone I talked with was disappointed with the fishing.

What Happened and Where Are We Headed Now?

The most graphic display of the changes that have occurred in the striped bass population can be seen in the "juvenile" or young-of-the-year index. There are several of these, including ones done for the Kennebec, Hudson, and Delaware Rivers and the Chesapeake Bay, both in Maryland and Virginia. The longest running, most established, and unquestionably the most important one is from Maryland. Essentially a long net is swept over the same sections of nursery areas for baby striped bass three times every year, and the number of small stripers is counted and then averaged at the end of the year to produce a single number that is thought to represent the success of that year's spawning. Not all of these baby fish live on and become part of the coastal migratory stock, but the percentage of those that do is relatively consistent. I personally put a lot of faith in the young-of-the-year-index as an indicator of future striped bass abundance, because over the years they have reflected what I have seen with my own eyes on the water.

You can see in the Maryland statistics from 1954 through 2020 that the spawning success increased from the 1950s through 1970, it declined to a very low level in the very early 1980s, it again hit a peak around 1995, and then it fell back to very low levels in 2019 and 2020. As fishery biologist, author, and retired charter boat owner David Preble from Rhode Island observed, a classic sign of a stock in trouble is when there is a pattern of decline in both the highs and the lows over a period of time. That pattern is certainly evident in the graph below. All of the population fluctuations we refer to throughout this book are reflected in the trends revealed in this graphic.

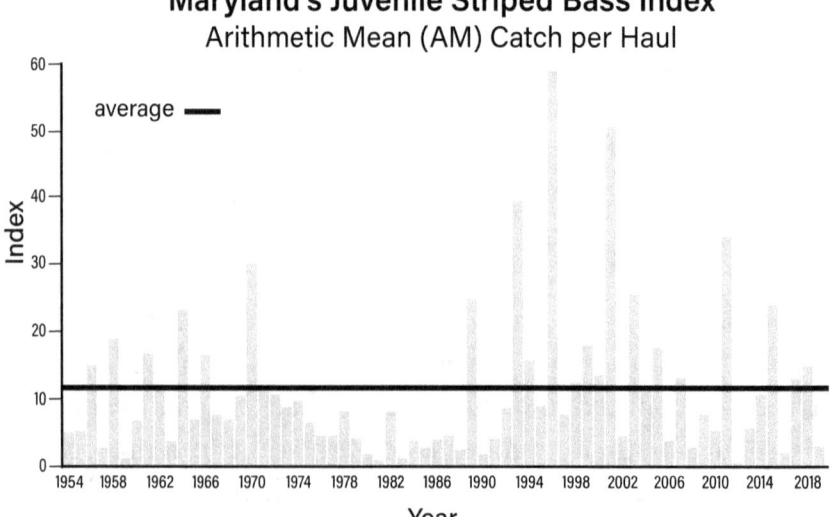

What exactly caused the striper population to decline so drastically in the 1970s? What caused it to increase in the late 1980s? What caused that recovery to stall and begin a decline again in the late 1990s (a process that has continued through at least 2020)? In the mid-1970s, when it became clear striper fishing had declined dramatically, people devised many explanations. I read all the information of the day that I could find, and I went to many of the meetings that were held. Some people even denied there was any problem.

I remember walking into a little tackle shop in Brunswick, Maine (the shop is now long gone). The owner, a crusty old salt, leaned over the counter and told me not to worry. His lobster fishing friends had seen big schools of stripers offshore.

"That is where they are," he said. "It was just a matter of the baitfish migrations or perhaps water temperature, and next year things would be as good as ever."

But they weren't.

Theories for the 1970s decline included poor spawning success due to acid rain releasing toxic aluminum derivatives from the soil in cultivated fields along the Chesapeake, the nefarious effects of sunspots, the evolutionary clock having run out on the species, overfishing, and more. What I also know is that, in 1985, Maryland shut down all harvesting of striped bass, and the coastal jurisdictions followed a similar but less drastic course in harvest reductions. And according to all the latest scientific statistics, the fishing mortality rate then decreased from a very high level to a very low level. Instantly, upon reducing the fishing mortality level, the stock started on the road to recovery.

It is generally conceded by the experts today that the 1970s striped bass population crash came from overfishing.

In the previous chapter I noted that in 1999 we were no longer seeing the schools of stripers on the surface we had seen as recently as 1997, and we never did see them again. At that point, it was clear to many of us fishing hard on a daily basis that the recovery had been cut off at the knees. What caused that to happen?

The short answer is that the Atlantic States Marine Fishery Council (ASMFC) allowed the liberalizations of both the commercial and recreational harvests to take place at a rate that quashed the population improvements that were underway, and it also caused the population to lose almost all of the larger older fish. This lack of large breeders caused the young-of-the-year production to become unstable. The recreational advocates fought catch liberalizations at every step of the way, but the commercial fishing industry continued to push for larger quotas. The longer answer starts with the next paragraph and ends a couple of pages from now with the sentence that reads, "This is why the Kennebec River went from a world-class fishery in 1994 to poor by 2000." I won't be offended if you want to just skip to there.

From the late 1970s I have followed the striped bass regulatory process organized by the ASMFC. The plans developed by the ASMFC are based on incredibly complex computer models that attempt to consider every variable and are constantly scrutinized for what is believed to be the most accurate and appropriate data. These plans assume what will happen to the population using all the most likely assumptions for things such as young-of-the-year production, recruitment to larger from smaller sizes, and fishing as well as background mortality rates. Then, after the fishing seasons passed, the ASMFC uses other data to calculate what actually happened and what the current status of the stocks is believed to be.

I believe the real-world scenario the striped bass management plan is trying to unravel is probably too complicated for existing science to explain accurately. This inaccuracy is further compounded by political pressure, largely from states with commercial fishing interests, to allow higher quotas by adopting overly optimistic interpretations of the forecast data.

I also believe that recreational catch-and-release mortality has been substantially overestimated, largely because it is subject to many variables that are hard to combine into an accurate summary of the activity. For instance, we know that, instead of the 9 percent mortality calculation used by the ASMFC, in some warm-water bait fishing the mortality is more like 25 percent, and we also know that in some cold-water, artificial-lure fisheries the mortality rate is more like 1 percent. I believe the big catches are made in the ocean during the cooler periods, when the fish are migrating, and they are made largely with artificial lures and that overall catch-and-release mortality is substantially lower than 9 percent. Beyond this, the recreational catch itself—to which the 9 percent figure is applied—is an estimate based on statistical survey data. This data is the best available, but that does not mean it is accurate. This uncertainty makes catch-and-release mortality a perfect catchall to blame for the inaccuracies of the management plan.

In 1995, Amendment 5 to the striped bass management plan was put in place. This ended Amendment 4, which had reopened the striped bass commercial fisheries under the dark cloud of the infamous Hambrook Bar counts we discussed earlier in the book. Under Amendment 5, the fishing mortality level was to gradually increase over three years from the assumed and then current .25 level to a level of .5, which was thought to be the maximum sustainable yield. This doubling of fishing mortality manifested itself as large increases in commercial quota and recreational fishing liberalizations. Also, under Amendment 5, the deal was struck to set the fishing mortality levels in the producer areas (meaning largely Chesapeake Bay) to reference a minimum size of twenty inches, but to use twenty-eight inches in the coastal fishery. The fixed reference points allowed bigger catches if higher minimum sizes were selected, and lower catches if smaller sizes were chosen. This is why states such as Massachusetts selected thirty-four inches rather than twenty-eight inches in their commercial hook-and-line fishery. One real effect, though, was to generate a huge amount of pressure on large breeder-sized striped bass.

We have now seen the ASMFC institute a slot limit for between twenty-eight inches and thirty-five inches in order to reduce the pressure on the few remaining fish that live to make it to thirty-five inches. Meanwhile, the Chesapeake Bay jurisdictions went down to eighteen inches rather than twenty inches, but they successfully argued for even larger quotas, because the smaller fish were thought to be more abundant.

The bottom line of all this is as the late Russell Nelson told me in the early 2000s, after the ASMFC had allowed all the increases in striped bass fishing mortality, "Any of these numbers could easily be off one way or the other by 50 percent or more." Russell had been the director of Marine Fisheries in Florida when they designated redfish as a game fish. Russell was a bit irreverent but smart as a whip, and unlike many fishery managers, he had no problem talking about the limitations of current fishery management science.

Under Amendment 5, the total striped bass fishery—both commercial and recreational, including estimates for commercial bycatch and recreational catch-and-release mortality—went from just over two million fish in 1994 to more than six million in 1997. These figures include no estimate at all for the commercial black market catch, yet in some years, convictions were made of groups of commercial fishermen with hundreds of thousands of pounds of illegal catches.

Clearly, in retrospect, a lot of the data and even the formulas used to calculate these statistics were inaccurate. And even though a lot of people involved in the process urged caution, those warnings went unheeded. The fishery managers were focused on allowing larger catches. Bigger quotas were what their commercial fishermen wanted, and it was the only standard for success that too many of the fishery managers understood. This is why the Kennebec River went from a world-class fishery in 1994 to poor by 2000.

What about the future? We still have calls from commercial interests in Chesapeake Bay to increase their quotas, and we have groups such as Stripers Forever calling for a moratorium on all harvesting of the fish, recreational and commercial. The trend line of the young-of-the-year-index has steadily declined since the early 2000s, and the spawning stock biomass is back to near where it was in the late 1980s during the moratorium. Right now, in April 2021, the ASMFC is rethinking the values of its striped bass management plans and preparing to construct Amendment 7.

Those of you who are reading this book years down the road will be able to find out exactly what did happen. I'm going to predict the ASMFC will continue to fiddle with the quotas and regulations but remain behind the curve. Nothing truly dramatic will happen until the situation is completely desperate.

Actually, the ASMFC is really not the right body to deal with the problem. Striped bass need to be designated as game fish. They are simply too important to the recreational fishing public to be beaten down by commercial fishing and the inevitable black market that accompanies it. It is a plain-and-simple fact that at every turn in the road of these management plans, the recreational interests have said no to bigger bag limits, and the commercial interests have clamored to be able to kill more fish.

If a few more states join Maine, New Hampshire, Connecticut, New Jersey, and Pennsylvania, then perhaps the federal government will see the wisdom in making striped bass America's saltwater game fish. If the commercial market for wild striped bass was ended, I am certain the fishery would then be managed much more conservatively, since great fishing that would attract and hold recreational participants would become the goal of management.

That is what happened in Florida and Texas when redfish were designated as game fish. The success of those fisheries and the recreational industry they support is legendary. Unlike redfish, though, stripers make large migrations up and down the Eastern Seaboard. Bass conserved in the Kennebec can be butchered in Massachusetts, New York, and Rhode Island, which is exactly what happened to John Cole's slammers.

Unfortunately, it looks as if the old ways are going to hang on for a while yet, and as Walter Fondren noted, "The great thing about managing these fisheries is that there is no finish line." Striped bass may not be game fish yet, but the benefits of that action can be ours whenever the recreational anglers really get behind that goal, and shift the political tide into their favor. One thing that is important to realize is that in no state where striped bass have been made a game fish has a commercial fishery ever been reopened.

www.ingramcontent.com/pod-product-compliance
Lightning Source LLC
Chambersburg PA
CBHW050159240426
43671CB00013B/2185